The Breads of France

N

BELGIUM

W. GERMANY

CALAIS

SS FRANCE

LE HAVRE

HONFLEUR

BAYEUX

CHARLEVILLE

LUXEMBORG

FRANKFURT

PARIS

BÉNODET

LE MANS

STRASBOURG

BRACIEUX

MONTBARD

DIJON

LA ROCHE-SUR-YON

WICHTRACH

ROCHELLE

SWITZERLAND

ANGOULÊME

GANNAT

VICHY

GENEVA

PAIN CUIT AU BOIS

ROCHEFORT-MONTAGNE

LYON

BORDEAUX

ROMANS

GRENOBLE

ITALY

MONTÉLIMAR

BAYONNE

Ghartzalaka

CAMBO-LES-BAINS

PALAIS

MONACO

CARCASSONNE

BEAUCAIRE

LIMOUX

SPAIN

CLAYTON

The Breads of France

AND HOW TO BAKE THEM IN YOUR OWN KITCHEN

By Bernard Clayton, Jr.

Introduction to the New Edition by Patricia Wells

TEN SPEED PRESS
Berkeley ~ Toronto

Ten Speed Press
P.O. Box 7123
Berkeley, California 94707
www.tenspeed.com

Distributed in Australia by Simon and Schuster Australia, in Canada by Ten Speed Press Canada, in New Zealand by Southern Publishers Group, in South Africa by Real Books, in Southeast Asia by Berkeley Books, and in the United Kingdom and Europe by Airlift Book Company.

Jacket and interior design by Betsy Stromberg
Photographs by Bernard Clayton, Jr.
Illustration on page ii by Jeff Clayton

Photographs courtesy, The Lilly Library, Indiana University, Bloomington, Indiana.

Library of Congress Cataloging-in-Publication Data

Clayton, Bernard.
    The breads of France and how to bake them in your own kitchen/by Bernard Clayton, Jr.
      p. cm.
    Includes index.
    ISBN 1-58008-389-7
    1. Bread—France. 2. Cookery, French. I. Title.

  TX769.C54 2002
  641.8'15'0944—dc21   2002023327

First printing this edition, 2002
Printed in China

1 2 3 4 5 6 7 8 9 10 — 06 05 04 03 02

To the French *boulanger*
for his hospitality and helpfulness
both at sea and ashore.

Breads at L'Hôtellerie de Relais, Bracieux.

CONTENTS

Introduction to the New Edition by Patricia Wells   xi

Introduction   xiv

Acknowledgments   xvii

PART I: ESSENTIALS OF FRENCH BREAD MAKING

Ingredients and How They Are Combined   3

Equipment That Contributes to a Perfect Loaf   12

Sources of Supply   20

Storing and Freezing   28

What Went Wrong?   29

PART II: THE BREADS OF FRANCE

RECIPES FROM PARIS

Pain Hawaiien Fauchon ❖ Fauchon's Hawaiian Bread   36

Pain aux Noix ❖ Nut Bread   38

Pain de Campagne Poilâne ❖ Poilâne's Peasant Bread   43

Croissants Briochés ❖ Crescent-shaped Brioches   46

Les Bagels de Jo Goldenberg ❖ Jo Goldenberg's Bagels   49

Ka' Achei Sumsum ❖ Salted Sesame Bagels   52

Galette Persane ❖ Persian Flatbread   55

Pain Complet ❖ Whole Wheat Health Bread   57

Pain d'Épice ❖ Spice Bread   60

Pain de Son—Régime ❖ Bran Diet Bread   62

Pain sans Sel ❖ Salt-Free Bread   63

RECIPES FROM LE HAVRE

Brioche Nanterre ❖ Nanterre Brioche Loaf   65

Brioche Parisienne ❖ Parisian Brioche Loaf   65

Brioche aux Raisins Secs ❖ Raisin Brioche Loaf   69

Brioche au Fromage ❖ Cheese Brioche Loaf   69

RECIPES FROM HONFLEUR

Pain de Campagne—Honfleur ❧ Honfleur Country Bread 74

Pain de Méteil ❧ Maslin Stone-ground Rye or Pumpernickel Bread 77

Brioche Mousseline ❧ Mousseline Brioche 79

Croissants Feuilletés ❧ Flaky Croissants 82

RECIPES FROM BAYEUX

Pain Brié Normande ❧ Normandy Beaten Bread 88

Pain Ordinaire de M Gautier ❧ M. Gautier's Loaf 90

RECIPES FROM BRACIEUX

Petits Pains au Lait—Sandwich ❧ Small Sandwich Rolls 96

Petits Pains au Lait ❧ Milk Rolls 97

Pain Seigle ❧ Rye Bread 100

Les Benoîtons ❧ Rye Rolls with Raisins 103

Brioche aux Pruneaux ❧ Brioche with Prune Filling 104

Petits Pains au Chocolat ❧ Chocolate-filled Rolls 106

RECIPE FROM ANGOULÉME

Brioche Vendéenne ❧ Vendéenne Brioche 110

RECIPES FROM BAYONNE

Gâteau au Maïs ❧ Corn Cake 113

Biscuits au Maïs ❧ Corn Biscuits 115

Taloa ❧ Corn Sandwich Muffins 117

Méture au Potiron Basquais ❧ Basque Pumpkin Bread 119

RECIPES FROM CAMBO-LES-BAINS

Gâteau Basque ❧ Basque Cake 122

Croissants Cambo ❧ Unlayered Croissants 125

RECIPE FROM CARCASSONNE

Galette de Dame Carcas ❧ Twelfth-Night Cake of Dame Carcas 129

RECIPES FROM LIMOUX

Gâteaux au Poivre ❧ Pepper Cakes 133

Pain de Régime Gluten ❧ Gluten Diet Bread 135

RECIPES FROM MONACO
Pain de Gruau ✤ Finest Wheaten Bread 139
Panettone ✤ Italian Panettone 143
Pain Italien ✤ Italian Bread 146
Pain de Mie de Monaco ✤ Monaco Sandwich Bread 149

RECIPES FROM SISTERON
Fougasse ✤ Ladder Bread 153
Pain de Seigle Sisteron ✤ Sisteron Rye Bread 155

RECIPE FROM BEAUCAIRE
Pain de Beaucaire ✤ Beaucaire Bread 157

RECIPES FROM GRENOBLE
Pain Ordinaire Carême ✤ A Daily Loaf 163
Pain de Campagne Madame Doz ✤ Madame Doz' Peasant Loaf 165
Petites Galettes Salées ✤ Little Salted Biscuits 169

RECIPES FROM THE RHÔNE VALLEY
Le Muffin de Montélimar ✤ The Muffin of Montélimar 174
Le Bun de Montélimar ✤ The Bun of Montélimar 175
Schneckes ✤ Currant Rolls 178

RECIPES FROM ROMANS-SUR-ISÈRE
Pogne de Romans ✤ Romans Loaf 181
Petits Pains au Beurre ✤ Small Butter Loaves 185
La Ficelle de Romans ✤ Small Braided Breads of Romans 187

RECIPES FROM GANNAT
Gâteau de Gannat ✤ Gannat Clabber Bread 192
Piquenchagne ✤ Pear Bread 195
Pompe aux Gratons ✤ Crackling Bread 197
Galette de Gannat ✤ Gannat Cheese Bread 200

RECIPES FROM ROCHEFORT-MONTAGNE
La Tourte ✤ Round Country Loaf 203
La Tourte de Seigle ✤ Rye Country Loaf 205

RECIPES FROM WICHTRACH

Weggliteig ❧ Button Rolls   211
Gipfelteig ❧ Swiss Croissants   214
Nussgipfel ❧ Nut-filled Croissants   216
Stolle ❧ Stollen   218

RECIPES FROM STRASBOURG

Kugelhupf ❧ Kugelhupf   222
Kougelhopf Blanc ❧ White Kougelhopf   226
Kougelhopf Complet Biologique ❧ Whole Wheat Kougelhopf   228
Stolle de Noël ❧ Christmas Stollen   230
Pain de Seigle Strasbourg ❧ Strasbourg Rye Bread   232

RECIPES FROM CHARLEVILLE-MÉZIÈRES

Pain de Ménage ❧ Family Loaf   237
Les Pistolets ❧ Split Rolls   238
Chapelure et Croutons ❧ Breadcrumbs and Croutons   241

RECIPES FROM THE S.S. *FRANCE*

Petits Pains S.S. France ❧ Rolls S. S. *France*   246
Brioches S.S. France ❧ Brioches S. S. *France*   249
Croissants S.S. France ❧ Croissants S. S. *France*   253

Glossary   257

U.S., British, and Metric Equivalent Weights and Measures   259

Index   262

INTRODUCTION TO THE NEW EDITION

I remember clearly the day in 1978 that Bernard Clayton, Jr.'s *The Breads of France* arrived in my New York City kitchen. Finally, a book to fire my passion for bread baking! And linked to that, a chance to fuel my ever-growing love of France, its people, and its sacred traditions. As a journalist, food writer, and ardent home cook and bread baker, I found this book to be a model for all my labors.

At that time in America, artisanal bread baking was in its fledgling stage. Bread was purchased in supermarkets and was white and often flabby. There was not even a school for professional bakers to be found in all of America! It's no surprise, then, that home bread baking has always been a tradition in the American kitchen. When I was growing up in Milwaukee, Wisconsin, my Italian mother baked bread about once a week, usually on Saturdays. The loaves were deliciously yeasty, crusty, and white. At other times, she treated us to thick and crusty rectangles of homemade pizza, topped with her own tomato sauce and plenty of spice. Whenever a special meal was planned, she prepared the soft and golden white rolls known as refrigerator rolls, since they were put into the refrigerator for the long, slow, cool rise that would give them a very special flavor and improved character.

I followed in her footsteps, and wherever I lived as an adult—El Paso, Texas; Madison, Wisconsin; Washington, D.C; and then New York City—I baked bread, even grinding my own wheat into coarse flour and working with sourdough starters.

So when *The Breads of France* arrived on my doorstep, I plunged in. With Clayton's book on my kitchen counter, I created beautiful bagels following instructions gathered at the famed Goldenberg delicatessen in Paris; reveled in the success of André David's giant Honfleur Country Bread; prepared his Mousseline Brioche, rising and baking the buttery, egg-rich dough in oversized coffee cans; delighted in the orange flour water–flavored Pogne or Romans Loaf from the Rhône Valley; and sampled the great variety of sweet kugelhupf from Alsace. For those of us who thought French bread was only baguettes, croissants, and brioche, the book was a true revelation.

In 1980, I moved to Paris, Clayton's book in hand. Instantly, it became a model, a bible of sorts. Clayton's journey from one end of France to the other was the result of two key factors: a passion for bread and a sense of disciplined accuracy. *The Breads of France* was clearly not a book that was churned out in a matter of months, but was the result of years of zealous research, all those long, sometimes endless, always adventurous drives through the back roads, hamlets, villages, and cities of France. Like any good researcher, he took the name of a specialty bread, went directly to the source, walked into boulangeries and poked around, asking question after question. He took copious, detailed notes, and then returned home to his Indiana kitchen and tested and tested and retested until the results were satisfactory. And we were the beneficiaries.

Clayton taught both American home cooks and, later, artisanal American bakers that the real secret of French bread baking is simple: The key quality is patience. He taught us how to give in to the bread's basic nature, so it would develop slowly, at its own pace, to become all that it could possibly be in terms of flavor, texture, color, and character. He taught us how to knead breads by hand, and how to give the dough body and suppleness. He did not skip a detail, and with his careful instruction, we home bakers soon knew everything there was to know about equipment, ingredients, special tips, and techniques. He didn't ask us to go out and build wood-fired bread ovens or invest a fortune in special stoves. He made us feel confident, at home in the most modest of kitchens, and allowed us to succeed, flawlessly, time and again.

As Clayton clearly points out, the French don't bake bread at home. Why would they? They need only reach out one arm, with a boulangerie on every corner, offering crusty baguettes, huge golden country loaves, sweet brioche, and tempting *pains au chocolat.*

As I look back, *The Breads of France* was very much a model for my own first book, *The Food Lover's Guide to Paris*. Clayton's book encouraged me to search out the famed French bread expert Raymond Calvel, professor of professional bread bakers in Paris. In fact, my first freelance article upon my arrival in Paris was about the bakers of Paris, and reading of Clayton's experiences in *The Breads of France* gave me the courage to knock on the door of famed Parisian bread baker Pierre Poilâne, with whom I spent many memorable moments. Today, his son, Lionel, is a close friend and still one of the most inspirational men I know.

Today in Paris, in France, and now in the world, the name Poilâne is synonymous with huge, healthy loaves of country bread. Each day, more than 3 percent of Paris's 10 million residents consume one of his wholesome loaves, spreading them with butter or jam, pairing them with oysters, or fragrant raw-milk cheeses.

Years ago, Lionel pointed out that three of our most precious foods, and those that best define France—bread, cheese, and wine—are all fermented foods. Bread begins with flour, water, and a touch of yeast. Cheese begins with milk and a fermenting agent, such as rennet. Grapes become wine by being pressed and, with the help of either natural yeasts in the air or a touch of yeast to move the process along, transformed into wine. Every loaf of bread, every cheese, every bottle of wine develops its special character through the careful, very personal, and particular intervention of man.

Clayton introduces us to these men. Men who create authentic corn muffins and pumpkin breads from Basque country, those famed for their Twelfth-Night Cake from Carcassonne, breads made with cracklings and pears, those studded with walnuts, stuffed with prunes, or topped with coarse salt. Our bread repertoire, and our knowledge of the depth and variety of loaves available to us, was expanded, and we were introduced to personal loaves from Paris and Le Havre, Normandy and Provence, Monaco and Strasbourg, Carcassonne, and Bayonne.

Clayton wrote this book in a day when breads in France were still largely regional and traditional. Since then, the country has gone from an era of tradition, into a modern moment when bakers seemed to be losing their touch, into what is now a glorious moment in France's bread history, when an entire cadre of youthful bakers all around the country have moved towards more organic, multigrain breads. What a feast Clayton would have if he covered the same territory again!

The changing status of boulangeries in my Provençal village of 5,000 is a good example: When Clayton's book was first published, the bread in our village of Vaison-la-Romaine was completely uninteresting, which is why I continued to bake my own bread—partially out of passion, partially out of necessity. In the 1980s, supermarkets were beginning to smother the small, independent merchants, as the French were embracing all that was new and modern.

Thankfully, by the 1990s, the clock seemed to have turned back to tradition, as exceptionally wholesome, organic breads were no longer seen as a rarity or a luxury, but began to be taken for granted again. At my favorite village boulangerie, Le Pains des Moissons, young baker Denis Lefevre regularly turns out more than twenty different 100 percent organic, artisanal loaves, ranging from a brioche-like *pain aux fruits confits*, or candied fruit bread, to an irresistible *pain au fromage*, a cheese bread that makes me think of Clayton's *Galette de Gannat*, about which he endearingly says, "There is a surprise in a slice of the *brioche au fromage*. The cheese bits will have melted, leaving glistening pockets." Who could resist such a thought?

Today, more than twenty years since its first publication, Clayton's work seems pleasantly naïve, his homespun character totally endearing, and the amateur black-and-white photographs almost appear to have been taken in another century. And that remains much of its charm; we trusted Clayton then and we can continue to have confidence in and gratitude for his work. Bread is forever, and will never go out of fashion. In America, we now have good artisanal bread in almost every city, ranging from energetic, independent bread bakers to entire chains dedicated to creating wholesome, delicious, varied loaves of bread for every time of day and every occasion. One can't help but wonder how many of them were originally inspired by Clayton's travels and labors in his own kitchen.

As I read through the book one more time, so many years later, it occurs to me that the book still offers me plenty of inspiration. I think I will go into the kitchen now and make the *Brioche au Fromage*, or Cheese Brioche Loaf. And I don't know how I ever overlooked his star-shaped *Pain Seigle*, his dense, moist rye bread, fragrant as a result of a long, double fermentation. And should the breads not turn out 100 percent perfect the first time, I can always fall back on one of Clayton's greatest statements, "There are no mistakes in bread baking, only more bread crumbs."

—Patricia Wells
Paris, France
January 2002

INTRODUCTION

The idea for this book grew during the dozen years we traveled by foot, bicycle, canal boat, Irish gypsy wagon, train, and car across Europe and the British Isles searching for the exceptional loaf of bread. While some traveling was done on writing assignments, most of the time my wife and I crossed the Atlantic on vacation, with no deadlines and free to go wherever we wished.

Out of these travels, and extensive trips to all parts of the United States, came an interest in bread making far more serious and rewarding than anything I could have imagined at the beginning. Back home at Indiana University, where I am an editor and writer, a published collection of bread recipes began to be a possibility. With the help of kind friends as tasters, I tested hundreds of recipes for American breads and European favorites that I had gathered on my travels. The final result was *The Complete Book of Breads* (Simon and Schuster, 1973).

It was an exciting decade of travel and writing but there seemed to be much more to say about baking—especially French breads. France had so much to offer, and we returned there again and again.

Home bakers were writing to ask for more recipes for the breads of France than I had provided in *The Complete Book of Breads*. The students in my baking classes were asking to be shown the techniques for such traditional French favorites as brioches and croissants. The more I thought about the range of French breads in different regions of France, the more eager I was to visit with the *boulangers* who might be willing to share their secrets with me.

One day it was decided—a book about the breads of France.

Unlike the U.S., which has a long tradition of preparing bread in the home—and there are thousands of recipes in countless cookbooks that attest to this—the French have no such tradition. For good reason. The *boulanger*, the baker, is just around the corner creating crusty masterpieces two and three times a day, and once on Sunday. The French need only to hold out a hand and the *boulanger* puts a delicious loaf of bread in it. Even for the countryman, the *boulanger* will oblige by driving to the farm in his mini-truck to slip a warm loaf of unwrapped bread into the mailbox out front. Or, he may walk up to the house and impale the unwrapped loaf on a long nail by the door, there to await the farmer's wife when she comes in from the fields.

Indeed, why bake?

The French *boulangers* with whom I talked were convinced that the French housewife would never bake bread. I could always be certain of a smile when I suggested that someday she just might try. There was a time, of course, when rural families baked peasant loaves once a week in their own ovens, but this, too, passed when good roads brought them closer to town.

In France, the baking secrets are with the *boulanger,* and I am happy to report that he did not hesitate to share them. Any artisan is pleased when his work is admired. The French *boulanger* is no exception. In this search, I beat a path to his door in cities, towns, and villages in all regions of France. I found him hospitable, helpful, and more than a little pleased that his bread would be re-created in a great many American kitchens.

Like many Americans, I once thought a loaf of French bread meant just one thing— a baguette, a long golden loaf, with crackly crust and a honeycomb of irregular holes inside. It has been an adventure to learn that there are dozens and dozens more French breads—from every part of France—reflecting the characteristics of their regions and the creativity and expertise of the *boulangers* who make them. They range from such highly regarded breads as *pain brié* and *pogne de Romans,* which have never moved out of their native regions, to the lovely croissant and brioche, which seem to belong to everyone.

Are the breads of France difficult to make?

No, and baking them can be the same rewarding adventure that home bakers have found in the wide range of breads in *The Complete Book of Breads.*

When that book was published, its enthusiastic reception by both new and experienced home bakers amazed and pleased me. It was apparent that bread making was providing a creative outlet and a sense of fulfillment that could not always be found in doing other things. It was clear that a great many people felt as I did that working with something as warm, alive, and responsive as bread dough could be satisfying and pleasurable.

Exchanging recipes is a long-standing tradition in American kitchens and, to many, my book called for recipes in return. I received dozens of old family favorites, often with a loaf of bread as well, and always with a note expressing delight with the book's step-by-step approach—instructions complete, and problems anticipated.

A young home baker in Montana wrote, "You never left me dangling, wondering what would happen next."

A home baker in Virginia, who had been making white bread for more than a quarter of a century, never dared to make a rye loaf because she didn't know how the dough was supposed to feel in her hands. She had heard that it had a different consistency than white. "You warned me that it would be sticky—and it certainly was," she wrote. "But I wasn't surprised. I knew what to expect and I never had as much fun in my life as kneading that first batch of rye dough. It turned out beautifully, as you said it would."

I had been with the university for several years as a writer and editor for the School of Business. Teaching and teachers were all around me, but I had never taught. However, after *The Complete Book of Breads* was published, I decided to adapt an explicit writing style to classroom teaching. It adapted with considerable success. While the first classes were held to ten students, the response was so overwhelming that ten times that number wanted to enroll, forcing the classes to move from my demonstration/test kitchen to a university research kitchen where large numbers could be accommodated.

"How precise is bread making?" students wanted to know. "How critical are the times given for kneading, or for raising the dough or for baking?"

Baking is a relaxed art. There is no step in the bread-making process that cannot, in some way, be delayed or moved ahead just a bit to make it more convenient to fit it into a busy schedule. If you are called away overnight just when the dough is rising in the pans, oil the dough surfaces, cover with plastic wrap, and slip the pans in the refrigerator to keep until you return. If the dough you are shaping gets stubborn, pulls back, and refuses to be shaped, walk away from it for a few minutes. It will relax, and so will you.

While it is a relaxed art, bread making is not necessarily a gentle one, especially kneading. Don't baby dough. Break the kneading rhythm by occasionally throwing the ball of dough down hard against the work surface. Wham! Don't gentle it! Smack it down hard!

This kind of kneading—aggressive yet relaxed—gives the dough the elastic quality that allows it to rise to more than double its original bulk. If the dough is not sufficiently conditioned by strong kneading, it could collapse when it expands in the heat of the oven.

The only time I pay strict heed to a schedule in the baking process is when the dough is in the oven. Normally, I never leave the kitchen during the bake period. If I must, I carry a small clock-timer to remind me when to return. I want to be in the kitchen to shift the pans so they will brown evenly, and to decide when it is the right moment to take the golden loaves from the oven.

There are two other questions often asked that will give heart to anyone considering the first loaf.

"How can anything so delicious be so easy to make?" and "Why didn't I do this before?"

ACKNOWLEDGMENTS

There was a moment one day in France when I felt capable of speaking fluent and flawless French only because of a tremendous desire to do so. My rapport and sense of belonging was so strong with Monsieur André David of Honfleur that for an instant I was sure I could will myself to communicate wholly and completely. I could not, of course. My French is passable in the writing department but it is only mediocre when spoken.

During many trips to France to research this book, I was met always with friendliness, understanding, and goodwill. While my French did improve, I would never have dared to go as deeply into such a specialized field as baking without the patience of friends in France and the help of fine interpreters and translators—especially Nancy Lane, who could detect a nuance a continent away.

To the *boulangers*, their charming wives, and scores of others who wanted to see this book written as much as I wanted to write it—*merci mille fois!*

In France and Switzerland, thanks in particular to:

Monsieur Gaston Bichet of Bracieux, whose charm was surpassed only by his talents as a chef and *boulanger*.

Monsieur Raymond Calvel, professor of baking at the national school for *boulangers* in Paris and author of *La Boulangerie Moderne,* from whose pages I took compass readings all along the way. Eyrolles, Paris, for permission to quote from *La Boulangerie Moderne.*

Monsieur and Madame Georges Coquet of Romans-sur-Isère, for recipes and help in learning to braid a *ficelle.*

Monsieur André David of Honfleur, for sharing his wisdom in many matters, especially baking.

Monsieur and Madame Bernard Gautier, for good breads and in admiration of Monsieur Gautier's coolness in front of the American visitor when the oven was exploding.

Monsieur Jean Grey of Grenoble, for leading the way to the ovens of Record II and then to the family home high in the mountains to be with Madame Doz and Monsieur and Madame Blanc Aimé.

Professor Thomas Kelly and Madame Georgina Frank of Strasbourg, for allowing me to use the Indiana-Purdue Overseas Study Program headquarters as my base in Alsace.

Walter LaBorie of Menton, my brother-in-law, for sharing my enthusiasm for this project, giving me the benefit of his considerable knowledge of food and drink in France and mapping my travels.

The editors of *Larousse Gastronomique,* for compiling an unsurpassed reference volume that helped clear up many questions.

Monsieur Louis Malleret of Gannat, for sharing his great knowledge of Gannatois culture, mores, and breads.

Monsieur Fernand Moureau, the *ancien boulanger* of Beaucaire, for many detailed letters written because, as he explained it, "I would like very much to see you succeed."

Monsieur and Madame Yves Ordonneau of Angoulême, for bringing work to an absolute halt so they could explain their recipe for the exceptional *Brioche Vendéenne.*

Messieurs Léon Tardy-Pandit and Yves Sauvignon of the S. S. *France,* for their recipes, technical help, suggestions, encouragement, and friendship.

Monsieur and Madame Albert Phillips of Monaco, for sharing recipes for breads that often go up the hill to the Palace.

Monsieur Pierre Poilâne of Paris, for his recipes, inspiration, and friendship over the years.

Monsieur and Madame Roger Rebolledo of Limoux, for their recipe for pepper bread and the patience to explain how it is shaped.

Monsieur and Madame Jean Pierre Scholler of Strasbourg, for introducing me to the French world of *pain de régime.*

Herr and Frau Rolf Thomas of Wichtrach, Switzerland, for showing me more than just the magnificent view of the Alps from the Bäckerei window.

Some breads and baking equipment in the author's studio kitchen.

My thanks also to Centre d'Information des Farines et du Pain, Paris; Ecole Nationale Supérieure de Meunerie et des Industries Céréalières, Paris; Secretary General R. Deroide and M. Jacques Luccioni, Syndicat Patronal de la Boulangerie, Paris; Gerard Escarpit, Soumoulou; Jo Goldenberg, Paris; Jouvin Bessière, Hôtel du Lion d'Or, Bayeux; Christiane Ullern, Syndicat d'Initiative, Honfleur; Richard Olney, Solliès-Toucas; Count and Countess Charles d'Andigne, Montélimar; René Dessagne, Allier-Magazine, Limoges; Monsieur Charamnac, Président du Syndicat des Boulangers, Limoges; Madame A. Bacharan, Carcassonne; and Monsieur Morel, Grenoble.

In the United States, my thanks to:

The *National Observer,* for permission to adapt my column on home-crafted baking pans for inclusion here.

Evelyn Gendel and Patricia O'Connell Read, who did so much to bring my earlier book, *The Complete Book of Breads,* to fruition and then, lo and behold, were there to give this effort their enthusiastic support from inception forward.

Sadonna Spurlin, a friend and a marvelous stenotypist with the mind and manner of an editor.

Harry E. Roach, my father-in-law, who spent most of a lifetime as the owner of an excellent bakery in a small northern Indiana town, and whose knowledge of baking has helped me immeasurably.

Joan Raines, author's representative and friend, who can move with equal ease from erudite matters to deadlines, editorial content, and all those things that prod, push, and propel an author into doing his best.

Finally, my wife, who shared these travels and these breads and who did so much to make doing this book a lot of fun.

—B. C., Jr.

PART I

Essentials of French Bread Making

INGREDIENTS AND HOW THEY ARE COMBINED

The glory of French bread is its simplicity. Flour, water, salt, and leavening are the basic ingredients of many doughs. But the way the ingredients are assembled, their proportions, and how the dough is shaped and baked differ considerably from shop to shop, and give each *boulangerie's* product its unique character.

One of the secrets of French bread baking is the *boulanger's* willingness to give the dough whatever time is necessary to allow it to develop taste and character. He will not rush it. He will not take shortcuts.

The recipes in this book reflect this concern for the proper development of the dough. They also reflect the care the *boulanger* gives every aspect of baking—from flour and leavenings to oven temperatures and humidity. Each *boulanger's* recipe has been taken apart, tested, and adapted to the American kitchen. The instructions in all of the recipes are divided into timed steps so that at no point are you left to guess what should be done next. The only surprise in this book is the pleasant and recurring surprise that it was you who baked the handsome loaf of bread just taken from the oven.

All recipes can safely be reduced by dividing in half. Don't bother to divide a packet of yeast, however. The action will be slightly more vigorous but presents no problem. One caution: be certain there is sufficient dough to fill an appropriate pan in the amount called for in the recipe or a less-than-attractive loaf may result.

Bread making may sound complicated—but it really isn't. Many students in my bread-making classes and many readers of my first bread book had never baked before. Yet they learned very quickly to make a variety of breads. In the process of learning, they have found it helpful to know some of the essentials of bread making as it relates to all breads but especially to the breads of France.

Flour

The French *boulanger* admires American white flour and wishes he could get more of it. He makes do with what he has, and he does very well with it, to be sure. Some *boulangers*—Monsieur Poilâne in Paris and Monsieur David in Honfleur—use special flours made from wheat grown according to their specifications. The wheat grown along the Normandy coast for Monsieur David, for example, is fertilized with the local seaweeds.

The flour in most of these recipes is not sifted. The amount of flour given is only approximate because flour varies greatly in its power to absorb moisture. Flour kept in a warm kitchen in wintertime will be dry and far more receptive to liquid than flour stored in a humid room in summertime.

In the latter stages of mixing dough, add additional flour sparingly. It is better to slowly add the last bit of flour to be certain the texture of the dough is just right rather than to overwhelm the dough with flour. If you do go beyond the point where the dough is soft and elastic, and the dough is hard, add water. The dough will accept it, though reluctantly.

The gluten content in flour is an important factor in baking. Gluten is a plant protein found chiefly in wheat flour. When kneaded, it forms an elastic network throughout the dough that catches the carbon dioxide gas thrown off by the yeast and expands the dough. The greater the gluten content of the flour, the more expansive the dough, and the larger the loaf. Most U.S. and Canadian white flours milled for commercial use have a high gluten content—11 to 14 percent—and are unexcelled for bread making. They are much prized in France to correct or improve French flour, which has a lower gluten content.

In North America, the flours milled from two types of wheat and a mixture of the two interest the home baker most. Soft wheat flour, low in gluten, makes a tender product and is used chiefly in cake flours and cake mixes. Hard wheat, grown in the Western prairie country of the U.S. and Canada, has a higher gluten content. It is milled into "bread" flour that produces loaves of greater volume.

All-purpose flour is a blend of hard and soft wheat flours, enriched and, in most cases, chemically bleached. It is a versatile flour that fills most of our baking needs.

So-called unbleached flour, which nevertheless is bleached by an aging process, is a blend but with more hard wheat flour added to give it the same baking qualities as the chemically bleached.

U.S. all-purpose flour is very close in its characteristics to French bread flour. However, French flour gets no chemical treatment whatsoever except for minute additions of ascorbic acid to the dough, which is allowed because of its relation to natural Vitamin C. Unbleached U.S. flour, therefore, has perhaps the closest affinity to French flour.

Some recipes in this book call for U.S. hard-wheat bread flour, the French *farine supérieure*.

In some recipes, alternate flours are listed. The first is preferred in the recipe but the second can be substituted with good results.

Whole wheat flour, which is made from the whole wheat kernel, is relatively easy to work and knead because it has its full quota of gluten. While any whole wheat flour may be used in these recipes, some of you will prefer whole wheat ground between stones because it gives the slice a rougher texture and has more fiber. The sharp edge of the bran in the flour cuts the gluten strands, reducing somewhat the size of the loaf compared with one made with the same volume of white flour. Graham and pumpernickel whole wheat are other varieties of stone-ground whole wheat flours.

Whole wheat flour contains the whole germ or fat portion of the wheat kernel. If it is to be stored for any length of time, whole wheat flour should be kept in the refrigerator or freezer to prevent rancidity.

Rye is a grain with little gluten in its makeup. Hence, most of the time, rye flour must be mixed with white or whole wheat flours to give the dough a gluten network to trap the fermenting gases. Rye flour is either white, medium, dark or rye meal, or pumpernickel. The one most commonly used in rye bread making is medium flour. Dark rye and pumpernickel are coarsely ground with bran particles left in. White rye, which is used to make a rye bread light in color, is seldom used in home baking.

Only in southern France, in and near the Basque region, is corn used in bread making. Most Europeans consider it "gross food," fit only for livestock. Nevertheless, the Basque breads made with cornmeal are delicious and can be made with either white or yellow cornmeal. There is no gluten in cornmeal, so batter made with it can be beaten until smooth without danger of toughening it.

Leavening

Almost all breads are leavened in one or more ways. Without leavening, bread would come out of the oven as flat as a Swedish baker intends *knäckebröd*, rye wafers, to be. Yeast is the most common leavening agent. Yeast cells, wild or cultivated, feasting on the natural sugars in the mixture, will produce carbon dioxide gas to raise the dough.

Yeast cells are introduced in some fashion into almost all French bread doughs. A Basque pumpkin bread and a cornbread, leavened with beaten egg whites, are the exceptions.

The *boulanger* has several choices as to how he will leaven a batch of dough. The first step in many French recipes is to make a "starter" or *levain*. This may begin with a simple mixture of flour, water, and yeast, called a *poolish*. Or, the *boulanger* may start with a piece of dough cut from the previous batch and use it to begin the fermentation action in the new mix. This is the *chef*. After the starter has begun to mature, the next step is to make a "sponge" by mixing the starter into a larger quantity of flour and water. This gives the yeast cells new life and they begin anew, doubling in number in about two hours. The *boulanger* may also use the "direct method" of adding the yeast to the other ingredients without prior fermentation. Or, he may decide to add the yeast to the *levain* to be certain the dough is strong and robust for some special bread he is about to make.

The *boulanger*'s heavy reliance on a starter springs from a long history of baking with a yeast that was less than certain. There is a parallel in several Western U.S. frontier recipes that call for *both* yeast and baking powder. The pioneer cook felt that one or the other was almost certain to work and if both leavenings happened to be alive and active, so much the better.

It is different today. The starter contributes more to the good taste of the bread than strength to the leavening. The *boulanger* now unabashedly uses yeast to revitalize the starter if it seems to need help. In fact, it is rare among *boulangers* who make bread with starters to do so with pure starter dough. Almost all of them depend on yeast as a booster. It is usually dissolved in water and added to the dough before the final kneading. While the *boulanger* uses large 1-pound ($1/2$-kilo) bricks of fresh yeast, we home bakers have a choice of instant dry yeast or fresh compressed cakes. In my kitchen, I use only dry yeast because the packets, either Red Star or Fleishmann's, are so readily available and so easy to store unrefrigerated.

Boulangers at Work

Strasbourg

Wichtrach

Bayeux

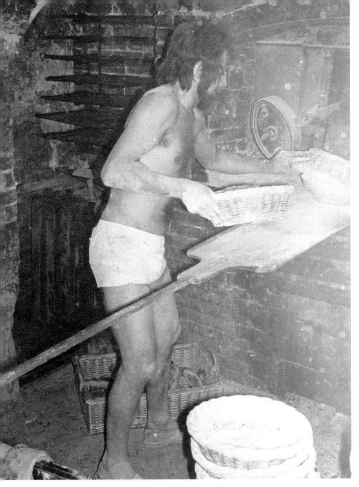

Poilâne's cellar oven at
8 rue du Cherche-Midi, Paris.

One of six ovens in the author's Indiana kitchen. It's a wood-burning favorite, but others
bake equally as well.

There is no need to "proof" this modern breed of finely ground yeast granules to prove that it is alive and viable, as bakers a few generations back felt they must do with all yeast. "Proofing" was a common practice. I have baked hundreds of loaves and never have I had yeast fail to work in the dough. Heat above 140° will kill it, of course. Cold will not destroy it, only slow its action down, and this can be to the home baker's advantage by stretching out the development time to fit a more convenient schedule.

Brewer's yeast is not a leavening agent. Known also as nutritional or primary yeast, it has been heat-treated and cannot be substituted for regular yeast. It is, however, an excellent source of biologically complete and digestible protein and is often used in baking.

Water Temperatures

The water temperatures in the recipes of this book were selected on the assumption that the ideal temperature of French bread dough is 75° and most home kitchens are close to this ideal temperature. The French *boulanger* may adjust temperature of the water to achieve the correct temperature for his dough. First, he determines the temperature of his workroom, which may be quite hot, and the temperature of the flour, which may be stored in another and cooler part of the building. He averages these two figures. If it is above 75°, he adds cool water. If it is lower, he boosts it with warm water. His formula is simple: room temperature plus flour temperature plus water temperature should be equal to three times the ideal temperature of 75°.

If room and storage temperatures vary greatly in the home kitchen, you may wish to make adjustments by using this simple formula.

Kneading

Although hand kneading has been supplanted by machinery for most French *boulangers,* the older ones have not forgotten the techniques.

First comes the *fraisage,* the mixing of the ingredients until every trace of water and flour has disappeared and the mass becomes dough. The dough is given a short rest while the *boulanger* cleans the bowl. The dough is then kneaded, and lifted up and thrown down against the work surface again and again until it is cohesive and elastic.

If the dough is too firm or inelastic after the first kneading, water may be added (*bassinage*). If, on the other hand, the dough is soft and slack, more flour is added.

Whether in France or in your kitchen, dough responds in the same way. When the dough is kneaded, gluten, a plant protein found chiefly in wheat flour, forms an elastic network to trap the carbon dioxide gases produced by the yeast.

Kneading should be done at a comfortable height that allows the arms to be fully extended, palms resting on the work surface. The rough mass is turned out of the bowl onto the work surface, which has been sprinkled lightly with flour. If the dough is sticky, begin by lifting and turning it with a dough scraper or dough knife. Add sprinkles of flour as needed. Fold the dough in half, push down hard against it with your hands, and at an angle away from the body. As you pull back, give the dough a quarter of a turn. Fold it. Push. Repeat the sequence—turn-fold-push.

Break this rhythmic pattern by frequently lifting the ball of dough above the table and bringing it crashing down against the work surface. Wham! This is a wholly satisfying action that alerts the household to the fact that bread is being made. Don't gentle the dough! Pummel and push it! Return to the cadence of push-turn-fold.

Vigorous action gives dough body and suppleness. It will be elastic when stretched. It will not stick when it is handled. It can be folded and pushed about, yet retain its ability to spring back.

I am glad to pass on this test I was shown in a Midwest farm kitchen to indicate when the dough has enough flour and has developed the proper texture. Hit the ball of dough with an open hand. Hold the hand on the dough for a count of ten. Lift off the hand. If the hand is clean—no dough particles clinging—the dough is about ready to put aside to rise, depending on the kneading time prescribed by the recipe. If dough sticks to the hand, add sprinkles of flour.

Rising

Dough comes of age when it rises. It has been pushed and shoved by hand or twisted under the dough hook of an electric mixer, and now comes the quiet time when it grows and matures. Now is the time for the yeast cells to multiply and give off carbon dioxide to expand and puff the dough.

The French baker allows his dough to rise at temperatures considered cool by most American home bakers—between 70° and 75°. It takes longer, true, but it gives the dough time to develop flavor. It can be speeded up in a warmer room, of course, but that is not the French way.

A heavy stoneware bowl is ideal for raising most doughs because it keeps a constant temperature during the long period when the dough is expanding. For the first rising, cover the bowl with plastic wrap. Pull it tightly across the top of the bowl and the dough will not lose moisture.

The doughs for most of the big robust French loaves with large, irregular holes in the slice should rise to two to three times the volume of the ball when first placed in the bowl.

There are two ways to determine if the dough has risen sufficiently. One is by watching it move up the side of the bowl to a place you have earlier determined is two or three times the volume, depending on the recipe. The other is to press one or two fingers into the dough near the edge. If the indentations remain, the dough has risen sufficiently.

After the dough has been punched down, formed into whatever shape and size loaves you want, and placed in the appropriate bread pans or held in cloths (to be transferred later to a baking sheet), it is allowed to rise again—expanding to three times its volume for the classic French mealtime bread. The dough is often covered with wax paper or a cloth during the second rising to prevent a "skin" forming.

While some place the bowl of dough in the oven to rise—heat turned on for *1 minute,* if electric, or by the heat of the pilot light, if gas—I prefer to leave the dough an additional ¹/₂ hour or so at room temperature to give it every opportunity to develop great flavor.

If the final rising of the shaped loaves has been allowed to go on too long (which may cause the expanded dough to collapse in the heat of the oven), turn the dough back onto the work surface. Knead briefly and reshape. No loss. Dough will double or triple in volume in about two-thirds of the usual time.

The Shape of Loaves

To most North Americans, French bread means a long loaf of crusty white or near-white bread to be cut into thick slices or broken off in big chunks to be eaten with a meal. To the French, their daily bread may be a round loaf as well as a long loaf, and there is increasing interest in whole-grain breads, health breads, and *pains de régime* (diet breads).

French breads may vary in weight from a big 4¹/₂-pound (2-kilo) loaf to a 2-ounce *petit pain.*

The most popular French loaf is long and cylindrical. It may be a 2-pound *pain ordinaire,* a 1-pound *baguette* or *bâtard,* or a ¹/₂-pound *ficelle* or *flûte.*

The long loaves may rise in long cloth-lined baskets (*bannetons*), or between folds of light canvas (*couches*) spread on the countertop, or in shallow pans with curved sides that go directly into the oven with the risen dough.

In my kitchen, I allow the dough for a variety of long and round loaves to make its final rise on a baking sheet, covered with a cloth. The loaves go directly into the oven on the baking sheet.

The country or peasant loaf is rugged, heavily crusted, and usually round. It is often raised in a round cloth-lined *banneton,* which the *boulanger* overturns to deposit the risen dough on a long-handled peel (*pelle*). In the *boulangerie,* it is thrust into the oven and the wooden peel is jerked from under the dough to drop it on the hot oven floor. The home baker can approximate the effect by overturning the risen dough onto a preheated baking sheet which goes into the oven, or onto a baking stone in the oven.

The *couronne* or crown loaf is raised in a basket into which a center tube has been woven (in appearance much like an angel food tin) and around which the dough is shaped.

The best-known country loaves are *pain de campagne* and *tourte.* There is also the ball-shaped *boule,* the *boulat* with flour sprinkled over the top crust, and the *miche.* The rolls or small breads (*petits pains*) come in an assortment of round and oval shapes. Some have topknots; the *pistolet* is pressed with a stick into a double roll before it rises.

While these are the most widely recognized of the breads of France, this book is devoted to dozens of others, regional as well as countrywide favorites, that come in many other shapes, including braids, crescents, and stalks of wheat (*épis*).

Dough Volume

We need not be concerned with measuring the volume of dough for a loaf of French bread that is to be baked on a baking sheet or baking stone. There is also considerable freedom in estimating dough volume for the long slender loaves to be baked in open-ended U-shaped French bread pans. The roll of dough fills less than half the volume of the pan. For a typical *baguette,* I place a long roll of dough weighing about 1 pound in an open-ended pan 16 to 18 inches long. If I am baking for a buffet at which smaller slices are desired, I will use $1/2$ or $3/4$ of a pound of dough in the same pan.

But the volume of dough placed in a rectangular bread pan must be more exact if it is to yield an attractive loaf. Too little dough will produce a stunted loaf, while too much can create a top-heavy loaf.

To avoid such problems, determine the total amount by weight or measure, then decide how many loaves of what size you wish to bake. Follow the chart.

	Pan Size	*Volume*	*Weight*
LARGE	$9 \times 5 \times 3$	3 cups	2 pounds
MEDIUM	$8^{1}/_2 \times 4^{1}/_4 \times 2^{1}/_2$	$2^{1}/_2$ cups	$1^{1}/_2$ pounds
SMALL	$7^{1}/_2 \times 3^{1}/_2 \times 2^{1}/_2$	$1^{1}/_2$ cups	1 pound
MINIATURE	$5^{1}/_2 \times 3 \times 2$	$3/_4$ cup	$1/_2$ pound
SUB-MINI	$4^{1}/_2 \times 2^{1}/_2 \times 1^{1}/_2$	$1/_2$ cup	5 to 6 ounces

EQUIPMENT THAT CONTRIBUTES TO A PERFECT LOAF

Work Surfaces

The ideal working surface is large enough for the assembling of all the ingredients, the mixing, the kneading, and the shaping. A space 2 feet by 2 feet is adequate for almost all bread making, reserving the right to move special doughs to the dining table (or even the floor) if need be. I made all the loaves in *The Complete Book of Breads* on a 2-foot-square formica countertop between the stove and the sink and on an 18 × 18-inch board in our trailer while traveling the U. S.

Formica is a good surface, but it can be scratched with a knife or dough scraper. Maple is my preference, but it must be cleaned thoroughly after each batch of dough. Stainless steel is very good. The height of the countertop or table is more important than its composition. It should be high enough to allow you to rest the palms of your hands, arms extended, on the top surface. If it is too low, a backache will result; too high, you cannot push down on the dough. You can push it away from you, but that isn't kneading.

Bowls

A loaf begins life in a bowl and, for this important event, the bowl should have several qualities. It should be easy to hold, large enough to accept all of the ingredients without their spilling over, heavy enough to maintain an even temperature during risings, yet not too large to go into the refrigerator when dough must be chilled.

It may take several bowls to do all of these things. Large ones and small ones. Stoneware, earthenware, and heavy ceramic bowls are my favorites, and I have collected a number of them. They also add touches of color to my kitchen. I follow antique shows and farm sales and have acquired a half dozen heavy crocks 9½ inches in diameter and 5 inches deep. These are ideal for two-loaf recipes. I also have one 18-inch giant in which I mix big batches of dough for country loaves.

Stainless-steel bowls, such as those used with an electric mixer, and plastic bowls are usable, certainly, although they reflect outside temperature change more quickly.

Electric Mixer

A large ball of dough made with five or six cups of flour will climb up the dough hook of my electric mixer with maddening persistence and try to work its way into the gears of the machine. I shower it with forceful language but nothing stops it unless I force the dough to remain below the wide metal collar with a rubber scraper.

If I am making a large number of loaves, I will allow the mixer to share the task, but then I must stand by the machine, scraper against the collar, while the dough is being kneaded.

Even when I use the machine, I still start the dough by hand, otherwise I cannot feel the texture of the dough. It never seems to spring to life in a machine with the enthusiasm it does when kneaded by hand. Part of this, I believe, is that the dough is deprived of the warmth of my hands. The cold dough hook gives nothing in return.

Yet, if for you kneading is a test of strength, use a mixer; if not, knead by hand.

Don't attempt to mix heavy doughs with a machine that is not guaranteed by the company to knead dough. Mixing and kneading put a strain on small motors and even my large machine gets hot during the few minutes it takes to knead a batch of dough. Do not use lightweight or portable or handheld mixers because the danger of damage is too great. They are fine for batters no thicker than pancake mixes, but that is all.

Dough Knife

Known as a *coupe-pâte* by the *boulanger,* a dough knife, dough blade, or pastry scraper is a rectangular piece of steel (about 4 by 5 inches), with a wooden handle that quickly becomes an extension of the arm as you work with French bread doughs. It is great for lifting and working soft doughs that are sticky during the early part of kneading. A thin, flexible blade is preferred over a heavy, stiff one. A 4-inch putty knife is an excellent substitute.

Rolling Pin

There are only a few doughs among French breads that need a rolling pin. Croissant, yes. The layering of dough and butter calls for a heavy rolling pin. My favorite weighs 6 pounds, has ball bearings in the handles, and rolls an 18-inch-wide swath. It just dares chilled dough and butter not to roll out as they should. The graceful, tapered French rolling pin is marvelous for many kitchen chores but it is almost too light for croissants.

Bannetons

The *banneton* is a woven basket, cloth-lined, in which the *boulanger* places dough to rise. It can be duplicated by shopping for a selection among round and rectangular wicker baskets sold for serving bread and rolls in all kitchenware departments. The round basket I use for one pound of *pain ordinaire* dough, for example, is 9 inches in diameter and 3 inches deep. The cloth inside the basket is tied to the bottom and around the top so it will stay in place when the dough is later turned onto the baking sheet. The cloth is tightly woven and heavy—duck, denim, or light canvas.

Couches

Dough for long loaves that will be baked directly on baking sheets, baking stones, or on the oven floor can be helped to retain its shape by an *apprêt sur couche,* as the *boulanger* calls it. This means placing the shaped dough for its final rising (*apprêt*) between folds of light canvas (*couche*). The long edges of the canvas are held in place by pieces of wood to force the dough to push up, not out. A pastry cloth or a length of duck or light canvas will make a couche for your dough.

Baking Sheet

A heavy baking or cookie sheet, silicone-coated, such as Teflon, is the best because it does not have to be brushed with oil each time before using. Cleanup is easy with only a swipe of a paper towel. Get the largest and heaviest sheet your oven will accommodate, leaving a 1-inch clearance on all sides for the flow of hot air to circulate. The heavier the baking sheet, the better it will retain heat when preheated, and the better it will duplicate baking on an oven floor. Some heavy-gauge dark steel baking sheets (26 by 17 inches) weigh more than 6 pounds! Excellent.

For hearth loaves and rolls, there is no need for a solid lip or bead around the sheet, but it is necessary for croissants, which may ooze butter that can drip to the floor of the oven and burn.

Baking Stone

New on the U.S. market is a baking stone made in two different shapes—a circle 16 inches in diameter or a rectangle 14 by 16 inches. It is a thick plate of light brown, heat-retaining composition stone that actually gets harder the more it is used. The $1/2$-inch-thick baking surface is on a $1/2$-inch raised platform of the same material and has channels molded into it to allow the heat to circulate freely. Move the bread to a new position on the stone at least once during the bake period to allow for temperature variations in your oven.

The stone weighs about 10 pounds and is heavy enough to closely duplicate the baking qualities of the brick floor of a French oven. Place it on the lowest oven shelf used for baking. The oven is also a good place to store the baking stone and it can even be left there when using the oven for other purposes.

Unlike a baking sheet that can be moved in and out of the oven to receive the dough, the preheated stone is better left in place in the oven and the bread taken to it. Pans or baking sheets containing dough can also be placed on the heavy stone to produce a thicker bottom crust.

A little cornmeal sprinkled on the surface of the baking stone is all that is necessary before slipping the shaped and raised dough onto it. It's fine for all breads except croissants, which may drip butter. It can be used as well for pizza and pie crusts.

The round stone is large enough to accept a large hearth loaf or two small hearth loaves, or three medium ($8^{1}/_{2} \times 4^{1}/_{2}$) bread pans plus a small one. The rectangular stone is only slightly larger in total area and will accept a total of four medium pans.

French Bread Pans

The loaf of *pain ordinaire* in the classic shape of a *baguette, ficelle, flûte,* or *bâtard* is baked in special pans or raised between cloths and baked directly on the hot oven floor. In France, the pans for two to six loaves are pressed out of a single piece of metal.

In the U. S., several firms are producing two-loaf pans. One of the oldest, based in Washington, D. C., has sold an unbelievable number of aluminum pans. Another U.S. manufacturer (Ekco) is producing a dark brown, silicone-coated pair that gives excellent results. (See Sources of Supply.)

For a number of years, I have been baking French loaves and long sticks of rye bread in pans that I fashioned in my workshop from stovepipe that I bought at Honey Jones's country store perched on a ridge road in the hills of southern Indiana. I didn't purchase the pipe, I must confess; Honey loved my whole wheat bread, so we traded.

The stovepipe pans cost less than a dollar or whatever a length of ordinary stovepipe costs at the moment at the local hardware store. Surprisingly, stovepipe did not go out of fashion along with high-button shoes, but is still much used in rural America and in city homes without central heating.

It is an excellent baking tin because it absorbs rather than reflects the heat.

Stovepipe can be purchased at most hardware stores and is sent from the manufacturers with the seam left open so a great number can be economically shipped stacked together. Don't snap the seam shut. Leave it open. The diameter of the pipe must be at least 10 inches, and most are considerably more.

Essentially, the procedure is to bend the stovepipe to form two troughs that will remain open-ended. With tin shears, cut the stovepipe to a length that will fit into the oven, with a 1-inch clearance at the ends. (My pans are 18 and 24 inches long.)

For the most convenient size, one that will bake two 1-pound loaves, make a cut the length of the metal 10 inches from one edge. Discard or reserve the other piece for a later project. Next, form a $^{1}/_{2}$-inch bead along the long edges by turning back the metal with pliers and beating with a hammer. A raw edge can be as sharp and dangerous as a razor. The ends, however, need not be beaded.

Holding it with both hands, press and bend the length of metal against the edge of a table to make two long troughs of equal dimensions. Viewed from the end, it will now resemble a soft or slouching W. Mold the roughly formed pan with your hands and form a somewhat flat surface on the bottom of each trough. It may look rough and ill-shaped, but the bread it holds will be slender and elegant.

There is also nothing better than an empty 1- or 2-pound coffee can for baking bread, especially the tall, cylindrical loaves such as *mousseline* brioche and *panettone.* First, it is readily available at no cost in any kitchen, if not yours then perhaps a neighbor's. Second, and most important, the printing on the metal absorbs rather than reflects the heat to give the loaf a handsome deep-brown crust. (Shiny aluminum allows only a light tan.) Last, the can is expendable, so if the bread should stick, cut out the bottom and push out the obstinate loaf.

To prepare a coffee can, wash, dry well, and grease lightly. Be certain the spare plastic lid usually fitted on the bottom is taken off. And as a precaution against dough sticking, at least to the bottom, drop a round of greased wax paper in the can. Most coffee cans have two indented rings around them, but the bread will shrink during baking so these are no problem.

For a yeast bread, fill the can a little more than halfway. Cover it with a piece of plastic wrap, let it rise to the edge of the can—no more. "Oven-spring"—the action of the heat on the yeast dough—will blossom it up, out, and over the edge like a mushroom.

A word of caution: Place the can on a lower rack so that the rising dough will not attempt to push its way through the roof of the oven.

Conventional Bread Pans

Don't discard your shiny aluminum bread pan because it doesn't brown bread as well as dark metal or Pyrex pans. When you turn out the loaf and find it less brown than you wanted, put it back in the oven—without the pan—for an additional 5 to 10 minutes. The crust will brown nicely.

The silicone-coated (Teflon) pans are excellent—they will produce a deep brown crust with no sticking.

Coups de Lame

The last act before the loaves are baked is the *coup de lame*—literally, the blow of the blade—the diagonal slit that gives French bread its distinctive appearance.

In France, a special set of blades or *lames* are used to make the cuts. The most common is a straight blade with a slightly curved tip. I find a single-edge razor blade perfectly suitable to make the classical *coups de lame.*

The angle of the cut influences the development of the loaf. To make the *coup de lame* the cutting edge of the razor blade is not drawn vertically hut at an angle toward the horizontal.

A long *baguette* (24 inches) may receive up to ten cuts with the blade. The shorter *bâtard* will get four to five.

One point the *boulanger* will insist upon is that no diagonal cut should start beyond the end of the cut above it or the dough between the two points will tear rather than fold open.

While the long loaves take diagonal cuts, many of the round loaves are given cuts in a tic-tac-toe grid design. The *pogne de Romans* is a *couronne* or crown that is cut in a triangle with the curving lines crossing over. Other round loaves are slit three times across the dough or are given a single cut that gives the effect of dividing the loaf into two pieces.

Peel

While the *boulanger* needs a peel (*pelle*) with a 10-foot handle to move breads in and out of the oven, home bakers can make do with a piece of thin wood, formica, masonite, or tough cardboard, about 18 inches long and 8 inches wide, to pick up dough raised between the folds of cloth (*couche*) and to lift it onto a baking sheet or baking stone. There is also a short-handled peel that pizza makers use, on which I will let a hearth loaf rise before carrying it to the preheated stone in the oven.

A peel is a necessity, certainly, if one has a deep oven in which the bread is baked directly on the hot oven floor. I have such an outdoor adobe oven, as well as one indoors of brick, both wood-fired. The indoor oven is only 30 inches deep, so I move the dough into it with a peel that has no handle.

Bread Knife

A sharp knife adds a touch of professionalism that a good loaf of bread deserves. A slice of bread is only as attractive as a knife will permit it to be. A dull knife can wreck the most beautiful bread, while a sharp knife can do wonders with a less-than-perfect loaf.

There are a number of excellent knives on the market. I use a stainless-steel Swiss knife. Now about ten years old, the knife has cut thousands of slices, has never been sharpened, and yet is as sharp as a razor. The secret is that I respect the blade and use it only for bread.

Atomizer

A fine spray of water into a hot oven from an atomizer (a window-cleaner bottle or plant sprayer) will substitute for a pan of water in the bottom of the oven to make steam. I prefer the pan because a spray of cool water against the hot light bulb in the oven can be a shattering experience. However, point away from the bulb and there should be no problem in creating a satisfactory blanket of steam.

Cooling Rack

While bread can be left to cool on a spare oven rack, the space between the bars is usually too great for the hot bread to rest without leaving unsightly depressions in the bottom crust. A woven metal rack, with $1/4$- or $1/2$-inch spacing, will give firm support to the bottom crust. A rack is also a good place on which to rest a loaf of frozen bread while it thaws. It will not sweat against the countertop.

Pastry Wheel or Cutter

A pastry wheel is simply a circular knife, good for both lightly marking the dough and cutting without pulling the dough askew. Some imported wheels are twins—a plain wheel on one arm and a *jagger* on the other. The latter will give a jagged edge similar to that made by pinking shears on cloth. Equally good is a pizza cutter.

Nut Grinder

Nuts can be chopped in a bowl or on a cutting board, but they may fly all over the kitchen. The blender chops them too fine. If your food processor does not have a grinder attachment, I suggest a small hand-operated nut grinder that is good also for the hard cheeses. There is a French one, Mouli, with three different cylinders.

Ovens and How They Work

OVEN TEMPERATURE

The oven is perhaps the most important piece of equipment in bread baking, and the correct oven temperature is one of the most important factors in producing a delicious loaf of bread. A loaf is no better than the oven in which it is baked. An oven too hot will burn the loaf. An oven too cool will not bake it. An oven just right will produce a master-piece! For several years, I have asked each of my students to test their ovens at home with a reliable thermometer, such as a Taylor columnar. We have discovered that almost all ovens are surprisingly inaccurate—by a wide margin! Ovens will vary as much as 100°. *too hot* to 150° *too cool*, a range of 250°.

Don't trust the oven thermostat, even one in a new stove. Keep it honest by investing in a thermometer. My ovens are checked regularly by servicemen, but even then I take a temperature reading *each time* I bake. Even an oven that is calibrated correctly today will slowly lose its accuracy over a period of several months of daily baking.

The uniformity of heat in ovens will vary from side to side and from back to front. To compensate for this, move the loaves once or twice during the bake period to expose them to various heats in the oven.

Ovens in my kitchen are heated with gas, electricity, and wood. After hundreds of loaves baked in almost identical Tappan gas and electric ranges, I have found almost no difference in the quality of the bread.

The adobe oven in my backyard and the oven built into my fireplace wall are designed for bread to be baked directly on the hot brick floor (after clearing away the wood ashes) as most of the hearth and unpanned breads are baked in France. Firewood is becoming scarce in France, however, and now most ovens are fired by gas or fuel oil. Nevertheless, the great Parisian *boulanger*, Monsieur Pierre Poilâne, continues to fire his ovens with fruit-wood—apple, peach, and pear.

Baking bread on the oven floor will ensure one special thing—a thick bottom crust.

I have also baked dozens of loaves on heavy ceramic tiles placed on my oven shelves to simulate a *boulanger*'s oven, but I have long since concluded that the danger of a shelf collapsing under the unstable weight makes it not worth doing. The difference between a loaf baked on a preheated and very hot baking sheet or baking stone and a loaf baked on a deck of hot tiles is so small as to be indistinguishable.

STEAM

The role of steam in baking thin-crusted, crispy loaves of *pain ordinaire* is multiple. Steam softens and protects the dough for a longer period as it rises than would be possible without the added moisture. Steam favors the growth of the *jet,* the bulge in the dough where it is split with the razor blade or *lame.* The moist oven helps to caramelize the sugar in the dough to give the crust a golden yellow color and an overall glossy appearance.

Most ovens in French bake shops are equipped with steam-generating devices. While a large commercial oven built of thirsty bricks demands immense amounts of steam or the heat will pull the moisture right out of the loaves, a home oven big enough for two or three loaves does not need water in that quantity. In fact, there is more danger of creating too much steam than not enough. Too much moisture will bleach the crust and cause the cuts to run together.

You must provide some steam at the beginning of the bake period, but when the heat penetrates the dough, steam is created naturally. Each loaf loses one or two ounces of water in the oven during the bake period. The moisture that fogs glasses (if you wear them) when the oven door is opened attests to this.

The most important thing about steam is to have it in the oven for a few moments before the bread goes in. Pour water into a broiler or shallow roasting pan placed on the floor of the oven. The steam will puff harmlessly through the cracks of the door to let you know that it is ready. Steam can also be created by spraying a fine mist of water into the hot oven with a kitchen atomizer. Aim away from the oven light bulb or it may shatter. All of the water in the pan should have boiled away about the time the crust begins to brown. If you are using an atomizer, don't use it from this point forward. The bread should finish baking in a hot, *dry* oven.

Some home bakers create steam by dropping a heated piece of heavy metal into the pan of water on the floor of the oven. This is dangerous and unnecessary.

SOURCES OF SUPPLY

There are two areas in which home bakers most often ask for guidance. One is where to find ingredients, especially flours. The other is how to locate various utensils in the *batterie de cuisine*.

Ingredients

FLOURS

Home bread baking has created such a stir in the milling industry that now almost all supermarkets have or will special-order all of the basic flours—all-purpose white, unbleached white, whole wheat (ordinary grind and stone-ground), rye (fine and stone-ground or pumpernickel), and cornmeal, white and yellow. Gluten flour, however, is found only in health food stores.

Bread flour may not be readily available in your part of the country. Many home bakers buy it in their communities from the big flour mills that supply commercial bakeries. Expect nothing smaller than 25-pound bags, however. But more and more bread flour, milled from hard winter wheat grown on the Western prairies, is coming into the retail market. The Great Valley Mills of Quakertown, Pennsylvania, carries both an unbleached hard white flour (North Dakota) and a hard whole wheat flour excellent for muffins and coarse loaf breads. Elam's has an enriched white flour, with wheat germ, that is made from hard wheat with 13 percent protein.

Most millers of unbleached flour use hard wheat, which makes it closely akin to bread flour in its baking characteristics. If you can't find bread flour, try unbleached white and then fall back on the commercial mill or order by mail. Ceresota is a source in the Midwest.

Be prepared to buy flour when you see it on the shelves. This is especially advisable in the late spring if you wish to have flour for summertime baking. Baking in many U.S. kitchens slacks off in hot weather and in anticipation of this many stores will cut back on stocks, and some flours may disappear for a time. Also, buyers for large stores and chains will often make a one-time-only purchase of a boxcar or two of a certain flour at a special price. And when it is gone, it may not reappear for months, or ever. If you aren't using the flour right away and have room in the deep-freeze, drop the bag of flour into a plastic bag and leave it in the freezer until you need it.

It pays to shop for price when buying flour.

Flours in 1- and 2-pound bags at premium prices (some are more than double the usual price per pound) may be purchased in health food stores, gourmet sections of department stores, and in special sections of supermarkets but they are no better than such national brands as Gold Medal or Robin Hood or store brands packaged for Kroger, A & P, Standard, and others.

If you have exhausted local sources, here is a list of suppliers:

Byrd Mill Company
P.O. Box 5167
Richmond, Virginia 23220

Byrd Mill flours are widely distributed in the U.S. and sold by mail order. The selection ranges from natural unbleached flour, whole rye flour, and oat flour to soy flour and old "tyme" yellow grits. Quality products, expensive.

Elam's Flours
Elam Mills
2625 Gardner Road
Broadview, Illinois 60153

Elam's red-and-yellow box is on shelves in supermarkets, health food stores, and gourmet shops. All basic flours, including a bread flour, but no mail order. Expensive.

The Great Valley Mills
Quakertown
Bucks County, Pennsylvania 18951

Stone-ground flours. Wide selection including unbleached, white, hard-wheat bread flour. Write for bountiful price list.

Arrowhead Mills, Inc.
Box 866
Hereford, Texas 79045

This famous mill in Deaf Smith County has a complete list of basic flours milled from organically grown grains. Impressive price list.

MALT SYRUP

Malt syrup or extract (*extrait de malt*) is a nutritionally valuable additive that has a peculiar and characteristic flavor that many find desirable, i.e., malted milk. Used extensively by the commercial baker, malt extract can be used at home in pies, cookies, candies, puddings, baked beans, chili con carne, and homemade vinegar.

Malt extract, a barley product, comes in 3-pound cans and is either plain or hops-flavored. The latter is used primarily in making beer, but some baking recipes call for it.

Blue Ribbon Malt Extract is one of the foremost products in the country and can be found in most large supermarkets, sometimes in the section devoted to home-brewed beverages. If you cannot find it, write to:

Premier Malt Products, Inc.
Milwaukee, Wisconsin 53201

BRAN FLAKES

Bran is the flaky brown outer coating of the wheat kernel and it has a nutlike flavor. It is often mistaken for one of several breakfast cereals with bran in their names. Bran flakes can be purchased in health food stores or in the larger supermarkets where some flours, especially those made with organically grown grains, are displayed in bulk.

EAU DE FLEUR D'ORANGER

The only unusual ingredient in this book is *eau de fleur d'oranger,* orange flower water, distilled from the blossom of the Alpine bitter orange. It is used in the delicious *pogne de Romans.* A product of quality, it is produced in France by Funel, *parfumeur-distillateur,* Le Cannet-Cannes, and distributed in the U. S. by Holly World Foods, Inc., 343 Oyster Bay Boulevard, San Francisco, California 94080.

Write to the San Francisco firm for the name of a retail outlet in your area or order the product direct from Jurgensen's Grocery Company, 601 South Lake Avenue, Pasadena, California 91109. Mr. K's in Los Angeles's Farmers' Market will ship anywhere in the U. S. Mr. K's, Shop 30, Farmers' Market, 6333 West 3rd St., Los Angeles, California 90036.

A 4-ounce bottle (enough for two batches) retails for about $1.80 (as of 1977).

BATTERIE DE CUISINE

There is a French utensil for every job in the French kitchen. Fortunately, however, there is an American substitute for each. The special French blades (*lames*) for slicing the surface of the French loaf can be replaced by a razor blade. The triangles cut by the rolling French croissant cutter (about $30) can be produced with a bit of calculation with a yardstick and a pastry wheel. A substitute for the French dough scraper is a 4-inch putty knife.

A rich source of information about everything for the kitchen is *The Cook's Catalogue,* Harper & Row, 1975. There is one notable exception—no French bread pans! There are Pullman pans (for *pain de mie*), mini-loaf, and black steel loaf pans, but nothing that resembles the long U-shaped pans in which the classic *baguette, flûte, ficelle,* and *bâtard* are baked.

Nevertheless, more U. S. manufacturers are coming out with a French-type bread pan—open-ended, curved bottom, and short enough to fit into the American home oven—and more stores are carrying them.

There are two American sources for these pans listed below, or you can make your own from stovepipe (see page 15).

For special bread pans as well as the ordinary ones, visit the kitchenware departments in large stores in your area or kitchen specialty shops that have sprung up almost everywhere in the past decades. My small city of 50,000 has a top-notch one (Goods, Inc.) that has or can get almost anything I need.

And don't overlook farm sales and antique shows. I discovered my wonderful 6-pound rolling pin of maple in a small antique shop in the country in southern Indiana. Some of my best blackened baking pans, which I use to make dark crusty loaves, came from farm sales where I have also found many of my best stoneware bowls.

When you are next in Paris visit the crowded store of E. DeHillerin, 18 Rue Coquillière, and browse through their fabulous stock of *everything* for the kitchen—the ultimate in the *batterie de cuisine*. (Take the Métro to Les Halles. DeHillerin is a block away.) Marvelous shopping for the kitchen, and the cafes nearby serve the best onion soup in Paris.

PANS

Stone Hearth, Inc., is the distributor for two fine, black, steel, open-ended pans (two loaves each); a narrow French (FRB-16) pan; and a broader Italian (ITB-16) one. Write or phone for name of your local outlet.

> Stone Hearth, Inc.
> 40 Park Street
> Brooklyn, New York 11206
> (212-491-4433)

Clyde Brook, a retired Air Force officer, has been producing an aluminum French bread pan (for two loaves) for several years. I wish it could be made of dark metal to give the crust a deeper shade, but when I use his pans, I end the bake period by turning the loaves over and exposing their bottoms to the oven's heat for an additional 10 minutes.

> Paris X
> 500 Independence Avenue, S. E.
> Washington, D. C. 20003

A fine but expensive bread pan from France that will bake three *baguettes* is distributed by a Ramsey, New Jersey, firm. Write for sales outlets in your community.

> Hoan
> 615 East Crescent Avenue
> Ramsey, New Jersey

BAKING SHEET

To simulate a commercial oven—intense heat on the floor when the bread goes in—I use a heavy baking sheet rather than a shelf full of tiles.

Most restaurant supply houses have them. Lockwood Manufacturing Company, Cincinnati, makes a heavy 5-pound sheet (18 × 26) for commercial customers and a smaller one (14 × 16) sold through a distributor, below. Write for names of stores in your area.

> Rowoco, Inc.
> 700 Waverly Avenue
> Mamaroneck, New York 10543

BAKING STONE

A baking stone (circular or rectangular), which gives intense heat to the bottom of the loaf much as a hot brick oven floor would do, can be found in most fine kitchenware shops. The stone retails for about $15. The round stone, which is ideal for pizza as well, can also be purchased with a wooden paddle or peel. Write for names of stores in your area or order directly from:

> Old Stone Oven Corporation
> 6007 Sheridan Road
> Chicago, Illinois 60660

BREAD KNIFE

A sharp knife in the kitchen is a blessing. One of the best for slicing bread is a Swiss blade, Victorinox #460-9, stainless steel, which is distributed in this country by a New York City firm. Restaurant supply houses and culinary departments of retail stores carry them. If you can't find a local outlet, write:

> R. H. Forschner Company
> 324 Lafayette Street
> New York City, New York 10012

The French care not how bread is transported—
only that it be crackling fresh!

Gannat

Grenoble

Paris

Gannat

Rochefort-Montagne

Near Soumoulou

Carcassonne

Paris

Storing and Freezing

Bread to be eaten within the next day or two should be kept in a paper bag, bread box, or bread drawer. Don't wrap it in plastic unless you want an especially soft crust. If the bread is to be used for toast, it doesn't matter. The toaster will crisp the slice.

Bread will not stale as quickly at room temperature as it will in the refrigerator. However, if you fear the loaf may mold, refrigerate it.

Bread will freshen simply by heating it in a 350° oven for 15 minutes.

If you are concerned that a whole loaf will stale before it can be eaten, freeze part of it to serve fresh at a later date.

Frozen bread keeps so well and freshens so marvelously that I freeze all bread even though I may plan to serve it within the next few days. I often bake on Wednesday and Thursday and freeze the loaves to be served on the weekend.

There is no loaf that cannot be frozen. While some breads seem to keep longer than others, I try not to keep any loaf frozen for more than three months because after that the bread loses its ability to bounce back.

To freeze, allow the loaf to cool before placing it in a medium or heavy plastic bag. Tie it securely with a wire wrap. Freeze. After taking the bread out of the freezer, allow it to thaw inside the unopened bag. Frost particles and ice crystals inside the bag represent moisture from the bread and should be allowed to be absorbed back. When the moisture has disappeared, remove the bread from the bag, place on a baking sheet, and put it in a 350° oven for 15 minutes.

Freezing dough is less than satisfactory. It can be done, of course, but you must watch it for hours as it thaws so that when it doubles in volume it can be shaped into loaves and placed in pans or on a baking sheet. Then, it must be allowed to double or triple in volume before putting it in the oven. Not worth the bother.

WHAT WENT WRONG?

Bread making is a forgiving art. While there are several things that can go wrong, there are far more things that can go right. Expect good things to come out of the oven, and they usually will.

Nevertheless, the most experienced home baker will have an occasional setback, a problem, a mishap, or whatever. I often forget the salt, which I later add when I discover the texture of the dough is not right. I make certain by tasting a bit of the dough. Yes, forgotten again. I dissolve the salt in a tiny bit of water, and knead it into the dough. I once had three pans of dough for cheese loaves actually in the oven, but barely, when I turned around to discover the three cups of shredded cheese still on the counter waiting to be added. I quickly got the pans out of the hot oven, dumped the dough out of the pans, and worked in the cheese. I had to let it rise again in the pans, but time was all that I lost. The bread was delicious.

Here are some of the things that can go wrong, and what can be done about them.

Too-Soft Dough

If the dough for the hearth loaf that you formed on the baking sheet spreads and slouches when it is supposed to rise, begin anew by working a small quantity of flour into the slack dough and kneading it aggressively. The combination of a little flour and the kneading will give the dough sufficient body to stand alone on the baking sheet. Test it by slapping your open hand against the ball of dough. Leave it there for a count of ten. If your hand comes away clean, the dough has enough flour.

Cannonball

I have made a number of these. Too much flour has been forced into the dough and it has lost its elasticity and suppleness. The ball is hard, firm, and unyielding. If you attempt to punch it down, it seems to punch back. Add water to soften it. This is a sticky process, but it can salvage the dough. Knead thoroughly again.

Salt?

If the dough is stringy, unresponsive, pulls away in strands, and doesn't get any better despite continued kneading, and, later, when the loaf is baked, the slice tastes flat, you probably have forgotten the salt. It happens. One test along the way is to taste a bit of dough during kneading to make certain you salted it.

Won't Rise

If the dough refuses to rise, you may have forgotten the yeast or it might have been killed if dissolved in water above 140°. Don't throw the dough away. Start a new batch but make certain the yeast is among the ingredients. After the new dough is mixed, blend the two doughs. There will be more than enough healthy yeast cells to go around.

Too High

If it is obvious that the dough rising in the pan or *banneton* is pushing too high, it probably will collapse when the heat of the oven forces it to stretch even further. Punch down the dough, reshape the loaves, and this time don't let the dough rise beyond the recommended volume, whether doubled or tripled.

Pans Too Big or Too Small

When the dough has risen in the pans, it may be obvious that the dough and pans are mismatched—too much dough in pans too small, or too little dough in pans too large. Either way, the loaves will be less than attractive. Turn the dough out of the pans, knead briefly again, reshape, and match to the proper size pans according to the dough volume chart on page 11. Most doughs in the conventional rectangular bread pans should rise about one half inch above the edge before they go into the oven. Cylindrical pans (coffee cans) are filled halfway and dough is allowed to rise to the edge before baking.

Pale Bottom

The top crust is a golden brown, but the side and bottom crusts are pale and appear not done when the loaves are turned out of their pans. Shiny aluminum pans are the worst offenders since they reflect rather than retain the heat. Return the loaves to the oven without pans for five minutes. They will get a lovely overall tan.

Hard Crust

If the crust is too hard and crispy, next time bake with less steam in the oven. A hard crust softens overnight if left in a plastic bag.

Soft Crust

If the crust is not thick or crusty enough, place a little more water in the broiler pan to generate more steam or give it an additional spray of water with an atomizer. A swipe with a wet pastry brush will also help a hard crust to develop.

Uneven Crust Color

Once or twice during the bake period, open the oven door and change the positions of the pans so the loaves are exposed evenly to temperature variations that occur in most ovens.

Poorly Baked

The dough was beautifully risen when it went into the oven, but it came out a disappointment. Bread must be baked at the recommended temperature. Test the oven with a thermometer. Never trust the thermostat to deliver the temperature it promises. An oven 100° too cool will not bake bread. An oven 100° too hot may burn it to a crisp.

Not Done

When you cut the first slice, it is obvious that the bread is moist and perhaps gummy. It is not done. It needs to be baked longer. Recap the loaf with the slice and put the loaf (or loaves) back into the oven for another 10 minutes. If not done then, five minutes longer. However, don't judge bread for doneness until it has cooled.

Shelling

When the bread under the top crust separates to form a tunnel down the length of the loaf, it is probably caused by one of two things. The top surface of the dough may have partially dried out during rising and later, in the oven, the heat could not uniformly penetrate the thick surface or "shell." Or, the oven temperature may have been too low and the dough expanded unevenly. For the next bake session, cover the dough with wax paper or foil during rising to prevent loss of moisture. Preheat the oven so the dough will get the full benefit of all of the heat at the outset. Use a thermometer beforehand to make certain the oven temperature is correct.

Layered Effect

If there is a layer of bread in the loaf just below the crust that is different in texture and color, it may be that you added too much flour too late in the kneading process, and it didn't get absorbed into the dough. Sprinkles of flour are no problem, but substantial amounts can be unless followed by additional kneading.

Assortment of breads in the author's Indiana kitchen.

PART II

The Breads
of France

RECIPES FROM PARIS

Where else to start a search for the breads of France but in Paris—one of the gastronomic capitals of the world? We had been there before, but never quite so single-mindedly in pursuit of *pain ordinaire* and the not so *ordinaire*. It was the latter that turned up most often. We found unusual breads in settings as varied as the breads themselves. Our paths led from an array of luxury food at Fauchon to the dark, damp wine cellar of a master baker's suburban retreat. A Jewish restaurant-deli in a less-than-grand section of Paris provided delicious bagels and a sharp contrast to the elegant *boulangerie* shaded by plane trees in Place Victor Hugo, where I found *pain d'épice,* made with wild honey and rye flour.

The Paris of Fauchon

Fauchon, one of the world's great food shops, is easily the number one food spectacle in Paris now that the ancient market, Les Halles, has been torn down and removed to the suburbs.

Find the riot of color that is the open-air flower market at Place de la Madeleine and you are very close to the two buildings that house Fauchon. It will not be difficult to spot. A dozen or more passersby will be at the windows, feasting their eyes on spectacular food displays put together by the store's two full-time decorators. No doubt a sleek limousine or two will be at the curb, waiting for an owner to browse and buy among hanging hams and sausages and pyramids of vegetables and fruits rushed there from gardens and orchards everywhere in the world. It is not an especially large place, but everything is absolutely tops—top quality and top price. Wholesale markets hold their best for the Fauchon buyer. If he doesn't want it, then it will be released for sale to others. Tucked in various displays are small plastic cards that proclaim, modestly, that this *asperge blanche* or that *orange* was grown and picked expressly for Fauchon.

Fauchon was the creation in 1886 of Monsieur Fauchon, who in the beginning refused to display or sell any food not a product of France. But two wars changed all that and today Fauchon, while resting its reputation solidly on French foods, has gone far afield to stock such exotic items as U.S. sweet corn, cranberry sauce, maple syrup, mincemeat, and California wines, which, three thousand miles away from home, are displayed alongside Bombay duck, Indian herbs, Mali mangoes, Spanish peppers, Scotch smoked salmon, Israeli avocados, and passion fruit.

The Fauchon annex across the street is a glorious salon dedicated solely to cakes, pastries, and ice cream. Here, if one gets lost among the mountains of cakes and banks of petits fours, he or she can take nourishment in stand-up elegance at one of the waist-high tables provided for those who have neither the strength nor the willpower to make it out of the door with his or her purchase.

In the main Fauchon store, midway between the vegetables and the *charcuterie,* a counter is given over to three breads that are *specialités de la maison.* One is Fauchon's

35

own creation, pain *hawaiien* (with coconut, of course). The other two are from the *boulangerie* of Monsieur Pierre Poilane, the city's most celebrated baker. Poilane provides a small round loaf, heavy with broken walnuts—*pain aux noix*. Also a big country loaf, so large for most city folks that Fauchon will sell you just a piece of it if you ask.

Pain Hawaiien Fauchon ❧ Fauchon's Hawaiian Bread

[FOUR 1-POUND LOAVES]

One must toast a slice of pain hawaiien *to fully appreciate the delicate blend of nuts and coconut, said the floor manager of Fauchon. He was lyrical about it. I could not disagree, yet there is a lovely and haunting aftertaste even in an untoasted bite.*

*In Hawaii, the nut would have been a macadamia, but the hazelnut (*noisette*) has much the same hard crunchiness and a unique flavor of its own. It is an able substitute and not nearly so expensive. Nevertheless, that afternoon in Paris a pound loaf of Fauchon's* pain hawaiien *was $3.75!*

INGREDIENTS	6 cups all-purpose flour, approximately
	1 package dry yeast
	1 tablespoon salt
	2 tablespoons sugar
	$1/2$ cup non-fat dry milk
	$1^1/2$ cups warm water (105°–115°)
	4 eggs, room temperature
	4 ounces (1 stick) butter, room temperature
	$1^1/2$ cups coconut flakes, packaged or fresh
	$1^1/2$ cups hazelnuts, coarsely ground (see note below)
BAKING PANS	Four small ($7^1/2 \times 3^1/2$) loaf pans, greased or Teflon.
PREPARATION	*Note:* Since much of the good taste of this bread rests on hazelnuts, they should be ground coarsely, preferably in a nut grinder, so that the particles are about the size of rice grains. Don't grind them so fine that they become like flour or they will disappear into the mixture.
	The nuts and coconut can be added after the first rising, rather than in the batter, but it is a little more difficult to get the dough to accept them.
12 minutes	In a large bowl, combine 2 cups of flour, the yeast, salt, sugar, dry milk, and $1^1/2$ cups of water to make a thick batter. Drop in the eggs, one at a time, and blend into the batter. Work in 2 more cups of flour. Break butter into several pieces and drop into the mixture. Blend with 25 strong strokes of rubber scraper or wooden spoon. Work in the coconut flakes and ground hazelnuts. Add remaining flour, $1/2$ cup at a time, to form a shaggy mass that can be lifted from the bowl.

Fauchon's Hawaiian Bread, an unusual Parisian recipe.

With fingers and scraper, clean the sides of the bowl and add particles to the dough.

KNEADING
7 minutes
Sprinkle the work surface with flour and turn out dough. With a rhythm of push-turn-fold, knead dough until it becomes smooth (excepting the nut and coconut particles, of course) and elastic. Add sprinkles of flour if dough is sticky, but don't over-flour or dough will become dense and difficult to work.

FIRST RISING
1 hour
Return the dough to the bowl, cover with plastic wrap, and leave undisturbed at room temperature (70°–75°) until doubled in volume.

SHAPING
15 minutes
Dough will weigh about 4 pounds—sufficient for four 1-pound loaves or a combination of others.

Turn dough onto floured work surface and with knife or dough scraper divide into number of loaves desired. Roll each piece into a ball and let stand for 2 or 3 minutes to relax dough.

Press each ball into a flat oval—as wide as the pan is long—fold in half, and pinch seam together. Tuck in ends and drop into prepared pan, with seam under.

SECOND RISING
1 hour
Cover with wax paper and leave at room temperature (70°–75°) to rise until dough has risen above the level of the pan edge—about 1 hour.

BAKING
400°
30 minutes
With razor blade, make one long slice down the center of the loaf with 4 or 5 short diagonal cuts radiating on either side, as fronds from the trunk of a coconut palm.

Place on middle shelf. When loaves have been in the oven 20 minutes, turn the pans around. Loaves are baked when golden brown with darker flakes of nuts and coconut in the crust. Larger loaves may need 10 additional minutes in oven.

Turn baked loaves out of pans. Brush top crust with melted butter and return to oven without pans for 5 minutes.

FINAL STEP
Place on metal rack to cool. Good toasted. Good cool. Good anytime.

Pain aux Noix ✻ Nut Bread

[THREE 1-POUND LOAVES]

Pain aux noix is dark, dense and delicious. With as many walnuts worked into the all-whole-wheat dough as it will embrace (more than ¹/₂ pound), a slice of this bread is a deserving companion at any meal. Toasted and served with cheese it is even better.

The Fauchon loaf, baked for the store in the celebrated boulangerie *of Monsieur Pierre Poilâne, is a small* boule, *a round loaf, but it can easily be made in other shapes and sizes to accommodate almost any need.*

Rather than sugar or molasses, malt syrup is added to impart a special sweetness, definitive but not cloying. The 100 percent whole wheat is responsible for the solid slice.

INGREDIENTS
1 package dry yeast
2¹/₂ cups warm water (105°–115°)
1 tablespoon plain malt syrup (not hop-flavored)
¹/₂ cup non-fat dry milk
2 tablespoons butter, room temperature
2 teaspoons salt
1 cup bran flakes, optional
4¹/₂ cups whole wheat flour (add 1 additional cup if bran flakes not used), approximately
2¹/₂ cups English walnuts, broken

Glaze:
1 egg
1 tablespoon milk

BAKING SHEET One greased or Teflon baking sheet.

PREPARATION
18 minutes

Sprinkle the dry yeast in a large bowl and add the warm water.
Blend in malt syrup, which is also an ideal nutrient for yeast and will quickly boost it on its way. Stir in dry milk, butter, and salt.

Note: Bran flakes will add a desired roughness to the texture, particularly if the whole wheat flour is finely ground. If whole wheat is stone-ground or pumpernickel, forget the bran flakes and add 1 additional cup of whole wheat flour.

Blend bran flakes (see note above) into the wet ingredients in the bowl. Add whole wheat flour, ¹/₂ cup at a time, until batter is thick and difficult to stir. Let it rest for 3 or 4 minutes while large flour particles absorb their fill of moisture. Cautiously add additional flour to make a mass that can be lifted by hand from the bowl. While whole wheat dough is not as elastic as a white dough, nevertheless it must not be made into a solid ball that cannot be kneaded. The tendency in working with 100 percent whole wheat is to add too much

Nut Bread from Paris, delicious with tea or coffee.

flour to overcome stickiness and then discover suddenly that the flour has absorbed all of the moisture—and the dough is hard. Sprinkles of white flour will help control the stickiness yet not over-flour the dough.

The nuts are to be added after the first rising.

KNEADING
6 minutes

Turn the ball of dough onto the floured work surface. Use a dough scraper or putty knife to help turn the dough and clean the work surface in the early moments of kneading. Keep light sprinkles of *white* flour between the dough and the hands and work surface. Bang dough down hard against the work surface to relieve the tedium of kneading.

FIRST RISING
1–1¼ hours

Return dough to washed and greased bowl, cover with plastic wrap and leave at room temperature (70°–75°) until dough has doubled in bulk.

SHAPING
10 minutes

Place dough on work surface and push it into a large flat oval. Pour half the nuts into the center of the dough and fold in. When they have disappeared, repeat with the balance of the nuts. Some of the nuts may have a tendency to fall out of the dough as it is worked. Keep pushing them back into the dough as it is kneaded and soon they will stay in place.

Divide dough into 3 equal parts (or the number of loaves desired). Let the dough rest 5 minutes to relax it before shaping.

With cupped hands, turn one piece of dough into a smooth ball, the cut surfaces pulled together under the ball.

Flatten the ball slightly with a gentle pat of the palm. Place on baking sheet, and repeat with other pieces.

SECOND RISING
50 minutes

Cover the *boules* with wax paper and leave them at room temperature (70°–75°).

BAKING
380°
35 minutes

Preheat oven 20 minutes before breads are to be baked. Brush loaves with egg-milk glaze and cut the top of each with 4 shallow (¹/₈ inch deep) cuts with a razor blade.

Place sheet on middle shelf of oven.

Halfway through the bake period, turn baking sheet around to equalize oven temperature on loaves.

Loaves are done when dark brown. Turn one loaf over and tap bottom crust with forefinger to determine if it has a hard, hollow sound. If so, it is baked.

FINAL STEP

Place loaves on metal rack to cool.

Good to eat cool, toasted, or reheated. Freezes well.

The Paris of Poilâne

Everything master baker (*premier boulanger*) Pierre Poilâne does, he does with a flair.

The big brass door-pull at his *boulangerie* at 8 rue du Cherche-Midi is wrought in the delicate shape of a sheaf of wheat. At home, Poilâne serves a delicious onion soup from a golden brown ceramic tureen for which his famous 2-kilo country loaf was the model. It is this loaf that has inspired countless imitations. Its decoration came about when Poilâne was asked by a Catholic sister to make something "not ordinary" for a special confirmation gift for a family. He created a large hearth-baked loaf decorated with a cluster of grapes resting on a large leaf, amidst twists of vine—all in dough. It has since become a Parisian favorite.

Flair.

Artists have long found Poilâne a marvelous subject and the walls of his shop and office are blanketed with photographs, oils, and watercolors of him in his cocky black beret and plain tradesman's smock.

Flair.

Poilâne once took us to lunch at Le Borghèse, an outstanding restaurant near his *boulangerie*. We moved as a royal procession down the street, hailing and being hailed all along the way by dozens of Poilâne's friends. It was raining lightly when we started and midway a downpour forced us to take refuge in a small bistro. The place was jammed at the noon hour but we could not continue until we drank a bottle of wine (compliments of the house) and had met everyone at the bar. Continuing on, we turned into the tradesmen's entrance of the Lutetia Concorde Hotel, past the staff dining room (where for a moment I thought we might be dining), through the kitchen, with waves and introductions to chefs and pot scrubbers alike, and, finally, to burst through the swinging doors into the restaurant and the arms of a beaming *maître d'hôtel*. Even without a drum roll it was a memorable entrance. The other guests stared as the *maître d'* embraced Poilâne, who was still in his beret and smock, and took from under Poilâne's arm the loaf of bread that he had brought for our lunch.

Flair!

My wife will never forget our processional to the restaurant that day when, with a loud cry, Poilâne stopped in the street, grabbed and kissed her when he discovered that she was the daughter of a baker!

Flair!

Late one afternoon we drove with Poilâne to Clamart, in the direction of Versailles, to visit his retreat in the suburbs where he goes when the pressures of being a celebrated *boulanger* get to be too much. From the street I could see only fruit and shade trees, untrimmed and overgrown with vines. The grass was high. It was obvious that the place received only minimal attention.

"If I kept the lawn cut, I would not have these," he said as he stooped to pick a handful of *fraises des bois,* the tiny wild strawberries that were growing half-hidden in the deep grass.

There was a small house among the trees, but its windows and doors were standing open and its sole function seemed to be as the repository for an impressive collection of wine and liquor glasses resting on a half dozen shelves. Poilâne picked up a number of glasses and several unlabeled bottles half-filled with liquids. He dismissed the house with a wave.

"We use it only as a place to keep dry in a storm and as a base for work in the garden," he said. He led us to a dilapidated wooden table standing on the lawn. Nearby was a water faucet on a short length of pipe rising out of the ground. He rinsed the glasses, then turned them upside down on the table to drain.

"Come," he said, and we fell in behind him as he walked to a rough wooden door on the face of a big grassy mound. Poilâne threw open the unlocked door, kicked away a pile of leaves from the threshold, and reached for a candle and match cached above the door. A short flight of steps led down into the darkness. I decided to hang back until Poilâne struck the match. No, he said, we all had to crowd into the dark cavern. The door was pulled shut and then, when Poilâne was satisfied the moment had arrived, the match was struck.

Champagne and wines! Hundreds of bottles.

Cases were on the floor and racks lined the sides of the large room. From floor to ceiling. Some bottles had been laid down only recently and the clean glass sparkled in the candlelight. But most were subdued under dust and cobwebs. Poilâne laughed when he caught my look of disbelief.

"Select one," he offered. No, I could not, I told him, for my knowledge of champagne and wines was so meager as to make any selection by me a silly gesture. Please. He ran his finger down a list stuck to the end of a bin.

"Ah, this is the one," he said, and reached for a modestly dusted bottle.

"For this occasion something special!" He handed me the bottle. Mouton-Rothschild. My first.

We climbed the stairs. Poilâne banged shut the door. I was disturbed that he did not lock it.

"No need, *monsieur,* for this is a very peaceful place. We have no problems."

Poilâne placed the champagne on the old table alongside the bottles he had brought from the house. We were to taste them all, he said. We should begin with the *anisette aperitif* that he had made the summer before. Very good. The glasses were rinsed under the water tap. This time we would taste the raspberry liqueur, white, followed (after a rinse) by another *framboise,* this one red. Both homemade and both good.

The sun had now gone down and it was cold in the damp garden. Poilâne talked about his life, which had been rich and full.

A toast, he said. The Mouton-Rothschild was poured.

"A grain of wheat is perfection in life. It lives, and it gives life. It has given me life, a rewarding life. *Merci.*"

The click of glasses was the only sound in the garden.

Flair.

Poilâne's celebrated design of grapes and wheat stalks.

Pain de Campagne Poilâne ❧ Poilâne's Peasant Bread

[ONE LARGE LOAF OR FOUR 1-POUND LOAVES]

By far the most famous of the more than a score of different breads made by Poilâne is the round 2-kilogram (4.4-pound) peasant loaf baked in the wood-fired oven in the cave-like basement of the boulangerie *built over the ruins of a fourteenth-century Gothic abbey at 8 rue du Cherche-Midi. The steep narrow steps, up which perspiring young men drag huge baskets filled each day with a thousand big thick-crusted peasant loaves, were cut out of the rock five centuries ago.*

Each of the big Poilâne loaves measures about a foot in diameter and is slashed across its domed top with the traditional and functional jets *that allow the crust to spread and the dough to expand.*

But Poilâne's most celebrated design, the one he created for a young girl's confirmation party, is the cluster of grapes, complete with twisted tendrils, resting on a large leaf. My execution of the Poilâne design sometimes looks like a stack of marbles on a small raft, but it's fun to do whatever the result.

I must have a model, so each summer I pick a grape leaf, a full cluster of grapes, and a handful of tendrils and arrange them in a circle about the size of the top of the Poilâne loaf. I sketch or photograph my creation and to this I refer long after the leaves have fallen and the birds have eaten the grapes. Another Poilâne design is the several stalks of wheat that are also on Monsieur David's country loaf at Honfleur.

Poilâne has his flour grown and milled in the south of France for his two boulangeries *(a newer one is in a Paris suburb), and while the flour is difficult to duplicate precisely in the U.S., the whole wheat starter in this recipe—developed in two stages—imparts a fermentation, flavor, and color that will delight peasant and prince alike. The bread recipe is Poilâne's; the starter recipe was developed with American flours in my kitchen to match his recipe as closely as possible. Poilâne approved it.*

INGREDIENTS   *Starter:*
1 package dry yeast
1 cup warm water (105°–115°)
1 tablespoon non-fat dry milk
1 cup whole wheat flour, fine or stone-ground

Sponge:
All of the starter
2 cups warm water (105°–115°)
3 cups all-purpose or unbleached flour

Dough:
All of the sponge
1 tablespoon salt
3 cups all-purpose or unbleached flour

BAKING SHEET One baking sheet, greased or Teflon. Or the bread may be baked in a twin open-ended baguette pan, if available.

PREPARATION While the time can be shortened in each of the following steps to fit into other schedules, ideally 2 days should be given to the full development of the starter and sponge, with baking on the third day.

FIRST DAY
12 minutes
Starter: In a medium or large bowl, stir yeast in warm water until the particles have dissolved. Add dry milk and whole wheat flour. Blend with 15 to 20 strokes of rubber scraper. Cover tightly with a length of plastic wrap and set aside at room temperature (70°–75°). Batter will rise and fall and continue to ferment and bubble during the 24-hour period.

SECOND DAY
10 minutes
Sponge: Turn back plastic wrap and pour warm water into the starter. Stir in 3 cups of all-purpose or unbleached flour. The batter will be thick. Re-cover and leave at room temperature (70°–75°).

THIRD DAY
20 minutes
Dough: Remove plastic wrap from bowl. Stir briefly and add salt. With large wooden spoon or rubber scraper, stir in additional flour, $1/2$ cup at a time. When the dough becomes dense and difficult to stir, work in flour with the hands.

    While this is an elastic dough, sufficient flour must be worked into the mass to enable the shaped loaves to rest on the baking sheets without slumping, as hearth loaves are prone to do.

KNEADING
10 minutes
Turn dough out of the bowl onto the floured work surface and let rest 3 to 4 minutes before kneading. If the dough seems slack, without body, or is sticky, throw down liberal sprinkles of flour to work into it during the early kneading. A dough scraper in hand is convenient for keeping the work surface free of the film that often collects while the dough is moist and sticky. Bang the dough down against the table to break the kneading motion, and, at the same time, to hasten the development of the dough.

FIRST RISING
$1^1/2$ hours
Wash and grease bowl. Drop dough in bowl and cover with plastic wrap. Leave at room temperature (70°–75°) until dough more than doubles in volume, about $1^1/2$ hours.

SHAPING
15 minutes
Punch down dough and turn it onto the work surface.

    For a large loaf, use all of the dough, about 4 pounds. If making a grape leaf or wheat stalk design, reserve 1 cup of dough.

    The dough can also be divided into smaller loaves.

    While the small loaves may be put directly on the baking sheet to rise, they will have better shape if first placed in cloth lined baskets (see *bannetons*, page 13) or wedged between folds of cloth (see *couches,* page 14). After the second rising, they are transferred to the baking sheet.

If long French bread pans are available, the dough may be placed in these to rise and to bake, without being transferred to a baking sheet.

In forming the ball of dough for the basket, pull the surface taut under cupped hands. Place the ball of dough in the basket with the smooth surface down and the wrinkled seam up. When the dough is turned onto the baking sheet, the smooth surface will be on top and the seam under.

In rolling a length of dough into a *baguette* or *bâtard,* keep it taut by striking the length of dough with the side of the palm two or three times as it gets longer. After making a crease down its length, fold in two (lengthwise) and continue rolling. This forces out air that is trapped in the dough that might cause unsightly bubbles in the bread, in addition to stretching the surface of the dough.

SECOND RISING
2 hours
Carefully cover loaves with wax paper or woolen cloth. Leave at room temperature (70°–75°) in a place free of drafts until the dough triples in volume, about 2 hours. The large cell structure so characteristic of French bread depends in a large part on this extra period of rising.

15 minutes
Shortly before the dough is completely raised, make top decorations, if desired.

Grape: Use leaf, cluster, and tendrils as model. Roll dough ⅛ inch thick for leaf, trace design, and cut with dough wheel, razor, or sharp knife. Work carefully to trace veins of leaf. Pinch off 2 dozen small pieces of dough, and roll into grapes between palms or on work surface. Carefully roll out long strings of dough to resemble tendrils. Reserve. They will be assembled on top of the risen loaf.

Wheat stalks: Instructions, page 76.

BAKING
425°
35–40 minutes
Preheat oven 20 minutes beforehand. Place a broiler pan on the bottom shelf. Five minutes before the bread is to go into the oven, pour 1 cup of hot tap water in the pan. Be careful of the sudden burst of steam. It can burn.

Uncover loaf or loaves, lightly brush with water, and position decoration. If no decoration, slice top with 5 or 6 parallel *jets* or cuts in one direction, turn loaf, and slice 5 or 6 parallel cuts in the other— a checkerboard pattern.

Place loaves on middle and top racks if both are needed, and change positions of loaves 20 minutes into the bake period.

The water should boil away about the time the loaves begin to take on color, so that the bread will have a hot, *dry* oven for a brown, crispy crust.

Loaves are baked when a light golden brown and hard and crusty when tapped with a forefinger. If the bottom crust of loaves in pans is not crisp, turn the loaves over in the pans and return to the oven for 10 minutes.

FINAL STEP Place on metal rack to cool. This bread is its best when cooled, which allows the baking process to be completed. Warming bread *after* it has cooled is another matter. But fresh out of the oven, it should be cooled or nearly so before it is introduced to the knife.

CROISSANTS BRIOCHÉS ✤ CRESCENT-SHAPED BRIOCHES

[FOUR DOZEN]

This recipe combines in a different way two French favorites—the croissant and the brioche. It is brioche dough rolled in a crescent shape for a fine breakfast roll. The thinner it is rolled (¹/₈ inch or less), the more delicate is the bread.

While the Poilâne bakeries produce a delicious croissant brioché, *the recipe below is by his fellow Parisian, Monsieur Raymond Calvel, famed as a professor of professional bread-baking courses in Paris.*

This brioche dough is also used to make the brioche aux pruneaux *(page 104), a braided loaf, each strand hiding a length of pureed prunes.*

INGREDIENTS 7 cups all-purpose flour, approximately
2 packages dry yeast
¹/₂ cup warm water (105°–115°)
10 eggs, room temperature
1 tablespoon salt
5 teaspoons sugar
¹/₂ pound (2 sticks) butter or margarine, room temperature

Glaze (optional):
1 egg
1 tablespoon milk

BAKING SHEET One or two baking sheets, ungreased or Teflon.

PREPARATION Pour 2 cups all-purpose flour in a large bowl and form a well to hold
18 minutes yeast and water. Stir and leave for 3 or 4 minutes until yeast is dissolved. Break 4 eggs into well, and with wooden spoon or rubber scraper, pull flour in from the sides. Beat vigorously to blend. Add salt and sugar. Blend. Stir in 2 cups flour and break in 4 more eggs. Cut butter into tablespoon-size pieces and drop into mixture. Stir with 25 strong strokes. Add remaining 2 eggs. Additional flour is added, ¹/₂ cup at a time, until dough is a solid mass that can be worked with the hands. It will be rich and buttery and easy to knead.

KNEADING 7 minutes	Turn dough onto dusted work surface. Knead with a strong 1-2-3 rhythm of push-turn-fold, adding sprinkles of flour to absorb the butter, if needed.
FIRST RISING 1¹/₂ hours	Place dough in bowl that has been washed but not greased. Cover bowl with plastic wrap and put aside at room temperature (70°–75°) to double in volume, about 1¹/₂ hours.
PUNCH DOWN 2 minutes	Turn back plastic wrap and punch down dough with extended fingers. Turn dough over; return plastic wrap.
SECOND RISING 1 hour	Let dough rise a second time, about 1 hour.
REFRIGERATION 30 minutes	Again punch down dough; place in refrigerator for 30 minutes to firm.
SHAPING 30 minutes	If there is dough for more croissants than you can bake at one time in your oven, divide and place in refrigerator until needed.

Dust work surface with flour. Roll out half or about 2 pounds (3 cups) of dough into a 36-inch-long rectangle, 10 inches wide—and no more than ¹/₈ inch thick. Very thin. The thinner it is the more delicate.

Don't rush the rolling. Allow dough time to relax or it will continue to pull back. When sheet of dough is at least 10 inches wide and *thin*—let rest for 5 minutes before cutting.

With razor, sharp knife, or pastry wheel (preferred) and a yardstick, trim sides of the rectangle. Cut sheet of dough lengthwise into two pieces, each 5 inches wide. Mark series of 5-inch triangles down the length of each piece and cut.

With the fingers, roll each triangle from the bottom edge toward the apex. Stretch the dough slightly as you begin to roll and hold the tip under a finger as you roll toward it. Stop when the point is toward you and tipped down. The point should be tucked under so it will not spring loose during baking. Place on the baking sheet and pull both ends down to shape crescent. Repeat for each, and place on sheet about 1 inch apart. When first batch is raised and baked, repeat with reserved dough.

THIRD RISING 25 minutes	Brush with egg-milk glaze and leave uncovered at room temperature (70°–75°) while oven is heating.
BAKING 420° 20 minutes	Brush with egg-milk glaze again just before pieces go into the oven. Croissants will be baked when deep golden brown. Watch carefully that they don't get too brown in hot oven.

In a large oven, croissants may be baked on lower and middle shelves. However, midway in the bake period, quickly exchange positions of baking sheets so each will have been exposed to the same temperature conditions.

FINAL STEP Remove from oven and place on metal rack to cool. Delicious warm or re-warmed. These freeze well.

The Paris of Jo Goldenberg

The bagel is seldom baked in the Jewish home. Almost always the small but substantial bread is bought in a bakery. I once asked a New York cab driver if his mother had a favorite bagel recipe. He slowed his cab to look in the mirror to see if my question was serious and, when he determined it was, he pulled to the curb, turned in his seat and gave me a ten-minute discourse on the Jewish bagel. The gist of it was that his mother, whom he considered to be one of the best cooks in all of New York, never baked a bagel in her life. It was he who got the bagels at the bakery down the block.

"And only water bagels," he called to me when finally he dropped me at the hotel. "Forget about your egg bagels!"

It was the first of many lessons about bagels.

The French feel the same way, i.e., leave the bagel to the baker. Of course, the French feel that way about all breads.

More than half of the half-million French Jews live in Paris—all of these at one time or another eat and shop at the large Jo Goldenberg restaurant-deli at 7 rue des Rosiers. It is two or three blocks from the Seine in one direction and the Place de la Bastille in another. A block below is the rue de Rivoli, lined with department stores, clothing shops, and sidewalk merchants.

Jo Goldenberg is a Paris institution in a neighborhood surrounded by four synagogues and half again as many Catholic churches (the Cathedral of Notre Dame is less than a mile away). The district is old, worn, and well past its prime. One should have a mission to go there, and Goldenberg was ours.

While the Goldenberg bagel is an exceptional bread, the restaurant food is ordinary, not sensational. At lunch, a handsome black-haired man, a Monsieur Beare, sat immediately alongside at one of a number of small tables stretching the length of the room. We talked. He had been born in Durban, where his grandfather had the distinction of having made the first matzo ball in South Africa. He knew the United States and had done graduate work at the University of New Mexico. Now he was with an engineering firm in Holland.

"The food here is not why I come to Paris," he laughed, "but the bagels will make the trip worthwhile. Surprisingly, there are not many places in Paris where one can get kosher food. This is one of the few."

Monsieur Beare was seated between us and two elderly women, small and fragile, the quintessence of old lace and lavender, and evoking a picture of a kitten playing with a ball of yarn before a fire. He was explaining to them in Yiddish what the three of us had been talking about. They smiled, and nodded in our direction and spoke softly to Monsieur Beare.

Monsieur Beare laughed. "They said you will like the bagels here."

LES BAGELS DE JO GOLDENBERG ❧ JO GOLDENBERG'S BAGELS

[EIGHT LARGE WATER BAGELS]

Bagels are as varied as the imagination will allow—onion, sesame seed, poppy seed, white, rye, salted, plain, whole wheat, caraway seed, and on and on. Bagel lovers are also fiercely partisan—water or egg!

This recipe is for a water bagel made with white flour. It is plain, with suggestions as to how it can be glamorized.

The technique suggested here for shaping the bagel is for the occasional home bagel baker. The professional would roll the dough into a length that would go completely around his open hand—plus enough to overlap. He would then roll the bagel back and forth under the palm to seal the edges. It is difficult for a tyro to maintain the same thickness over the whole length of the bagel. (Mine look like a sleeping bag that has not been shaken out for several days.)

The easy way to achieve a highly professional-looking bagel is simply to push a hole through a ball of dough and gently work it into a bagel with smooth sides. Warning: never use a cookie or doughnut cutter! Tradition frowns on it. If you do, don't mention it when someone praises your perfectly shaped bagels.

INGREDIENTS
1¹/₂ cups warm water (105°–115°)
2 packages dry yeast
3 tablespoons sugar
1 tablespoon salt
3¹/₂ cups all-purpose flour, approximately
2 quarts boiling water
1 tablespoon malt syrup or sugar

Glaze (optional):
1 egg white
1 tablespoon water

CONTAINER
Four-and-a-half-quart pan for simmering hot water in which to drop bagels to cook in first stage of their development.

BAKING SHEET
Baking sheet, greased or Teflon, sprinkled with cornmeal.

PREPARATION
12 minutes
The early part of this preparation can be done with an electric mixer.
In a mixing bowl, pour water and yeast. Stir to dissolve and leave for 2 or 3 minutes until yeast is creamy. Stir in sugar and salt. Add 2 cups of flour and beat at low mixer speed for 1 minute—turn to high for 3 minutes. Stop mixer and add balance of flour; stir with wooden spoon or rubber scraper to make a thick batter. When it becomes difficult to stir, work soft dough with hands.

Author's own technique for shaping a bagel.

KNEADING
4–8 minutes

Place under a dough hook for 4 to 5 minutes, adding flour if dough sticks to the sides of the bowl. Bagel dough must be firm, so add flour sufficient to make it solid when pinched with fingers.

If kneading by hand, do so with strong 1-2-3 rhythm of push-turn-fold. Add flour if dough is sticky or elastic. Bagel dough must be firm. Knead for 8 minutes.

FIRST RISING
1 hour

Return dough to clean and greased bowl. Cover it tightly with plastic wrap and leave undisturbed at room temperature (70°–75°) until double in volume.

During this period prepare water in large (4½-quart) pan. Bring to a boil and add 1 tablespoon malt extract or sugar. Reduce heat and leave at a simmer.

SHAPING
15 minutes

Turn dough onto flour-dusted work surface and punch down with extended fingers. Divide the dough into 8 pieces, about 4 ounces each. Shape each into a ball. Allow to relax for 3 or 4 minutes before flattening with the palm of the hand. With the thumb, press deep into the center of the bagel and tear open with the fingers. Pull the hole open and smooth the rough edges with the fingers. It should look like a bagel!

Place bagels together on the work surface.

SECOND RISING
10 minutes

Cover bagels with wax paper and leave at room temperature only until dough is slightly raised, about 10 minutes. A *boulanger* calls this "half-proofed." If they go beyond half-proof, the bagels may not sink as they should when first dropped into the hot water. If by chance the bagels go beyond this point—no problem. Proceed as if they sank even though they are floating. Only a professional bagel maker would appreciate the nuance.

BOILING
4–5 minutes

The water should be simmering. Gently lift one bagel at a time with large skimmer and lower into the hot water. Do not do more than 2 or 3 at a time. Don't crowd them. The bagel should sink and then rise after a few seconds. Turn bagel over once during the 45 seconds it is in the hot water. Lift out with the skimmer, drain briefly on a towel, then place on prepared baking sheet. Repeat with all of the bagels.

Thanks to the malt syrup or sugar, the bagels will be shiny as they come from the water.

BAKING
450°
35 minutes

This is the time to give the bagels glamour with different toppings. To top with salt, onion bits, or sesame, poppy, or caraway seeds, brush bagels with egg-white-and-water glaze and sprinkle.

Place on baking sheet and bake on middle oven shelf.

When bagel tops have a light brown color, turn them over to complete baking. This will keep bagels in a rounded shape without the sharp flatness of baking on one side. Remove from oven when brown and shiny.

FINAL STEP Place on metal rack to cool. Bagels are versatile. Split and toast for a sandwich or breakfast. However, if bagels are to be kept longer than a day, they should be frozen. Thaw enough to slice in half, then heat in a 350° oven or open and toast.

Shaping the dough for salted sesame bagels.

Ka' Achei Sumsum ❧ Salted Sesame Bagels

[ABOUT TWO DOZEN SMALL BAGELS]

A sumsum *made its appearance in a small sidewalk café not far from Jo Goldenberg's. Full name:* ka' achei sumsum, *a small salted sesame bread traditional with Syrian Jews on a Sabbath morning over coffee, whether in Paris or Syria. I had mine with tea, and it was equally good.*

The sumsum *is not sweet, but it is rich with butter. Roll out a piece of dough 6 inches long—curl it around the index finger and let the tip of one end rest on the tip of the other. That's a* sumsum.

INGREDIENTS 2 packages dry yeast
$^{1}/_{2}$ teaspoon sugar
1 cup warm water (105°–115°)
1 teaspoon salt
3 cups all-purpose flour, approximately
8 ounces (2 sticks) butter or margarine, melted
1 beaten egg, to brush
$^{1}/_{4}$ cup sesame seeds, to sprinkle

BAKING SHEET One baking sheet, greased or Teflon.

PREPARATION
18 minutes
Stir together yeast, sugar and warm water in a mixing bowl. Allow the yeast to dissolve and become frothy, about 8 minutes. Stir in salt and 1 cup of flour. Blend. Pour in melted butter (warm but not hot). Beat 40 to 50 strokes to thoroughly blend ingredients. Add the balance of the flour, $^1/_2$ cup at a time, stirring first with utensil and then working in the flour with the hands. It is a rich dough and will soon lose its stickiness.

KNEADING
8 minutes
Turn the dough onto the floured work surface and knead aggressively with a rhythmic motion of push-turn-fold. The dough will become soft and elastic.

RISING
2 hours
Because of its richness it takes about 2 hours for the dough to double in bulk in the bowl. Cover with plastic wrap and leave at room temperature (70°–75°).

SHAPING
12 minutes
Divide the dough into 24 equal pieces and roll each into a tight ball. Set aside. Roll the first ball under the palm of the hand into a 6-inch length. Press the ends into points.

Form the piece into an overlapping circle on the baking sheet. Place the index finger down against the sheet and wrap the length of dough around it—letting the end overlap on the top of the piece underneath. Press the ends gently to join.

Repeat for the other pieces, and place 1$^1/_2$ inches apart on baking sheet.

The *sumsums* baked, a Parisian bread that originated in the Middle East.

REST 20 minutes	Preheat oven to 375° while the *sumsums* are brushed with beaten egg and sprinkled liberally with sesame seeds. Try poppy seeds on some for an attractive variation. Don't cover.
BAKING 375° 35 minutes	Unlike the conventional bagel that is first cooked in boiling water, the *sumsum* goes directly into the oven. They are done when a bright golden yellow and firm when pressed.
FINAL STEP	Allow to cool on metal rack. Delightful served with coffee or tea—or anytime. They keep very well in a bread box. Also freeze well.

The Paris of Place Victor Hugo

All of the things that are elegant about Paris can be found in and around Place Victor Hugo, 16ᵉ *arrondissement*. One-, two-, and three-star restaurants are scattered up and down the ten avenues and streets converging on the Place. Avenue Victor Hugo is one of the main arteries coming through from the great Parisian park and forest, the Bois de Boulogne, and going on to the Arc de Triomphe. There are two or three banks on the circle with the one owned by the Rothschilds just around the corner. In the center, there is a towering water fountain, and there is deep shade over most of the Place cast by a small forest of plane trees.

There are two standout establishments on the Place for generating traffic. One is the Bureau de Poste, the post office, and the other, two doors away, is La Petite Marquise, one of the 1,200 *boulangeries* in Paris, and certainly one of the finest.

As you come out of the Bureau de Poste, you are immediately aware, and pleasantly so, of the smell of warm bread and pastries being carried on the gentle breezes moving around the Place. You are drawn as if by magic to the display windows of La Petite Marquise. It is not sorcery. It is the work of an electric fan placed in the basement window, fronting the Place, pouring out the fragrance of hot breads being created there by the *boulangers.*

The personality of La Petite Marquise, *la maison des produits naturels,* "the house of natural products," is reflected in the credo printed on the card given to each customer.

"Milling done between stones, and products grown without chemical fertilizers or insecticides.

"By rustic methods of agriculture and manufacture, we obtain products of a biological value unique in the world: whole-meal flour, bread made with starters, honey bread, gingerbread, butter, natural vinegar, cheese, preserves, eggs, farm produce, vegetables, noodles, walnut oil, prunes, nuts, wine, country pastries, honey, germinated wheat, fruits, candy, natural olive oil, fruit juices, cereals. . . ."

If all of this does not convince a customer, there are small signs tucked among the loaves announcing that everything is "made with eggs which we sell, butter which we sell and flour which we sell. All of these products are of the highest biological quality."

GALETTE PERSANE ✤ PERSIAN FLATBREAD

[THREE ROUND FLATBREADS]

Three fermentations *or risings of dough made with unbleached and whole wheat flours and a portion of wheat germ make this flatbread* idéal pour un régime, *ideal for a diet. It is so good, so crusty, and so wheaty that I consider it ideal for any diet.*

In this adaptation of La Petite Marquise's fine loaf, there is no sugar. There is, however, 1 tablespoon of olive oil.

INGREDIENTS
Starter:
1 package dry yeast
1 cup cool water (70°–75°)
1¹/₂ cups whole wheat flour, stone-ground preferred

Sponge:
All of the starter
1 cup cool water (70°–75°)
1¹/₂ cups whole wheat flour, stone-ground preferred

Dough:
All of the sponge
2 teaspoons salt
¹/₂ cup cool water (70°–75°)
1 tablespoon olive oil
¹/₃ cup wheat germ
2¹/₂ cups unbleached flour, approximately

BAKING SHEET
One baking sheet, greased or Teflon.

PREPARATION
5 minutes
24 hours
Starter: Sprinkle yeast in water in a small bowl and stir until it is dissolved. Pour in whole wheat flour and blend to make a thick batter. Cover the bowl with plastic wrap and leave at room temperature (70°–75°) for 24 hours. During this time batter will rise and fall as it ferments.

5 minutes
12–24 hours
Sponge: Into a large bowl, pour all of the starter. Add water and whole wheat flour to make a thick batter. Cover bowl with plastic wrap. This should be left to mature a minimum of 12 hours. The longer the period, up to 24 hours, the more robust the flavor will be.

10 minutes
Dough: Remove plastic wrap and stir down the sponge which will be light and puffy. Add salt, water, olive oil, and wheat germ. Blend with sponge. Add unbleached flour, ¹/₂ cup at a time, stirring it in with a large wooden spoon or rubber scraper. When the batter gets too heavy to stir with the utensil, sprinkle with flour and work it with the hands. When the dough is a solid body, lift from bowl.

KNEADING
7 minutes

Drop dough on work surface that has been sprinkled lightly with flour. Knead with a strong push-turn-fold motion. Add sprinkles of flour if the dough is sticky.

Now and then lift the dough above the table and bring it down hard with a crash! It's good for the gluten. This will be a solid dough and, unlike all-white dough, it will not be very elastic.

FIRST RISING
1¹/₄ hours

Return dough to the large bowl (washed and greased) and cover with plastic wrap. Leave it at room temperature (70°–75°) until dough has doubled in volume.

SHAPING
10 minutes

Three pounds of dough will make 3 round loaves 6 inches in diameter. Punch down dough and knead to press out the bubbles. Divide the dough and shape into balls. Allow them to rest for a few moments. Press one ball flat with the palm of the hand—about 6 inches in diameter and ³/₄ inch thick. Place on baking sheet. Repeat for the other pieces.

SECOND RISING
40 minutes

Cover the *galettes* with wax paper or a cloth and leave at room temperature (70°–75°) until double in volume, about 40 minutes.

BAKING
425°
40 minutes

Preheat oven 20 minutes before baking. With sharp razor, slash 4 deep cuts (¹/₂ inch) across the top of the loaf. Make 4 more deep cuts in the other direction (90°).

Place on middle shelf of the oven.

When loaves are light golden brown, tap bottom crust with forefinger, and if it sounds hard and hollow, the bread is baked.

FINAL STEP

Place on a metal rack to cool. To serve, break the *galettes* along the deep cuts.

Persian Flatbread, a crusty, nutritious *pain de régime.*

Pain Complet ❖ Whole Wheat Health Bread

[THREE BRAIDED LOAVES]

A favorite bread of health food enthusiasts is pain complet—*the complete bread. Whole wheat, of course. This version of La Petite Marquise's* pain complet *is fashioned into a favorite form—*nattes *or braids. It begins with a starter, which may be left to develop flavor for two or three days. One-fourth cup of honey gives it just a touch of natural sweetness. These basic ingredients (no shortening) easily qualify it as a* pain de régime, *a loaf for the diet-conscious.*

INGREDIENTS

Starter:
2 cups warm water (105°–115°)
¹/₂ cup non-fat dry milk
1 *teaspoon* dry yeast
3 cups whole wheat flour

Dough:
All of the starter
¹/₂ cup warm water (105°–115°)
2 teaspoons (balance of package) dry yeast
¹/₄ cup non-fat dry milk
1 tablespoon salt
¹/₄ cup honey
1 cup all-purpose flour
2 cups whole wheat flour, approximately

Glaze:
1 egg, beaten
1 tablespoon milk

BAKING SHEET

One baking sheet, greased or Teflon.

PREPARATION
10 minutes
12 hours
or longer

Starter: At least 12 hours beforehand, pour water, milk, yeast, and flour into a large bowl and stir to blend all of the ingredients. Cover with plastic wrap and leave at room temperature (70°–75°) for 12 hours or overnight. Longer fermentation develops a more pronounced wheaty flavor.

12 minutes

Dough: Remove and save plastic wrap. Stir down starter. Pour in water, yeast, milk, and salt. Stir to dissolve and add honey. When blended, add 1 cup all-purpose flour and beat with 25 strong strokes before stirring in whole wheat flour, ¹/₂ cup at a time. Don't rush. Let each addition of whole wheat absorb its full quota of moisture before continuing. If all of the flour is dumped into the mixture at once it may suddenly become too dense and firm. When it is a solid mass but soft, scrape down sides of bowl and turn out onto flour-dusted work surface.

KNEADING
6 minutes

This may be sticky in the beginning, so toss down liberal sprinkles of flour on the work surface and work it into the dough. A dough scraper is handy to keep film of dough scraped off work surface. Knead with a strong 1-2-3 motion of push-turn-fold until ball of dough is smooth and elastic.

Whole wheat braids appeal to Parisian health food and diet enthusiasts.

FIRST RISING
1¹/₄ hours

Wash and grease bowl and drop dough into it. Cover tightly with plastic wrap and leave at room temperature (70°–75°) until it doubles in volume.

SHAPING
20 minutes

Turn dough onto floured work surface and knead briefly to press out gas bubbles. Prepare the braids or *nattes* by dividing the dough into 3 large pieces—and dividing each of these into 3 smaller pieces. Roll the pieces into balls and allow to rest for about 3 minutes.

Form the strands to be braided by pressing down and rolling each ball with the palm. As a strand lengthens, place both palms on it and gently roll it back and forth while exerting a slight outward pull with both hands; not too much or the dough might tear. If a strand pulls back, move to others and return when it has relaxed.

Individual strands will be about 12 to 14 inches long. Place 3 strands parallel. Braid from the center. Pinch the ends of the strands together tightly and complete braid on the other end. Place the completed braid on the baking sheet. Repeat for the other 2 loaves.

SECOND RISING
40 minutes

Cover braids with wax paper and leave at room temperature (70°–75°) until nearly double in volume. If ends should spring open, carefully pinch together again.

BAKING
380°
45 minutes

Preheat oven 20 minutes before bake time.

Uncover braids and brush with beaten egg-milk glaze. Place baking sheet on middle shelf of oven. At end of 30 minutes, turn baking sheet around so loaves will be exposed equally to temperature variations.

Braids are done when bottom crusts are deep brown and loaves sound hard and hollow when tapped with a forefinger.

The braids are fragile when they come from the oven so slip a spatula under each braid when you work it loose from the baking sheet and carry it to test or cool. It may stick if glaze has run onto the baking sheet.

FINAL STEP

Place braids on metal rack to cool. This is delicious toasted—or anytime.

PAIN D'ÉPICE ❦ SPICE BREAD

[TWO SMALL LOAVES]

While it smacks of gingerbread, pain d'épice *is a traditional French bread made with honey rather than molasses, and the flour is rye and white. There are four spices, a touch of rum, almonds, currants, and orange rind.*

The honey I use is from California—a mixture of avocado and clover—and, according to the label, is raw, organic, unfiltered, and uncooked. It is also delicious! But the product of any bee is as good in this bread.

Pain d'épice *improves with age, so don't plan to slice it (despite the temptation after the wonderful baking aroma) for at least 2 or 3 days. It will keep for several weeks in the refrigerator, and several months frozen. A fine bread to serve thinly sliced with coffee or tea or a glass of wine.*

INGREDIENTS
1 cup hot tap water (120°–130°)
1 cup honey
$^1/_4$ cup sugar
1 pinch salt
2 teaspoons baking soda
1 teaspoon baking powder
$^1/_4$ cup rum, or water to substitute
$1^1/_2$ teaspoons ground anise seeds
1 teaspoon cinnamon
$^3/_4$ teaspoon ground ginger
$^1/_4$ teaspoon ground cloves
2 cups rye flour
$1^1/_2$ cups unbleached white flour
1 teaspoon orange rind, grated
$^2/_3$ cup chopped almonds
$^1/_2$ cup currants or raisins (if the latter, chop fine)

BAKING PANS
Two small ($7^1/_2 \times 3^1/_2$) loaf pans, greased.

PREPARATION
15 minutes
In a large bowl, pour hot water over honey. Add sugar, salt, baking soda, and baking powder. Stir to dissolve and blend.

Pour in rum (if desired) or water to substitute, and add anise seeds, cinnamon, ginger, and cloves. Add 1 cup of rye and 1 cup of white flour, stir. When ingredients have been blended, add the additional 1 cup of rye and $^1/_2$ cup of white flour. The batter will be thick but smooth.

Add orange rind, almonds, and currants. Stir 25 strokes to blend thoroughly, but don't overbeat. Set aside while preparing pans.

Preheat oven to 400°.

FORMING
8 minutes

Grease pans, line sides with wax paper (not the ends), and grease paper. Leave 1-inch tab projecting to pull out loaf later.

With large spoon and rubber scraper, fill pans ³/₄ full. If the dough sticks to the scraper, dip in water. Fingers are also good to pat the dough into the corners of the pans.

BAKING
400°
10 minutes
350°
50 minutes

Place loaves on middle shelf. After 10 minutes, reduce heat to 350°, and continue baking for 50 minutes. Loaves will rise about 1 inch above sides of pans. They will be deep brown when baked. There will probably be a large crevice running the length of each loaf. This is good. Test with cake pin or metal skewer. Thrust into center of the loaf— if it comes out with no particles sticking to it, the bread is done.

FINAL STEP

Place pans on metal rack. Turn loaf on its side and gently tug free with the paper tab. Repeat for the other loaf. When loaves have completely cooled, wrap tightly in aluminum foil or place in plastic bag to age for several days. Bread keeps exceptionally well and is an ideal gift for sending to friends overseas, on the other coast, or around the corner.

Pain d'Épice, a honey-sweetened spice bread to serve with wine or coffee.

Pain de Son—Régime ❧ Bran Diet Bread

[TWO MEDIUM LOAVES]

This moist and brown-flaked loaf is much too good to be left only to those on a diet. At a buffet, for instance, it is great with a slice of cheese or a spread. It has an appealing nutty flavor.

While it has somewhat the taste of a fine pumpernickel, it is made without sugar or molasses. It depends entirely on the natural sugars in the bran and flour for its light touch of sweetness.

While bran is processed into a number of breakfast cereals, this bread is made with the brown, flaky outer covering of the wheat kernel just as it comes from the miller, and which you can find at health food stores.

Be forewarned that 4 cups of bran flakes absorb an inordinate quantity of liquid.

INGREDIENTS
5 cups all-purpose flour, approximately
4 teaspoons salt
1 package dry yeast
$3^1/_2$ cups warm water (105°–115°)
4 cups (8 ounces) bran flakes

BAKING PANS
Two medium-size ($8^1/_2 \times 4^1/_2$) baking pans, greased or Teflon.

PREPARATION
12 minutes
In a large bowl, pour 2 cups all-purpose flour, salt, and yeast. Add water, stir to dissolve yeast. Allow to rest for 3 minutes. Add bran flakes, 1 cup at a time, stirring well to blend all the ingredients (about 25 strokes). Add balance of all-purpose flour, 1 cup at a time. Stir with wooden spoon or rubber scraper until flour absorbs the moisture and the mass can be worked with the hands.

Allow dough to stand for 5 minutes to be certain bran has absorbed full quota of moisture.

KNEADING
8 minutes
Be prepared to use liberal sprinkles of flour to control stickiness.

Turn dough onto floured work surface. In the beginning, it may be helpful to turn and work dough with pastry scraper or putty knife. Slowly the flour and bran will begin to work together and become less sticky.

It will never have the easy elasticity of white dough because of the bran and its higher moisture content. However, don't allow dough to become a solid ball with the addition of too much flour. Dough will be somewhat soft and elastic at end of kneading period.

FIRST RISING
$1^1/_2$ hours
Place ball of dough in greased bowl and cover with plastic wrap. Leave at room temperature (70°–75°) until double in volume, about $1^1/_2$ hours.

SHAPING
10 minutes

Remove plastic wrap from bowl, punch down dough, and turn onto dusted work surface. Divide ball of dough into two pieces. Form the loaves by pressing each ball with the palm to form a flat oval, roughly the length of the baking pan. Fold the oval in half, pinch the seam together, tuck ends under, and place seam down in pan. Repeat for second piece.

SECOND RISING
1¼ hours

Cover the pans with wax paper and place in an undisturbed place at room temperature (70°–75°) until dough has reached edge of pan. The dough will rise slowly because of its dense nature.

BAKING
380°
45 minutes

Preheat oven 20 minutes before baking.

Remove wax paper. With razor blade or sharp knife, cut design on top crust of each loaf.

The top crust will be light brown when baked. For a richer color, brush with egg-milk glaze before placing in oven.

Turn pans end for end midway in the bake period. To test for doneness, turn one loaf from pan and tap bottom crust with forefinger. If hard, bread is done.

Crust may be given deeper color by returning to the oven without pan for an additional 10 minutes.

FINAL STEP

Remove from pans and place on metal rack to cool. Freezes well.

PAIN SANS SEL ❦ SALT-FREE BREAD

[TWO SMALL LOAVES]

Salt-free bread at times leaves more than salt to be desired. The French have taken steps to correct this by adding potato and milk to give pain sans sel *good texture and flavor yet remaining within the boundaries of a* pain de régime, *a diet bread.*

This recipe is for two loaves; one of these can be salted to appeal to the non-dieter in the house. It is simple to do. One buttered pan is sprinkled with salt before the dough goes in, and, later, the top crust is sprinkled as well.

Both are low-key, certainly, but good breads nevertheless.

INGREDIENTS

1 package dry yeast
2 cups warm water (105°–115°)
¼ cup non-fat dry milk
⅓ cup potato flakes (or ¼ cup mashed potato)
4 cups all-purpose flour, approximately

Glaze:
1 egg
1 tablespoon water

$^1\!/_2$ teaspoon salt, to sprinkle, if desired

BAKING PANS Two small ($7^1\!/_2 \times 3^1\!/_2$) or one large (9×5) loaf pan, greased or Teflon. The Teflon would need to be greased, of course, if it is to be sprinkled with salt.

PREPARATION
12 minutes In a large bowl, stir yeast into the water and allow the particles to dissolve. Add dry milk and potato. Stir in the flour, $^1\!/_2$ cup at a time, first with a large wooden spoon or rubber scraper, then work dough with the hands. When dough can be lifted from the bowl, place on work surface.

KNEADING
7 minutes Knead with a vigorous 1-2-3 motion of push-turn-fold. The dough will have a slightly different feel about it because it has no salt, but this will have no effect on the kneading. If the dough is sticky, toss down small sprinkles of flour.

FIRST RISING
1 hour Place dough in bowl and cover tightly with a length of plastic wrap and leave at room temperature (70°–75°) until it has doubled in volume.

SHAPING
10 minutes Punch down dough and turn onto floured work surface. Divide into two pieces and set aside for a moment while the pans are prepared.
　　If one loaf is to be salted, sprinkle its greased pan with salt.
　　To form the loaves, knead the dough briefly to push out the bubbles. Press dough into an oval the length of the pan. Fold the dough in half, pinch seam together, and place in the pan, seam down. Repeat for other pan, but without the salt, of course.

SECOND RISING
45 minutes Cover with wax paper and leave at room temperature (70°–75°) until dough rises to the edge of the pans, about 45 minutes.

BAKING
375°
35 minutes Preheat oven 20 minutes before baking.
　　Brush tops with egg-water glaze. On the loaf in the salted pan, sprinkle salt, preferably coarsely ground.
　　Place loaves on the middle shelf of the oven.
　　After 30 minutes, the loaves should be golden brown. Take one from the pan and tap bottom crust with forefinger. If it sounds hard and hollow, loaf is done. If not, return to oven for 5 minutes longer.

FINAL STEP Place on metal rack to cool. These are handsome small loaves, and a thoughtful gift for someone on a salt-free diet.

RECIPES FROM LE HAVRE

To the transatlantic ship passenger, now so few in number, Le Havre is remembered as a huge terminal where one could step directly aboard the special boat train to Paris. While the appealing resort towns of Honfleur, Deauville, and Trouville are nearby, Le Havre is a big and busy industrialized port city that would appear at first glance to have few appeals to the casual visitor. Near the invasion coast of Normandy, the city took a horrible pounding by the Allied air force during World War II, and most of it has been built from the rubble up. Le Havre rebuilt with vigor and enthusiasm, but it has taken the trees along wide Avenue Foch three decades to soften the hard, straight lines of post-war architecture.

Food is another matter. Chefs off the big ships have had a salutary effect on the city's cuisine, as have the other well-traveled natives of Le Havre. The town is especially fond of brioche—in all of its forms. Within a block or so of the big city market, Halles Centrales, on rue Voltaire, I hungrily window-shopped in front of the *boulangeries* of M. Quertier, M. Leprettre, M. Portier, and M. Duchemin. I could not pick a favorite *boulangerie* or brioche. The customers, however, seemed to lean toward a lovely braided loaf with raisins, if the number of loaves displayed in the windows could be considered a reliable gauge.

BRIOCHE NANTERRE ✤ NANTERRE BRIOCHE LOAF
AND
BRIOCHE PARISIENNE ✤ PARISIAN BRIOCHE LOAF

[ONE LOAF OF EACH]

*Brioche is often thought of only as a small breakfast bread (*brioche à tête *is the classic), when in reality it is an extremely versatile dough that can be used in a range of breads from hors d'oeuvres to* Brioche Nanterre *and brioche parisienne. The latter two are full-size loaves, made from the same dough but shaped in two different fashions.*

The Nanterre *is made by placing 6 or 8 balls of brioche dough in a zigzag pattern along the bottom of a loaf pan. They rise to fill out the pan in the same overall pattern. The* parisienne *is made by placing 9 or 10 short lengths of brioche dough side by side across the pan. They rise in identical sections that can be broken off and served.*

Usually the dough is made the night before, punched down twice, and left in the refrigerator before shaping the loaves the following day. This process can be foreshortened to 6 hours.

INGREDIENTS 5 cups all-purpose flour, approximately
2 teaspoons salt
2 packages dry yeast
1 tablespoon sugar
$^1/_3$ cup non-fat dry milk
1 cup warm water (105°–115°)
5 eggs, room temperature
$^3/_4$ pound (3 sticks) butter, room temperature

Glaze:
1 egg
1 tablespoon milk

BAKING PANS Two medium-size (8$^1/_2$ × 4$^1/_2$) loaf pans, greased or Teflon.

PREPARATION
15 minutes
In a large bowl, stir together 2 cups of flour, the salt, yeast, sugar and dry milk. Form a well in bottom of bowl and pour in water. With large wooden spoon or rubber scraper, slowly pull in flour from the sides to make a soft batter. Crack and drop in eggs, one at a time, blending each into the flour-yeast mixture. While the dough is still a thick batter, cut butter into several small chunks and drop into the bowl and blend. When butter has been absorbed into the mixture, add additional flour, 1 cup at a time, until dough can be worked with the hands.

KNEADING
7 minutes
Turn dough onto work surface that has been dusted with sprinkles of flour. The dough will be elastic and soft (later the refrigerator cold will harden it). Break the kneading rhythm by occasionally dropping the ball of dough forcefully onto the work surface. If the dough continues to be sticky, add light sprinkles of flour.

FIRST RISING
1$^1/_2$–2 hours
Place dough in bowl, cover tightly with plastic wrap, and leave undisturbed at room temperature (70°–75°) until dough has doubled in volume.

PUNCH DOWN
2 minutes
Turn back plastic wrap and punch down the risen dough with the fingers. Turn ball of dough over, and replace covering.

SECOND RISING
1 hour
Leave covered dough at room temperature for about 1 hour.

PUNCH DOWN
2 minutes
Turn back plastic wrap and punch down dough with fingers, as above.

REFRIGERATION
6 hours
or overnight
Re-cover bowl and place in refrigerator to allow dough to develop and chill.

Brioche Nanterre (left) and *Brioche Parisienne* (right) before and after baking.

SHAPING
30 minutes

Place the chilled dough on floured work surface and divide into two pieces.

For the *Nanterre,* cut off 6 or 8 pieces of dough, each weighing about 2 ounces or about 2^1/$_2$ inches in diameter when rolled into a ball.

Shape each into a ball and place in the bottom of the prepared pan in a zigzag pattern. They can be pressed tightly together if necessary to fit.

For the *parisienne,* cut off 9 or 10 pieces of dough, each weighing about 2 ounces. Fashion each into a roll or cylinder 4^1/$_2$ inches long (the width of the pan) and about 1 inch in diameter. Lay parallel and tightly together across the bottom of the pan.

THIRD RISING
2^1/$_2$–3 hours

Cover the pans with wax paper and leave them at room temperature (70°–75°) until the pieces have doubled in volume, about 2^1/$_2$ hours. The lengthy rising is necessary to allow the dough to come to room temperature after having been refrigerated.

BAKING
380°
35 minutes

Twenty minutes before baking, preheat oven.

Brush tops of loaves with egg-milk glaze. Place on middle shelf of oven.

Turn the pans around midway through the bake period to compensate for temperature variations in the oven.

Handle the hot brioche loaves carefully when testing for doneness because they are fragile along the lines where the pieces of dough have been joined. They will firm up when cool.

When done, each loaf will be a light golden brown, and the bottom crust will sound hollow when tapped with a forefinger.

If the bread is done but needs more color, put back in the oven *without* the pan for 5 to 8 minutes.

FINAL STEP

Place on metal rack to cool—remembering to handle the hot loaves with care until they cool.

BRIOCHE AUX RAISINS SECS ❧ RAISIN BRIOCHE LOAF
AND
BRIOCHE AU FROMAGE ❧ CHEESE BRIOCHE LOAF

[ONE BRAIDED LOAF OF EACH]

Le Havre would not be Le Havre if one did not see braided brioche loaves in a dozen windows on a walk through the inner city. Most of these would be brioches aux raisins secs, *with a number of* brioches au fromage *to be found here and there.*

These two fine loaves can be made by dividing the brioche dough into two equal pieces—adding diced-up Gruyère or Swiss cheese to one portion, and 1/2 cup of currants or raisins to the other. Each is braided and given an egg-milk glaze to produce a rich, deep brown crust. Each is delicious. Each is Le Havre.*

There is a surprise in a slice of the brioche au fromage. *The cheese bits will have melted to leave tiny glistening pockets.*

INGREDIENTS
1 package dry yeast
1 cup warm water (105°–115°)
3$^1/_2$ cups all-purpose flour
1 teaspoon sugar
1$^1/_2$ teaspoons salt
6 ounces (1$^1/_2$ sticks) butter, room temperature
4 eggs, room temperature
$^3/_4$ cup ($^1/_3$ pound) diced Gruyère or Swiss cheese
$^1/_2$ cup currants or raisins

Glaze:
1 egg
1 tablespoon milk

BAKING SHEET One baking sheet, greased or Teflon.

PREPARATION
15 minutes

The dough will be divided into two portions—one for the cheese and the other for the currants or raisins—after the mixing and before the first rising. This is an easy dough to prepare in a heavy-duty mixer.

In a mixing bowl, sprinkle yeast into warm water. Allow to dissolve and become creamy, about 5 minutes. Stir in 1$^1/_2$ cups of flour, and the sugar and salt. Beat in the electric mixer 2 minutes at medium speed, or for an equal length of time with a large wooden spoon or rubber scraper. Add the butter in small pieces and continue beating 1 minute. Stop the mixer. Add eggs, one at a time, and the remaining flour $^1/_2$ cup at a time, beating thoroughly with each addition.

The dough will be soft and sticky and must be beaten until it is shiny, elastic, and pulls from the hands.

MIXING
10–20 minutes

If mixing by hand, turn the dough onto the work surface. With dough scraper or putty knife, lift and turn dough—again and again. Use the hands to lift the dough and crash it down against the table top. It will cling to the hands and utensil in the beginning, but after 12 to 15 minutes of active kneading, dough will begin to pull away from the hands as it is worked.

If using a heavy-duty mixer, beat at medium speed for 10 minutes.

DIVIDE
5 minutes

When the dough is glossy and elastic, divide into two bowls. Stir currants or raisins into one, and cheese into the other.

FIRST RISING
2–3 hours

Cover the bowls with plastic wrap and leave at room temperature (70°–75°) until dough has doubled in volume.

REFRIGERATION
5 hours
or longer

Do not stir down before placing in the refrigerator for a minimum of 5 hours or overnight. The rich dough must be chilled before it can be shaped.

SHAPING
15 minutes

Take one of the two doughs from the refrigerator. It will be cold and hard but will become easier to handle after it has been kneaded for a few moments. Divide dough into 3 pieces and roll each into a long strand of 12 to 16 inches. Don't rush the dough or it may tear if lengthened too quickly. Move from strand to strand to allow pieces to relax. When strands are completed, place them parallel and braid from the middle, carefully pinching the ends together. Turn bread around and complete the braid.

Place the braid on the baking sheet and repeat for the second bowl of dough.

SECOND RISING
1–2 hours

When both braids are completed, brush with egg-milk glaze and set aside *uncovered* until dough has doubled in volume.

If the dough had been chilled for a long period in the refrigerator it will take longer for it to warm and rise. (My overnight dough in the refrigerator has an inside temperature of 45° when I take it out, and it is 2 hours before it climbs to 70°.)

Brush the loaves with glaze again midway through the rising period.

BAKING
400°
40 minutes

Preheat oven 20 minutes before baking the brioches.

Give the brioches a final brushing with the glaze, and place the baking sheet on the middle shelf of the oven. Halfway through the bake period, turn the baking sheet around.

Brioches are done when a deep golden brown. The large braids are fragile when hot, so it is better to test doneness with a cake testing pin or metal skewer rather than to try to turn one over to thump.

If the skewer comes out of the loaf clean and free of particles, the braids are done.

FINAL STEP Carefully slide loaves off sheet onto metal rack with the aid of a spatula. They will become firm when cool. A fine gift is half of a raisin loaf and half of a cheese loaf, wrapped together. Unforgettable—in sentiment and in taste!

RECIPES FROM HONFLEUR

The windows of Monsieur André David's two *boulangeries* in the small Normandy fishing port of Honfleur, tucked into the protected estuary leading from the English Channel to the mouth of the Seine, are major tourist attractions. They rank with the town's fine museum of great seascapes by native son Eugene Boudin and old St. Catherine's church and bell tower, which was too heavy for the wood structure so the ingenious carpenters built it on the ground alongside the church.

The pièce de résistance for the traveler is the Vieux Bassin, the old inner harbor, filled with fishing and pleasure boats and with what appears to be an equal number of artists along the quays standing or seated before easels recording the scene. One David *boulangerie* is across from a small park in the very heart of the traffic flow, while the principal *boulangerie* (where all of the baking is done) is several blocks uphill where shops and stores are less touristy and more establishment.

Monsieur David is recognized as one of the great *boulangers* of France, so it is small wonder that his shops attract throngs of tourists and townspeople alike. The most impressive sight is the window filled with big husky four-pound country loaves stacked like cordwood, each loaf decorated with stalks of wheat, fashioned from dough, of course. In other windows are a score of other breads, and if one is puzzled as to the name of each, Monsieur David has thoughtfully arranged in the center window a large board on which each bread baked by him is displayed in miniature and identified with a legend underneath. Should one wish to know which bread goes with the fish and which with the soup, Monsieur David has developed a guide explaining precisely the proper choice.

Prominently displayed in the windows also are the International Gold Medal for baking won by his father at Brussels in 1934 and the first prize, the *coupe de France*, won by him in a national competition among *boulangers* and *pâtissiers* in Paris in 1971. The latter prize was awarded for a basket of long-stemmed roses that brought gasps of disbelief and delight from spectators when they learned that the basket and flowers were not fresh from the garden but warm from the oven.

The talent in the David *boulangerie* has not only created the prize-winning roses, but recently a large birdcage and doves for a wedding party of a thousand guests. At Easter, the bakers make hundreds of baby chicks and rabbits and they will special-order such fanciful things as a sunburst or a turtle. Anything that can be done with bread, David can do.

Monsieur David, however, does have a special affection for one particular bread, *pain brié*, the centuries-old Normandy specialty.

"We think it came to us from Spain where it is baked in the south, in the province of Málaga. Legend has it that a Spanish sailor swam to our coast from a ship lost at sea and gave us the recipe and taught us the unusual technique required to make it a good loaf.

"For a reason I can't fathom," said Monsieur David, "*pain brié* has never become popular in other regions of France. It remains ours exclusively.

"While it is a remnant of the past, *pain brié* is not about to disappear. To the contrary. It is being discovered all over again by people who love good bread and it is growing in popularity.

"It goes especially well with our famous shrimp and equally famous Normandy butter. The fact that it keeps well for several days is another plus."

The key to good *pain brié* is the unusual beating that follows the kneading, which makes the dough smooth and dense. In the David *boulangerie,* as in the one in Bayeux, the dough is held in a metal basin and pounded mechanically under a heavy metal hammer. In earlier days, the beating was done by hand with a smooth length of wood. It can be done now by the home baker with a tapered rolling pin. Large batches of dough were too much for a stick of wood, thus a special two-man apparatus was designed, one of which has been restored in Honfleur's small but excellent regional historical museum, off the Vieux Bassin.

In the hands of an operator, an eight-foot wooden arm hinged to a heavy wooden table was brought crashing down again and again on the big ball of *brié* dough. An assistant sat on the low table to move the dough to a new position each time the arm was lifted.

As Monsieur David said, "It is a very old method of making bread and it is certainly one of the best since it is still so appreciated."

The Bayeux and Honfleur recipes for *pain brié* are so similar that I have combined them in the one recipe on page 88. It reflects the best of the techniques found in both places.

Monsieur David does not like the trend toward what he calls "plastic bread" that is gaining a foothold even in France. Yet, he admits he cannot be overly sentimental about the old ways and expect to stay in business. The best fuel for the oven, he feels, is orchard wood—apple, cherry, peach, etc.—because it gives bread an undefinable flavor impossible to get in a modern gas- or electric-fired oven. He has had to forgo wood, however, because of its inflated cost. His shop will bake with wood on occasion, but only for special quality products that can "tolerate" the high prices.

Premium flour for the David *boulangerie,* on the other hand, is organically grown especially for him by farmers near the ocean who fertilize their fields with kelp taken from the sea. No chemicals.

Despite this special care with his own flour, Monsieur David does not think too highly of most French flours.

"Our standards for flour, unlike U.S. and Canadian flours, are not strict, and consequently do little good.

"It takes a master baker," he said, "to cope with the idiosyncrasies of French flours!"

Monsieur David is such a baker.

Pain de Campagne—Honfleur ❧ Honfleur Country Bread

[FOUR 1-POUND LOAVES OR ONE LARGE HEARTH LOAF]

Monsieur David's pain de campagne *is a husky, rough country loaf that begins with a starter enriched with honey. The yeast loves it!*

While the bread baked in his Honfleur boulangerie *is made with a special flour milled expressly for him from wheat grown along the Channel coast and fertilized with seaweed dragged from the sea, the combination of the two flours in this recipe closely parallels his.*

Monsieur David makes big *loaves—18 inches to 2 feet across—larger than most families could use and store. There are about 4¹/₄ pounds of dough in this recipe, enough for a big country loaf—or four small-to-medium loaves. A large loaf has one marked advantage, however; it provides a wide canvas for an unusual piece of art work—wheat stalks of dough baked on the crust! The technique is described in this recipe.*

INGREDIENTS *Starter:*
1 tablespoon honey
1 cup warm water (105°–115°)
1 package dry yeast
1 cup bread or all-purpose flour, approximately
1 cup whole wheat flour

Dough:
All of the starter
2 cups warm water (105°–115°)
1 tablespoon salt
2 cups whole wheat flour
2–3 cups bread or all-purpose flour, approximately

BAKING SHEET One or two baking sheets: greased and sprinkled with cornmeal, or Teflon. Number of sheets depends on number of loaves made and size of oven.

PREPARATION *Starter:* In a large bowl, dissolve honey in 1 cup warm water and add
8 minutes yeast. Stir to dissolve and let rest until creamy. Add ¹/₂ cup each white and whole wheat flours to make thick batter. Add balance of two flours to make a shaggy mass that can be worked with the hands. Knead for 3 minutes. Toss in liberal sprinkles of white flour if slack or sticky.

4 hours Cover bowl with plastic wrap and then leave it at room temperature
or overnight (70°– 75°) for at least 4 hours. Left overnight it will develop even more flavor and strength.

10 minutes *Dough:* Pour 2 cups of warm water (105°–115°) over starter. Stir with large wooden spoon or rubber scraper to break up dough. Add salt.

Master baker André David has won national honors for creative baking; here he decorates his famous Honfleur Country Bread.

Place 2 cups each of white and whole wheat flours at the side of the mixing bowl—and add equal parts of each, $1/2$ cup at a time, first stirring with utensil and then working it with the hands. It may take slightly more white flour to make a mass that is not sticky. Lift from the bowl with the hands.

KNEADING
8 minutes

Place the dough on floured work surface and begin to knead the dough aggressively with a strong 1-2-3 motion of push-turn-fold. Once in a while, lift the dough high above the work surface and bring it down with a crash to speed process. Do this 3 or 4 times and then resume kneading. Dough will be moist, solid, and a pleasure to work.

FIRST RISING
3–4 hours

Return the dough to the bowl (washed and greased), cover tightly with plastic wrap, and leave it at room temperature (70°–75°) to double in volume, about 3 hours.

SHAPING
10 minutes

Push down dough and turn out on well-floured work surface. Divide dough into desired number of pieces and shape with cupped hands into tight balls. Reserve 1 cup of dough to make wheat stalks later, if desired. Place on baking sheet and press tops down to flatten slightly.

SECOND RISING
2$1/2$ hours

The loaves are left under wax paper to *triple* in size, about 2$1/2$ hours at room temperature (70°–75°).

DECORATING
15 minutes

Wheat stalks: These need a large round hearth loaf that measures at least 12 inches across to do the stalks justice.

Shortly before the loaf or loaves are completely raised, divide the reserved cup of dough into 3 pieces. Roll each into a long strand 12 to 14 inches long. Place them parallel and, beginning 4 inches from one end, braid to that end. Turn strands around and separate to make it convenient to cut the wheat design on each. With sharp-pointed scissors, make small cuts down 5 inches of strand—alternating right, center, and left—to create grains of wheat protruding from the stalk before harvest. Leave remainder of stalk uncut and bare. Repeat pattern for each strand. Lightly brush top of the loaf with water and carefully position the wheat decoration. Fan the upper stalks apart.

BAKING
425°
50 minutes

Preheat oven 20 minutes before baking and place broiler pan on the bottom shelf. Five minutes before the bread goes in the oven, pour 1 cup hot tap water in the pan to create a moist, steamy oven.

Place the loaves on the middle shelf. Midway through the bake period, shift loaves to balance the effect of the oven's heat.

Loaves are done when golden brown. Bottom crust will sound hard and hollow when tapped with a forefinger.

FINAL STEP

Place on metal rack to cool before serving. Freezes well.

Pain de Méteil ❧ Maslin Stone-ground Rye or Pumpernickel Bread

[TWO LONG HEARTH LOAVES]

In earlier times, pain de méteil *or maslin was an endeavor to upgrade the appearance of dark, all-rye bread by adding an equal portion of precious white flour. The result was, and is, a loaf of simple, forthright, substantial bread. Now it is made because it is good bread, not because it is all there is available.*

Although this loaf has as its base an overnight starter, the sourness is not as assertive as it is when it is made with molasses or sugar (as in Jewish rye). This bread relies entirely on the natural sugars in the flour, and it has a very pleasant sweetness about it.

While pain de méteil *can be made with finely ground medium rye flour, the loaf better reflects its peasant origins with stone-ground or pumpernickel flour. It goes especially well with meats, soups, and leafy salads.*

INGREDIENTS *Starter:*
1^1/$_2$ cups stone-ground rye or pumpernickel flour
1 package dry yeast
1^1/$_2$ cups warm water (105°–115°)

Dough:
All of the starter
1 cup warm water (105°–115°)
1 tablespoon salt
3 tablespoons vegetable shortening
1 cup stone-ground rye or pumpernickel flour
2^1/$_2$ cups all-purpose flour, approximately

Glaze:
1 egg
1 tablespoon milk

BAKING SHEET One greased or Teflon baking sheet.

PREPARATION
5 minutes
6 hours
or overnight
Starter: In a small bowl, mix rye flour, yeast, and warm water. Stir until blended. Cover bowl with plastic wrap and put aside at room temperature (70°–75°) for a minimum of 6 hours or overnight.

10 minutes *Dough:* Pour all of the starter into a large bowl and stir in the 1 cup of water. Add salt and shortening. With a large wooden spoon or rubber scraper, blend in the cup of rye flour. Stir the batter 25 to 30 strokes to mix the ingredients thoroughly. Add white flour, ^{1}/$_2$ cup

at a time. Stir with utensil until it gets too heavy to move and then work with the hands. This will be a sticky dough (thanks to the rye flour) until the white flour begins to take over. When dough is a shaggy mass and can be worked with the hands with a minimum of stickiness, lift from the bowl. Clean particles from the sides of the bowl and add to the flour.

KNEADING
6 minutes

Sprinkle work surface with flour and turn dough onto it. Dough is heavy and dense, but it will become elastic and less sticky as the kneading proceeds. Add liberal sprinkles of white flour to control moisture. Occasionally lift the ball of dough high and throw it down hard against the table top to help develop the formation of the gluten in the dough.

FIRST RISING
2 hours

Clean and grease the large bowl. Turn ball of dough into it. Cover tightly with plastic wrap and leave at room temperature (70°–75°) until dough has risen to double its volume. Dough may also be tested for adequate proof by pushing a finger into the edge of the dough. If the indentation remains, the dough is sufficiently risen to shape.

SHAPING
5 minutes

Turn dough onto work surface and divide into 2 pieces. Knead each briefly to press out the bubbles. This dough will keep its shape well so there is no need for concern about placing it in a *banneton* or *couche*.

SECOND RISING
50 minutes

Place the 2 loaves on the baking sheet and cover with a length of wax paper to keep a crust from forming on the loaves too early.

BAKING
400°
50 minutes

Preheat oven 20 minutes before baking.

Remove wax paper and brush loaves with egg-milk glaze. With sharp knife or razor blade, slit each loaf with 5 or 6 diagonal cuts, about $1/2$ inch deep.

Place on the middle shelf of the oven.

Thirty minutes later, turn the loaves on the baking sheet to expose them equally to temperature variations.

Bread is done when the loaves are a light golden brown and bottom crust sounds hard and hollow when tapped with a forefinger.

FINAL STEP

Place the two loaves on a metal rack to cool. *Pain de méteil* freezes well and holds its maximum freshness for 4 to 6 weeks. Thaw in the plastic bag to allow moisture collected as ice crystals to be absorbed by the loaf. Remove from bag to heat at 350° for 15 minutes.

Brioche Mousseline ❧ Mousseline Brioche

[TWO TALL, ELEGANT LOAVES]

Brioche mousseline *is a spectacular loaf, and delicious.*

The dough is allowed to rise to the very edge of a cylindrical container (a coffee can, most likely), a paper collar is tied around it, and in the oven the dough rises to a splendid height—twice as tall as the pan itself.

The only caution: be certain that the shelf on which the pan sits in the oven is low enough to allow the dough to rise without poking its head into the oven top!

INGREDIENTS

Starter:
1 package dry yeast
$^1/_2$ cup warm water (105°–115°)
1 cup all-purpose flour, approximately

Dough:
4 cups all-purpose flour, approximately
6 eggs, room temperature
4 tablespoons warm water (100°)
3 tablespoons sugar
$1^1/_2$ teaspoons salt
12 ounces (3 sticks) butter, room temperature

BAKING PANS
Two 1-pound coffee cans, or a combination of other size cans if you desire. Cut 2 strips of heavy brown paper 8 inches wide and long enough to encircle cans—to tie on as collars after dough is partially risen. Also small fluted brioche pan in the event there is more dough than needed for selected cans. Butter cans, brioche pan, and brown paper strips.

PREPARATION

10 minutes
2 hours

Starter: In a small bowl, dissolve yeast in water and put aside for 3 or 4 minutes until creamy. Stir in flour to make a shaggy loaf of dough and knead for about 3 minutes. Cover with plastic wrap and leave in undisturbed place at room temperature (70°–75°) for 2 hours.

15 minutes
Dough: The starter is left in reserve while the rest of the dough is prepared.

In a large bowl, measure 2 cups of flour and make a well in bottom to receive eggs. Break in one at a time, stirring with wooden spoon or rubber scraper to pull flour in from the sides. Add 2 tablespoons water, the sugar, and salt, and blend to make thick batter.

On a length of wax paper, knead butter with dough scraper or spatula to make it soft and pliable. Blend butter into the batter. Add the remaining 2 eggs and 2 tablespoons of water and beat into the thick batter.

Stir the rest of the flour into the batter, $1/2$ cup at a time, until dough is a soft ball that can be worked with the hands. Lift from the bowl.

Place dough on floured work surface, press it into a flat oval, and place starter in the center. Fold over edges of the larger piece and knead to incorporate the white starter dough with the yellow egg-and-butter dough.

KNEADING
8 minutes

Knead the two doughs until they have been blended into a solid light-yellow mass, with no swirl of contrasting dough distinguishable. With the help of a dough scraper or putty knife, dough will be easy to work although it is somewhat sticky or tacky even in the final stages of kneading. Light sprinkles of flour will help. The dough will become firm when it is cooled in the refrigerator.

FIRST RISING
3 hours

Place the dough in a greased bowl, cover with plastic wrap, and leave at room temperature (70°–75°) until dough has *more than doubled*. Under the covering, the dough will be light and puffy.

REFRIGERATION
2 hours
or overnight

Allow at least 2 hours in the refrigerator to chill the dough so that it can be more easily worked. (An overnight chill will require a longer rising in the mold but it will work perfectly well, nevertheless.)

SHAPING
15 minutes

It may be best to have a trial run to fill a coffee can exactly $2/3$ full. The dough in this recipe weighs about $3^1/2$ pounds. Dough for 1 can will weigh $1^1/2$ pounds, or 3 pounds for both of them. This leaves a small piece of dough for a separate pan, a small fluted brioche tin, for example.

Turn out dough after determining how much dough is needed and re-butter can. Fill both buttered cans $2/3$ full.

Collars are to be attached later when dough reaches edge of can. If there is an excess of dough, prepare an appropriate pan in which to bake it.

SECOND RISING
varies 1–2 hours

Cover cans and optional pan with wax paper and leave at room temperature (70°–75°) until dough rises to edge. The time will vary depending on how long the dough has been left to cool in the refrigerator. If left overnight, rising may take up to 2 hours.

BAKING
375°
1 hour

Preheat oven 20 minutes before baking.

Tie paper collar on each coffee tin with length of string. Dough will rise 4 or 5 inches above edge of can, so make allowances!

A tall pan may dictate the bottom shelf in a small oven. Midway in the bake period, turn cans around so they are exposed equally to temperature variations.

Brioche is done when crust is deep brown. Thrust a cake-testing pin or metal skewer into the dough. If the pin comes out clean, bread is done.

Untie and remove collars but let bread stand for 10 minutes before removing. If bread is difficult to budge, hold can firmly in one hand, grasp top of brioche with hot pad held in the other hand, and slowly work back and forth to twist loaf out.

FINAL STEP Place on metal rack to cool. While this loaf is a handsome upright piece, it should be turned on its side to slice. Freezes well for a period of up to 6 weeks for maximum freshness when thawed and reheated.

Brioche rising in coffee can with paper collar.

Voilà! The elegant brioche is twice its original height.

CROISSANTS FEUILLETÉS ❧ FLAKY CROISSANTS

[EIGHTEEN LARGE PIECES]

While the croissant dates from 1683 when Austria was at war with Turkey, for its first 200 years this famous bread was simply a triangle of rich dough rolled and bent to resemble a crescent. In the early 1900s, an inspired Parisian boulanger *made it with puff pastry and thereby made it doubly attractive and doubly delicious. By 1920, it was the rage in France and on practically every breakfast table. It has been growing in popularity abroad ever since.*

In making a fine croissant, the French boulanger *would underscore these points:*
- *There should be as little rising as possible during the process in which the dough is turned four times to increase the layers of butter and dough. If the dough is left to relax between turns for more than 15 minutes, place it in the refrigerator to slow the leavening action of the yeast.*
- *To assure tender dough, kneading should be as short as possible. Consider it sufficiently kneaded when all of the ingredients have been blended and the dough is smooth.*
- *The first rising of the dough should be "sufficiently long but not excessively so." If the rising is overly long, the yeast will have eaten most of the sugars in the dough and the croissant will not taste as sweet.*
- *If there is a choice, however, it is always better to reduce the amount of yeast and increase the rising time.*
- *One pound of butter will layer 5 to 6 pounds of dough.*
- *Butter produces the best croissants—finer, softer and with greater keeping ability than those made with margarine. On the other hand, croissants made with margarine are usually more flaky and hence more attractive (at least in the* boulanger's *eye). For the commercial baker, half butter and half margarine gives excellent results.*
- *Place a moist cloth over the dough during rests both in and out of the refrigerator so it will not crust.*
- *Steam is not necessary if the croissants are glazed with egg and milk. Croissants brushed only with water should also have a broiler pan of water in the oven for additional moisture.*

INGREDIENTS   7 cups all-purpose flour, approximately
1 package dry yeast
$^1/_4$ cup tap water
2 cups milk, *cool* (60°–70°)
1 teaspoon salt
2 teaspoons malt syrup
$^1/_2$ cup sugar
$^1/_2$ pound (2 sticks) butter or margarine, to fold into dough

Glaze:
1 egg
1 tablespoon milk

BAKING SHEET There is the possibility that fat may cook from the croissants and run onto the floor of the oven unless there is a lip on the baking sheet. One can be improvised with aluminum foil spread over the sheet.

PREPARATION
12 minutes

In a large bowl, place 2 cups of flour and make a well in the center. Dissolve yeast in $1/4$ cup of water poured in the well and let stand for 3 or 4 minutes until yeast is frothy. Pour in milk, and add salt, malt syrup, and sugar. Blend with 25 strokes.

Beat in additional flour, $1/2$ cup at a time, blending first with a large wooden spoon or rubber scraper and then with the hands when the dough can be formed into a ball.

KNEADING
3–4 minutes

Sprinkle flour on work surface and turn dough onto it. Knead only enough to smoothly blend the dough—no lumps, no bumps. The secret of this croissant is a tender crust from dough that was kneaded very little.

FIRST RISING
$1^{1}/_2$ hours

10 minutes

Place dough in bowl, tightly sealed with plastic wrap, for about $1^{1}/_2$ hours at room temperature (70°–75°).

During this interval, knead and work the 2 sticks of butter (at room temperature) with a putty knife or dough scraper to shape it into a rectangle 6 × 8 inches, $1/2$ inch thick.

Another secret of a fine croissant is to achieve the same consistency and firmness in the butter as there is in the dough. No more, no less. This may mean putting the butter in the refrigerator for a few minutes or longer. If both dough and butter seem soft and sticky, place in the refrigerator. Don't let the butter get too cold and hard or it will break into pieces as the rolling pin moves to stretch the layered dough.

LAYERING

10 minutes

If the kitchen is cool—70° or less—the "turns" can be done with a minimum of refrigeration. If, however, the butter breaks through and is soft, place the dough in the refrigerator—and patch the spot with a sprinkle of flour.

Roll the dough into a 10 × 12-inch rectangle. Let it rest in this position for 5 minutes so the dough will relax for the next step—the addition of the butter.

TURN 1
10 minutes

Place the rectangle of butter on the lower $2/3$ of the dough. Fold the top $1/3$ over half the butter. Lift the bottom $1/3$ up and fold over as for a letter. The layers will be dough, butter, dough, butter, dough.

TURN 2
8 minutes

Lightly flour the work surface and the dough. Roll the dough into a rectangle 6 × 12 inches and about 1 inch thick. Fold in thirds as for a letter. Let rest for 10 minutes.

If the room is warm, the dough may be placed in the refrigerator during this brief period.

TURN 3
4 minutes

Position the dough on the floured work surface so it can be rolled lengthwise with the seam. Roll into a 6 × 12-inch rectangle and fold in thirds, as for a letter.

TURN 4
4 minutes

Again roll the dough into a 6 × 12-inch rectangle. Fold into thirds again. There are now 55 layers of dough in this final turn.

REFRIGERATION
1¹/2 hours
or overnight

Wrap dough in a moist cloth and chill in the refrigerator before shaping, about 1¹/2 hours. If the dough is to be left overnight, also wrap wax paper around the damp cloth so the refrigerator does not pull out the moisture (as a frost-free machine will do).

SHAPING
25 minutes

Dust work surface with flour. With rolling pin, work dough into a sheet 24 inches long, 10 inches wide, and about ¹/4 inch thick. Stretching and patting with the hands will help form the rectangle. With a yardstick, divide the dough into two long strips, each 5 inches wide. Allow dough to relax before cutting or it may pull back. Mark each strip into triangles—5 × 5 × 5 inches—and cut with a pastry cutter. Place the triangles to one side. (If only half of these can be baked at one time, place the others on wax paper, cover, and reserve in the refrigerator until the oven is available.)

To shape each croissant, gently roll cut dough with the rolling pin from the base of the triangle to the apex—pressing the piece larger and thinner. Let the piece relax while others are rolled.

With the thumb and index finger of each hand, hold the ends of the base and roll toward the top of the triangle—with slight pulling to elongate the dough as it is rolled. The tip or tongue of the croissant will be on the inside and pointed down. It is not tucked under the body of the croissant but left free to rise as it wishes.

As the croissant is placed on the baking sheet, position the ends into a crescent. Repeat with each and place about 1¹/2 inches apart.

SECOND RISING
1 hour

Give the croissants the first of 3 glazings with egg-milk mixture. Leave at room temperature (70°–75°) *uncovered*. Thirty minutes later, brush croissants for a second time.

BAKING
400°
20 minutes

Preheat oven 20 minutes before baking croissants.

Brush croissants for the third time with glaze and place on middle shelf of oven. Bake until they are a golden brown. The French like theirs baked a deeper brown, an additional 5 minutes. If they are to be frozen for later use, take from oven when only a light brown.

FINAL STEP

Place croissants on a metal rack to cool but, ideally, serve while warm. To freeze, package in a plastic bag after cooled. Place them in the freezer where they will not get bumped around as they are fragile and can be broken even when frozen. Thaw in bag and return to a 400° oven for 8 to 10 minutes until rolls are golden brown.

RECIPES FROM BAYEUX

Bayeux, less than ten kilometers from the Normandy invasion beaches, was the first French town liberated by the American forces in World War II. It is a lively, friendly place, rich in both medieval and modern history (but not at all stuffy about it) and, overall, a thoroughly pleasant place to revisit.

We had been there five years earlier, when in the Gautier *boulangerie*, I had discovered a number of valuable baking techniques that I have much prized. I had failed, however, to get from Bernard Gautier the recipe for a singular loaf made in Normandy, *pain brié*. Ingredients are only flour, water, salt, and yeast, but it is the manner in which the texture is developed that sets it apart from other French breads. The *boulanger* uses a special motor-driven machine that pummels the yeast-raised dough with a heavy iron hammer. The dough is cradled in a metal basin that revolves slowly under the blows.

Pain brié and the fascinating machine were never long out of my mind and I was returning to Bayeux to learn to make it. Also, in the intervening years I had learned that *pain brié* might be pictured in the fabulous Bayeux tapestry, the 228-foot band of linen, 20 inches high, embroidered almost 900 years ago to tell the story of the conquest of England by the Duke of Normandy in 1066.

Confirming the presence of the *pain brié* in the magnificent tapestry was relatively easy to accomplish. On the other hand, the visit to the Gautier *boulangerie*, to put it mildly, was a real blast!

Under glass in the Musée de la Tapisserie, Bayeux's most celebrated treasure is a precise document of the clothes, ships, arms, customs, and food of the period. The bread is there—carried above the head of a servant shortly after the Norman forces landed at the English Channel town of Pevensey. The bread is shaped like a *couronne* or crown, and the man who holds it is sandwiched between a forager killing a sheep and one carrying a pig. They are on their way to a banquet honoring the Duke of Normandy.

"Every child in Bayeux grew up knowing just how *pain brié* was carried to England, along with everything else in the tapestry," explained Monsieur Jouvin-Bessière, owner of the Hôtel du Lion d'Or, a delightful old coaching inn only a few feet away from the *boulangerie* where I would go the following day. "After all," he continued, "it was every teacher's favorite place to take her class on a rainy afternoon. It seems to me that I walked along its length a hundred times."

The actual making of *pain brié* was another matter, I was to discover the following 3:30 A.M. when I presented myself at the *boulangerie* after an eerie passage across the darkened courtyard, the small sounds of my heels against the rough stone cobbles echoing back and forth across the distance. The massive iron gate leading out of the courtyard onto the street was locked but I had been briefed in the procedure to open it. I was to push a button hidden under a bush, a bell would ring somewhere in the distance, a light overhead would go on, the lock would click, and I could shoulder my way out.

As promised, the lock clicked and I found myself on rue St. Jean. Ten paces away, a slit of light led me to the *boulangerie* door that had been left open for me.

But from the moment I stepped out of the dark and into the bright lights of the *boulangerie*, I sensed that something was wrong. Every shop has its rhythms and work sounds, and if everything is functioning as it should, the result is a melody. This room had none of that. Only an ominous silence. A crew of bakers stood behind Bernard Gautier staring at the still smoking remains of an electric motor that moments before had powered the gas burner for one of the two big ovens.

"*Monsieur*, there is nothing that so grips the heart of the *boulanger* than to have his oven grow cold while all around the dough is growing, growing . . ." He waved his hand at the cabinets along the walls filled with loaves demanding to be baked in a short while.

"You will pardon me," he said, and darted out of the room to return a few moments later with a replacement unit that had been stored in the attic. Quickly, the motor was hooked to the blower that vaporized the fuel oil and shot it into the fire chamber under the oven. The blower worked but the spark mechanism that ignited the flame would not function.

In the meantime, three bakers, desperately trying to keep up with the rising tide of dough, were putting aside dozens of loaves.

French bakers are nothing if not ingenious. Bernard flew around the room opening wide all the doors and windows so that the cool night air could pour into the room and retard the dough. He positioned an apprentice with a wad of paper and a match and instructions to ignite the torch and come running the moment he was called. The vapor hissed into the chamber. Bernard shouted, and the boy ran with the flame. With a roar the oven was back in business.

A minor complication had developed, however. Because the oven was controlled thermostatically, it cycled off each time the oven temperature reached the optimum. When the oven cooled slightly, the blower cycled on to spray fuel oil. Each time, the young man would leave his station among the croissants to race the length of the room with his flaming torch to repeat the lighting procedure.

This strange routine had settled into a pattern of sorts, with loaves being hustled into the now-hot oven as fully baked loaves were coming out, when the town's electrician, who had been called from his bed for this emergency, came into the room. He was short, fat, old, and sleepy. A battered cap was pulled down to his ears.

He did not look happy as I watched him take the cover off a box jammed with wires and begin to poke among them with his screwdriver. Suddenly, a shower of sparks illuminated the room the instant before all the lights went out. All motors stopped, including those in the ovens. For a moment there was an exquisite silence. Then the old man started to yell that he couldn't be blamed for the lousy wiring. Someone changed the fuse and with the lights back on, the electrician insisted on demonstrating to Bernard exactly what had happened when he thrust the screwdriver into the wires. "*Voilà*," he said, and gave the wires a poke. A shower of sparks shot over him as the room went black for the second time. Again, the old man yelled it wasn't his fault. Again, the scramble to replace the fuse.

The ailing oven was coasting for the moment when the electrician walked to the switch box and pushed a bank of buttons. He obviously was not aware that one he pushed had started the oil burner, which, without the boy with the torch, was sending a vapor cloud into the hot chamber and overflowing back into the room. With a shout, one baker pointed at the fog collecting at his feet and lunged for the switch. Too late. With a mighty VOOM the vapor exploded, sending a tongue of flames licking across the floor.

Fortunately, it was a small explosion and the only thing damaged was the old man's pride. He was now using French words not in my dictionary.

Bernard Gautier simply looked resigned, a show of remarkable restraint, I thought. I was acutely aware, too, that I had not brought an abundance of good fortune that morning to the *boulangerie*. I picked up my notes and camera and walked out into the first small light of morning. I would return later. When I closed the hotel gate behind me and moved across the courtyard, I could hear the electrician's voice coming through the open skylight, still protesting that the bad wiring was not his doing!

At breakfast, Monsieur Jouvin-Bessière wanted to know how the reunion with Monsieur Gautier had gone.

"It must have been a success," he said, before I could reply. "Our bread delivery was a little late this morning and a few of the loaves looked as though they had been forgotten in the oven."

"Yes, the reunion was a bit out of the ordinary, but informative," I hastened to add.

Bernard Gautier was all smiles when I returned to the *boulangerie* for my *pain brié* lesson later in the day.

"That was the only explosion. All of the bread got baked and the wiring has been repaired. Some of the bread was more crisp than usual but I don't think the customers will mind."

When we parted, Bernard looked at me with a grin—"But one more night like that and I will be on the plane with you to America. I promise!"

Ancient machine in M. Gautier's *boulangerie* beats on *pain brié* dough.

PAIN BRIÉ NORMANDE ❧ NORMANDY BEATEN BREAD

[TWO LOAVES]

A long kneading period plus a hard beating produces an unusually dense dough with what the boulanger calls a "tight crumb." Brie is probably the heaviest of the yeast-raised breads to be found in France. It is served by the Normans with their famous Normandy shrimp and Normandy butter.

It is unlikely that there is a mechanical brié or beating machine in the United States, so the home baker must fall back on the first instrument used to make this bread—a wooden club. This can be a long, tapered French rolling pin, a heavy dowel, a length of broom handle—anything that can be held comfortably in the hand and brought down with hard whacks against the brié dough for no less than 10 minutes.

This recipe reflects the best of the techniques I found at Bayeux and Honfleur. The recipes are so closely related in the Normandy brié tradition as to be indistinguishable one from the other.

The overnight starter is more than the usual bowl of sour batter. It is a small ball of kneaded dough left overnight to develop flavor and become the leavening agent for the brié dough itself.

INGREDIENTS *Starter:*
2 cups all-purpose flour, approximately
3/4 cup warm water (105°–115°)
1 teaspoon dry yeast

Dough:
All of the starter
3/4 cup warm water (105°–115°)
1 tablespoon salt
2 1/2 cups all-purpose flour, approximately

BAKING SHEET One greased or Teflon baking sheet.

PREPARATION *Starter:* The night before, place 2 cups of flour in bowl and fashion a
10 minutes well to hold the water. Sprinkle yeast over water. Stir carefully to dissolve. Pull flour into center with wooden spoon or scraper until it forms a stringy ball. Work dough with fingers, adding heavy sprinkles of flour if sticky.

8 hours Knead for 2 or 3 minutes. Place in a small greased bowl and cover
to overnight with plastic wrap. Leave at room temperature (70°–75°) overnight or at least 8 hours to allow it to develop flavor.

10 minutes *Dough:* Punch down the starter, shape into a ball, and drop in a large bowl. Pour water around ball and add salt. Stir water and salt to dissolve.

While the starter in water may at first appear to be elastic and unresponsive, it will quickly dissolve with the addition of 1 cup of flour. Stir to blend and beat 75 strong strokes. Add more flour as needed to make an unusually dense dough. Allow the ball of dough to pick up all the flour it will as you work it with your hands.

KNEADING
18 minutes

This is an unusually long stretch of kneading to get the dough to accept the maximum amount of flour. Stop anytime during the kneading process and walk away for a few moments. Ask a friend to help.

BEATING
10 minutes

This can be fun. Call in several friends. Place the dough on a work surface that will not be shaken by a prolonged beating. Select a wooden instrument for the job. I use a tapered French rolling pin about 20 inches long, but on occasion I have tried hitting with the side of a Chinese meat-axe. It worked.

Work out a pleasant rhythm. Beat across the mass of dough from one side to the other. Overlap the dough and begin again. Try the other hand. The dough will become velvety.

SHAPING
5 minutes

Divide the dough into 2 pieces. The traditional *brié* shape is a round loaf, slightly elongated. Place dough on baking sheet.

Pain brié dough responds to beating by rolling pin.

RISING   Cover loaves with wax paper and leave undisturbed at room temper-
1 hour   ature (70°–75°) to rise. When risen, make 6 or 7 deep slashes across
the loaf radiating from the elongated ends.

BAKING   Preheat oven to 400°. Place loaves in oven. After ¹/₂ hour, look at breads
400°   and turn baking sheet to shift position of loaves. Fully baked *brié*
50–60 minutes   loaves may remind one of heavily striped melons—dark crust with
light stripes running lengthwise.

     Turn one loaf over and tap bottom crust with forefinger. A hollow,
hard sound means the bread is baked.

FINAL STEP   Place on metal rack to cool. *Brié* is marvelous sliced thin and served
with crab or shrimp hors d'oeuvres. Because of its unusual texture,
brié will stay fresh for several days. Freezes well. When thawing *brié*
(or any other bread), do not take out of plastic bag until after moisture has gone back into the loaf. Unwrap and place in 350° oven for
15 minutes.

PAIN ORDINAIRE DE M. GAUTIER ❧ M. GAUTIER'S LOAF

[ONE, TWO, OR THREE FLAT LOAVES]

Monsieur Bernard Gautier and his crew of boulangers *did imaginative things with*
pain ordinaire *dough. Two loaves in particular were favored by Gautier customers*
along with the traditional long loaves. Each of these was a rectangular loaf, about
2 feet long, 10 inches wide, and no more than 3 inches thick. Just before it went into
the oven, the top of one loaf was cut with parallel slashes, about 1¹/₂ inches apart, the
length of the bread. These raised to become long crusty cuts. The other loaf was deco-
rated with the dimpled imprint of the boulanger's *fingers pressed deeply into the raised*
dough on its way into the oven. (I have also seen M. Gautier do both to one loaf!)

     The beauty of this rectangular shape is the dividend of extra crust for crust lovers.

     These Bayeux loaves are too large for the home oven, so I have scaled them down
to a more manageable size.

INGREDIENTS   One batch, about 2¹/₂ pounds, of *pain ordinaire* dough (page 163).

BAKING SHEET   One baking sheet, greased or Teflon.

PRIOR STEPS   Here are the steps and times for the dough before the loaves are shaped:

       Prepare Dough   18 minutes
       First Rising   2 hours

SHAPING   Remove plastic wrap and punch down dough. Turn out on lightly
12 minutes   dusted work surface and knead for a moment to press out the bubbles.

(Opposite) Unusual forms of *pain ordinaire* provide extra crust for crust lovers.

The dough will be light, elastic, and a joy to work.

This batch can be made into longer or smaller loaves. A party might dictate the larger size, while two persons would find several smaller loaves more appropriate.

All sizes are made in the same way. With rolling pin and fingers, roll and stretch the dough into a rectangle about 1 inch thick. One pound of dough should make a rectangle 6 × 8 inches; the entire batch, an 8 × 18-inch shape.

SECOND RISING
60 minutes

Place shaped loaves on prepared baking sheet. Cover loaves with wax paper. If there is a tendency for the paper to stick to the dough, elevate over dough by resting paper on small water tumblers.

BAKING
450°
400°
45–60 minutes

Twenty minutes before baking, preheat oven to 450°. Five minutes before baking, pour $^1/_2$ cup water in broiler pan placed on lower shelf or bottom of oven.

With a razor blade or *lame*, make parallel cuts, $^1/_2$ inch deep, the length of the loaf and about $1^1/_2$ inches apart. For a dimpled loaf, press the fingertips of one hand deeply into the dough at several points to make a pattern. Or, as M. Gautier does, both cut and dimple! Place baking sheet in oven, which will be moist with steam generated by high heat. Reduce oven heat to 400°. Halfway through the bake period, shift baking sheet so loaves are exposed equally to the oven's temperature variations. The larger loaf will require an additional 10 to 15 minutes in the oven.

When baked, loaves will be golden brown with crispy crust both top and bottom. Turn over one loaf and tap with forefinger. If it is hard and sounds hollow, bread is done.

FINAL STEP

Remove from oven. Place on metal rack to cool before slicing. This bread freezes well, but will stay fresh only for about a day. Don't throw dry bread away. It makes great crumbs and croutons (see *chapelure*, page 241).

RECIPES FROM BRACIEUX

The *aventure de Bichet* has many of the elements of a fairy tale. Deer and boar roam the heart of the deep forest where a many-turreted castle stands, its hundreds of rooms empty and cheerless. For more than a hundred years, no princess has lived there. But a few kilometers away, just beyond the high stone wall that circles the forest, there is a small inn filled with laughter and happiness and all of the rooms are taken by people who have come from great distances to be served delectable dishes by the smiling little chef.

But this is not a storyteller's yarn. Both the castle and the inn are real places in the Loire valley and the chef, Monsieur Gaston Bichet, though not a big man (five feet, five inches), enjoys a very large reputation that has gone far beyond the small town of Bracieux, on the edge of the 13,000-acre Parc National, where sits the great Château de Chambord. Bichet has hosted not only princes and princesses, but in 1962 President Dwight D. Eisenhower and his grandson, David, lunched there to give the Hôtellerie Le Relais its finest hour.

Chambord, the largest and most pretentious of the Loire *châteaux,* has 440 rooms and 365 chimneys, and it is such an overpowering yet impersonal experience that walking a few minutes later into the cool, shaded courtyard of the small Le Relais, where ring-necked doves in a cote by the entryway call a low greeting, is an enchanted happening. The day we arrived, a buzzing swarm of bees had taken refuge just above the outside door to the dining room, but rather than discomfort the bees, guests were invited into the dining room in a roundabout way through another door.

Or this measure from a notation in the guest book—"I never had wild boar before so I can truly say it is the best wild boar I have ever eaten. P.S.: I will come back anytime there is wild boar on the menu!"

For several centuries, Le Relais had been a coach relay point for fresh teams between Paris and Bordeaux. Paris was six days in one direction, Bordeaux fourteen in the other. In 1870, the last coach to pull into Le Relais was a *diligence,* a big vehicle that transported a dozen passengers and was hitched to five horses. Years later, Bichet found a similar coach in Tours, restored it himself and parked it alongside the inn where it quickly became the focus of attention of travelers driving south from Chambord.

There was a pixie's touch in the lobby that Bichet had transformed into a museum of sorts dedicated to this golden age of travel. Several sets of oiled leather harness, trimmed in polished brass, hung from pegs on the stair rail. Long coach horns, unblown for a hundred years, were strung from the ceiling. A pair of hip-high leather boots stood by the dining room door as if the driver had slipped out of them just a moment before on his way to lunch. His long-handled whip stood against the doorsill. There was a bird's nest among the harness straps, and a sly wink in the eye of the mannequin dressed in the *postillon's* black woolen suit and red-trimmed top hat. The left half of his mustache had slipped to give him a less-than-sober look.

Remarkable display in front of dining-room fireplace of M. Bichet's country inn.

Bichet, to my delight, was also a master baker. It was spring. The big fireplace in the dining room was cleaned for the season, and decorated and lined with leafy boughs and wheat sheaves on which rested big husky loaves of *pain de campagne*. The hearth was covered with more loaves—round, long, fat, slender, braided, and twisted—to give the arresting effect of a treasure of breads flowing from a brick cornucopia.

Gaston Bichet was not to the country born. The son of a Tours hotel owner, he had earned his chef's toque in the Park Hotel in London, the Majestic in Paris, and Shepheards in Cairo. (Many years later he was to be asked by his government to help with food service at the French Pavilion at Expo 70 in Japan.) When France was overrun by the Germans in World War II, Bichet was conscripted to do farm work, but he prevailed upon the enemy to allow him to be a cook and, as a consequence, spent the rest of the war in a small Leipzig hotel until he was freed by U. S. troops.

He and Madame Bichet decided after the war that they wanted what every hôtelier dreams about—a small country inn. Bracieux, midway between two famous *châteaux*, Chambord and Cheverny, had a lot going for it. For sale was the shabby Le Relais, which had fallen on hard times after having been abandoned first by the horse-drawn coach and then its successor, a narrow-gauge railroad.

"The next fifteen were the best years of my life," Bichet said.

"There were only a few autos, some trucks, and none of those terrible motorcycles. Only bicycles and horses. It was good for the ears—the clop-clop of horses' hooves or the whistling of a happy man going past on his bicycle.

"There had not been much food during the war and now it was possible to eat again. Imagine what it meant. Everyone was happy. Everyone fell in love with food all over again. People came to Le Relais to stay days, not just for an hour or so. It was not all rush, rush!

"At first, summer was our only season for tourists. In the winter, the wealthy hunters came down from Paris. That was exciting. For a while there was only small game in the big Chambord forest because during the war the German officer corps, which had taken over the *châteaux*, treated it as their private hunting preserve. They killed all of the boar and deer. They left nothing but rabbits, squirrels, and a few birds. But the park was restocked and gradually the big animals returned to be hunted in numbers. More and more hunters came to stay with us. They loved good food. It was a happy time.

"But that, too, has changed. Now we have no more rich hunters; only tourists all year long. Boar and stags are shot at Chambord in government-controlled hunts, but the men come and go so quickly that we never see them.

"And the autos and the trucks," Bichet's happy face clouded. "They have spoiled the country. No more clop-clop. No more whistling. Now we must even close our windows to keep out the noise."

The Bichet cuisine was top-notch, but not elaborate. He ran the dining room with a young man to help serve and the kitchen with a neighbor woman who came in during the dining hour. Bichet advised, counseled, and took orders in German, English, Spanish, and French, and then darted away to prepare the dishes himself in a kitchen dominated by a big scrubbed-oak table and a wood-fired range. He came to the table at least once during each course to inquire as to how it was being enjoyed.

"I like it best when I am at the tables talking to pleasant people like yourselves who like good food but who are not fanatical about it. I have worked all day preparing it and now I have the joy of knowing that you like what I have created.

"Too many people eat too much food, served in too many courses. The French and Germans especially; the Americans less so. I like to serve a few simple dishes rather than have a guest goggle-eyed and glutted by the time a fourth, fifth, or sixth course is brought to the table."

We had just finished a platter of white asparagus cut in the garden less than an hour before (course 1), filet of beef with a light pepper sauce and fresh green beans (course 2), and wild strawberries with cream (course 3). A white wine, of course, and all in perfect harmony. I was neither goggle-eyed nor glutted.

Guide Michelin had never given Le Relais a star.

"Why, I don't know. We are listed only as a comfortable place to dine (two crossed knives and forks), but no stars. But a star would not bring happiness, I can assure you. It brings . . ." and he searched for the word ". . . wicked people who write nasty notes to *Michelin* about the smallest mistake or fancied slight. They have no sense of humor, these people. They see themselves as inspectors general for *Michelin*. No, I like it this way."

PETITS PAINS AU LAIT—SANDWICH ❧ SMALL SANDWICH ROLLS

[ABOUT THIRTY SMALL AND EIGHT LARGE ROLLS]

Because it has only 1 teaspoon of sugar, this au lait *or milk dough is unexcelled for sandwiches as it does not have an undue influence on a filling, whether fish, fowl, or fromage.*

A roll made from 1 ounce of dough—about the size of a golf ball before it rises—is about a 3-bite sandwich; it can easily be made smaller (1 bite) or larger (a meal) to suit the needs of the buffet or picnic.

The dough can be made with an overnight starter or from scratch (and a long first rising). Both develop flavor.

INGREDIENTS	*Starter:* 2 cups all-purpose flour 1^1/$_2$ cups warm water (105°–115°) ^{1}/$_2$ cup non-fat dry milk 2 packages dry yeast *Dough:* All of the starter 2^1/$_2$ cups all-purpose flour, approximately 2 teaspoons salt ^{1}/$_4$ pound (1 stick) butter, room temperature 1 teaspoon sugar 2 eggs, room temperature
BAKING SHEETS	One or two baking sheets, greased or Teflon.
PREPARATION 10 minutes 6 hours or overnight	*Starter:* In large bowl, place 2 cups all-purpose flour, water, non-fat dry milk, and yeast. Stir to blend. Cover tightly with plastic wrap and leave at room temperature (70°–75°) overnight or a minimum of 6 hours. *Note:* If you wish to forego overnight starter, combine starter ingredients as above, put aside for 5 minutes, and proceed with the next step.
15 minutes	*Dough:* Stir down starter and add 1 cup all-purpose flour, the salt, butter, sugar, and eggs. Beat vigorously 25 strokes. Add additional flour and work with hands until dough is a shaggy mass.
KNEADING 8 minutes	Turn dough onto flour-dusted work surface. This is an easy dough to work because of the butter and eggs. Add additional sprinkles of flour to control stickiness and to achieve a firm but elastic ball of dough. Knead with a strong push-turn-fold action, occasionally picking up the dough and bringing it down forcefully against the work surface.

FIRST RISING
1¹/₂ hours
or overnight

Place dough in bowl. Cover tightly with plastic wrap. Ideally, dough should be given several hours for the first rising. Minimum time: 1¹/₂ hours. Overnight for optimum development.

SECOND RISING
1¹/₂ hours

Punch down the dough and allow to rise for a second time, about 1¹/₂ hours.

SHAPING
20 minutes

Turn the dough onto the floured work surface. With knife or pastry blade, cut the dough into uniform pieces. Shape each roll by rolling under the cupped hand. Press down hard to force the various surfaces to blend together. Dough will respond to force!

THIRD RISING
45 minutes

As you shape the rolls, place them on the baking sheet about 2 inches apart so they won't touch when risen. Cover and let rise for 45 minutes. If the oven cannot take all the rolls at one time, allow the balance of the dough to continue rising until the first load goes into the oven. Shape additional rolls, cover, and leave to rise on the work surface until baking sheet is available. Transfer risen rolls carefully.

BAKING
375°
20–25 minutes

Place baking sheet in the oven. After 25 minutes, turn sheet around to compensate for temperature variations in the oven. Outer rolls may be done before those inside and may be removed earlier. Shuffle others around.

FINAL STEP

Place on metal rack to cool. Delicious when served with just a trace of warmth. May be broken or cut open to butter or fill.

PETITS PAINS AU LAIT ❧ MILK ROLLS

[EIGHTEEN TO TWENTY ROLLS]

The dough for these fine petits pains au lait *or milk rolls of* qualité supérieure *is left for at least 4 hours to rise leisurely, then is punched down and given another 1¹/₂ hours to rise. The master* boulanger, *Monsieur Bichet, explained the slow rising is responsible for a fresher, softer, and tastier roll. For this reason, he uses only a very small amount of yeast mixed with cool water to slow the leavening process.*

This basic dough is used also for several rolls and small braided breads. They can be rond *or* navette *(elongated). A cross may be cut with scissor points across the* rond, *or a series of 4 or 5 snips may be made down the length of the* navette *to achieve a sawtooth effect. Rolled into long strands, the dough can be braided into tresses or* nattes, *pigtails.*

INGREDIENTS
4 cups all-purpose flour, approximately
2 teaspoons salt
¹/₄ cup sugar
¹/₃ cup non-fat dry milk

1 ¹/₂ cups *cool* water (60°–70°)
1 *teaspoon* dry yeast
¹/₂ cup (1 stick) butter, room temperature
1 egg, room temperature

BAKING SHEET One baking sheet, greased or Teflon.

PREPARATION
12 minutes
Stir together in a large bowl 2 cups of all-purpose flour, the salt, sugar, and non-fat dry milk. Make a well in the center of the dry ingredients. Pour in water and add 1 teaspoon dry yeast. Stir and leave for a moment until yeast is dissolved. Pull in flour from the sides of the bowl to make a soft batter. Cut butter into several small pieces and drop into bowl. Add egg. Stir together until smooth. Add rest of flour, ¹/₂ cup at a time, stirring first with a wooden spoon or rubber scraper until dough is a rough shaggy mass. Work in additional flour with the hands if dough is sticky.

KNEADING
7 minutes
Knead with the 1-2-3 motion of push-turn-fold, tossing down additional sprinkles of flour if the dough continues to be sticky. Break the kneading rhythm by occasionally throwing the dough down hard against the work surface. Knead 7 minutes (about 5 minutes with dough hook).

FIRST RISING
4 hours
or overnight
Place the dough in a greased bowl, cover with plastic wrap, and leave in an undisturbed place at room temperature (70°–75°) for a minimum of 4 hours, or overnight. The dough will more than double in volume and push forcefully against the plastic.

SECOND RISING
1¹/₂ hours
Remove plastic wrap, punch down, and deflate dough. Replace cover and leave for 1¹/₂ hours.

SHAPING
20 minutes
Divide the dough into 2-ounce pieces, each roughly the size of a large egg. Roll each into a round ball. Let stand to relax the dough as you move to the other pieces.

Here are three basic shapes for milk rolls.

Rond: Roll a piece of dough under a cupped hand, pressing firmly to shape into a tight ball. Place on baking sheet and repeat for desired number.

Navette: The name is also applied to a weaver's shuttle, which this roll somewhat resembles. Roll a piece of dough first into a tight round and then under the flattened palm into an elongated form, perhaps 4 inches in length. Place on baking sheet and repeat for others.

Tresses: The braiding technique for this attractive roll is explained by Monsieur Coquet, *La Ficelle de Romans* (page 187).

Petits pains in interesting shapes make excellent sandwich rolls.

THIRD RISING
50 minutes
Carefully cover shaped rolls with pieces of wax paper and leave at room temperature (70°–75°) until nearly double in volume.

BAKING
375°
25 minutes
Twenty minutes prior to baking, preheat oven. Uncover rolls and leave on baking sheet to cut.

Rond: May be cut with single razor stroke across top of roll or snipped twice with scissor points to form cross.

Navette: May be cut lengthwise with one razor stroke or snipped 3 or 4 times down center of roll—one cut immediately following the other—to give a sawtooth effect.

Tresses: Leave as is.

Place baking sheet on middle oven shelf. After 15 minutes, turn sheet end for end to balance heat distribution. Rolls are baked when golden brown and bottom crust is dark brown and hard to the touch.

FINAL STEP
Place on metal rack to cool. Delicious with just a trace of warmth still in them. Will keep for several days in bread box or for several months frozen. A box of a half dozen or more makes an excellent gift.

PAIN SEIGLE ❧ RYE BREAD

[THREE 1-POUND LOAVES]

There are several unusual things about this typically French loaf of rye bread. There are two starters. The first is boosted into life with a small portion (1 teaspoon) of yeast, which begets a larger starter or sponge, which, in turn, begets the dough. Unlike most other rye loaves, which get most of their flavor and color from dark molasses or brown sugar (and even chocolate), there is no sugar in this recipe.

Fermentation is what rye flour does best—one whiff of the batter bubbling under the plastic wrap pulled over the bowl will tell you just how potent this brew is.

It is a pity that another of rye's characteristics is its stickiness, which often discourages the new home baker from preparing one of the truly fine loaves. Use a dough scraper as an extension of your hand to work and knead the dough in its early stages. Later, with your hands, keep a sprinkle of rye or white flour between the dough and the hands and work surface.

Caraway seeds are synonymous with rye bread to many, but not among the boulangers with whom I have talked in France. However, there is no reason a sprinkle of caraway seeds in the dough or across the crust could not be added if that is part of your rye flavor.

This is also the dough for a delicious rye roll studded with raisins, le benoîton. *Directions for using a portion of this recipe for rolls follow on page 103.*

INGREDIENTS   *Starter:*
1 cup rye flour
1 *teaspoon* dry yeast
1 cup warm water (105°–115°)

Sponge:
All of the starter
1¼ cups warm water (105°–115°)
1 cup all-purpose flour
1½ cups rye flour

Dough:
All of the sponge
½ cup warm water (105°–115°)
1 tablespoon salt
2½ cups rye flour, approximately
1 cup all-purpose flour

Glaze:
1 egg yolk
1 tablespoon milk

BAKING SHEET One baking sheet, greased or Teflon.

PREPARATION *Starter:* At least 12 hours before preparing, mix flour, yeast, and water
15 minutes in a small bowl, cover with plastic wrap, and put aside in an undisturbed
5 hours place at room temperature (70°–75°) for not less than 5 hours. More
time, up to 24 to 36 hours, will give a slightly more fermented taste
to final dough.

15 minutes *Sponge:* Remove plastic wrap and stir down starter. Add warm water
7 hours and all-purpose and rye flours. Blend well and re-cover bowl for minimum of 7 hours at room temperature (70°–75°). As for the starter, a
long rising period is desirable if you like your rye tangy and flavorful.

15 minutes *Dough:* On bake day, pour all of the sponge into a large bowl. Add
warm water, salt, and 1 cup each rye and all-purpose flours. Stir to
develop a heavy mass that will cling tenaciously to scraper or wooden
spoon. Add the additional rye flour until it is a shaggy mass that can
be turned out on the work surface.

KNEADING A basic rye dough does not need the longer kneading that an all-
5 minutes white dough demands. Use a dough scraper or putty knife to turn
and knead dough through its earliest period. Throw down liberal
sprinkles of flour if moisture breaks through the surface of the
dough. Continue kneading and working the dough. It will gradually
lose its stickiness and become soft and elastic. In a rush to overcome
the stickiness, don't overload the dough with flour so that it becomes
so heavy and dense it defeats the leavening effect of the yeast. But
don't skimp on flour so that the dough is slack and cannot hold its
shape on the baking sheet.

FIRST RISING Place the dough in a greased bowl, cover tightly with plastic wrap, and
40 minutes leave at room temperature (70°–75°).

SHAPING Uncover bowl and punch down dough. Turn onto a flour-dusted work
15 minutes surface and knead for a moment or two to press out the bubbles.

(Rye breads take several forms in France. Monsieur Bichet favored
eight cuts with a razor radiating from the top of a round loaf. In the
oven, the bread expanded beautifully along these lines. He also circled
the top third of a raised round loaf with a razor cut that gave an attractive accent to its roundness.)

Divide the dough, which will weigh about 3 pounds, into 3 pieces.
(See instructions on *les benoîtons*, page 103, if you want to put aside
a portion of this dough for raisin rolls.) Shape each of the 3 pieces
into a round ball, pulling down with cupped hands to keep the surface of the dough taut.

SECOND RISING
25 minutes

Place each loaf on the baking sheet and cover with wax paper. Put in an undisturbed place at room temperature (70°–75°).

BAKING
400°
45 minutes

Uncover loaves. For star effect, make 8 radiating cuts about $1/4$ inch deep from the top of the raised loaf down the sides to within an inch of the baking sheet.

The other design is created by cutting a circle around the top of the round loaf with a razor blade—about $1/4$ inch deep.

Brush loaves with egg-milk glaze and place in oven.

Midway through baking period turn the baking sheet around so that the loaves are exposed equally to temperature variations in the oven.

Bread is done when the bottom crust sounds hollow when tapped with the forefinger.

FINAL STEP

Place on metal rack to cool. Freezes well. Sliced, it makes a fine sandwich companion with ham, beef, or cheese. Goes well with soups, too.

This typical French rye bread, slashed before baking, expands to a star shape.

LES BENOÎTONS ❧ RYE ROLLS WITH RAISINS

[TWO DOZEN ROLLS]

Should this small rye bread appeal to you, use the entire recipe (about 3 pounds of dough) for pain seigle *(page 100) to fashion 24 of these raisin-filled rolls. They freeze beautifully for later use.*

I often bake two rye loaves and then add raisins to one-third of the dough to make 8 of these rolls. The egg yolk-milk glaze can be used for both.

INGREDIENTS Rye dough (page 100)
$1/2$ cup of raisins for each pound of dough

Glaze:
1 egg yolk
1 tablespoon milk

BAKING SHEET One greased or Teflon baking sheet.

PRIOR STEPS After you have decided on the amount of prepared rye dough (8 rolls per each 1 pound of dough), soak an appropriate amount of raisins in water for 10 minutes. Rinse and pat dry with paper towel. Flatten dough and spread raisins over top. Fold dough over the raisins and knead. Continue until raisins have worked through the dough and are well distributed.

SHAPING
5 minutes
Divide the dough into 2-ounce pieces and roll into balls.

RISING
1 hour
Place balls on baking sheet, flatten slightly, cover with wax paper, and allow to rise at room temperature (70°–75°) until about double in size.

BAKING
400°
25–30 minutes
Preheat oven 20 minutes before baking.

Remove wax paper, brush each roll with egg-milk glaze. With a sharp razor, cut an X across top of each. The roll will begin to open like a small blossom. Place in oven. Look at them after 15 minutes and turn bake sheet around to give balanced heat to all rolls. They are done when they are well browned on the bottom and feel solid when pinched slightly.

FINAL STEP Place the rolls on metal rack to cool. Especially good when served warm or when warmed over for later serving at breakfast, brunch, or with a mid-morning cup of coffee. These rolls freeze well.

An unusual brioche, prune-filled, in braided and rolled shapes.

Brioche aux Pruneaux ❦ Brioche with Prune Filling

[ONE LARGE BRAIDED LOAF AND ONE SMALL ROLLED LOAF]

On a bicycle ride out of Bracieux to a seldom-visited château at Villesavin, we cycled by a boulangerie *at the junction of three country roads. In the window was a braided loaf that had been cut in several pieces revealing an almost black filling in each of the lovely yellow strands.*

"Pruneaux," said Madame when I asked her what it was.

"Delicious," said my wife when she tried a slice of it at our luncheon stop a few miles down the road. Brioche aux Pruneaux was not cheap: 20 francs per kilo or about $2.50 a pound.

INGREDIENTS *Prunes:*
Three dozen prunes

Dough:
One-half batch, about 2¹/₂ pounds, of dough prepared for *croissants briochés*, page 46, will make 1 large braided loaf with enough left over for a small rolled loaf.

Glaze:
1 egg, beaten
1 tablespoon milk

BAKING SHEET One baking sheet, greased or Teflon.

PRIOR STEPS *Prunes:* A day ahead pour boiling water to cover 36 prunes in medium bowl and leave to cool overnight. Seed prunes and put through medium blade of grinder, food mill, or blender. Reserve puree.

Dough: Here are the steps and times for dough (page 46) before shaping:

Prepare Dough	18 minutes
Kneading	7 minutes
First Rising	1^1/$_2$ hours
Punch Down	2 minutes
Second Rising	1 hour
Refrigeration	30 minutes

SHAPING
30 minutes

Dust the work surface with flour. Roll dough and stretch with fingers into a rectangle—24 to 28 inches long by 10 inches wide. Dough will be about ^{1}/$_4$ inch thick. Allow dough to relax 5 minutes before shaping or dough will pull back when cut. The dough will not be cut until after the prune puree has been rolled inside.

Place a line of prune filling (about 3 tablespoons) across width of dough, leaving a 1-inch margin at the bottom and a ^{1}/$_2$-inch margin on either side. Carefully lift bottom edge over filling and press into bottom dough—and snug against the filling. Roll dough so there will be a 1-inch overlap. Cut off rolled piece with knife or pastry wheel. Pinch seam and ends tightly to close. Roll gently back and forth, if necessary, to shape strand. Leave with seam down while proceeding with other braids.

When the 3 strands are completed, lay parallel, with seams down, and braid from the center. Turn braid around and finish from the middle. The ends may try to pull apart. Moisten dough with wet fingers and pinch together tightly. Place on baking sheet.

Use balance of puree in remaining dough. Spoon puree as above. Roll dough into a single loaf. No braids. Pinch seam to seal or it may unroll like a scroll in the oven. Place on baking sheet.

Filling placed on dough—a first step in shaping *Brioche aux Pruneaux.*

THIRD RISING	Cover with wax paper and leave at room temperature (70°–75°) for
30 minutes	1/2 hour. A longer rising might tear the braid apart. Preheat oven.

BAKING	Brush loaves with egg-milk glaze. Place in oven. Watch carefully dur-
400°	ing the last 10 minutes of bake period. Cover with foil or brown sack
25 minutes	paper if loaves brown too quickly. The braid is fragile when hot, so don't turn it over to check for doneness. If braids are a deep rich brown and a strand feels solid under the finger, loaf will be done.

FINAL STEP	Allow braid to cool 15 minutes on baking sheet before transferring to metal rack. Handle with care while warm. A deliciously different coffeecake-style of bread. It goes well with coffee, tea, or a glass of wine.

===========

Petits Pains au Chocolat ❦ Chocolate-filled Rolls

[ONE DOZEN ROLLS]

Little known in the U.S., the petit pain au chocolat—*an ingenious packaging of a sweet in a soft and delicate roll has been beloved by French children for generations. Clutched in a hot little hand, the warmth can only soften the totally protected chocolate and make it even more desirable. Schoolboys often sit on them a few minutes before recess to hasten the melting process.*

French boulangers *wrap dough around a slender bar of chocolate made expressly for these rolls. A spoonful of chocolate "bits" is an excellent substitute.*

INGREDIENTS	*Dough:*
	One half batch of dough prepared for *petits pains au lait* (page 96). While these are made with *au lait* dough, an even richer *petit pain au chocolat* can be made with *brioche* dough (page 249).
	1 cup semi-sweet chocolate bits

BAKING SHEET	One baking sheet, greased or Teflon.

PRIOR STEPS	Here are steps and times for the *au lait* dough (page 96) before rolls are shaped:

Prepare Dough	12 minutes
Kneading	7 minutes
First Rising	4 hours or overnight
Second Rising	1 1/2 hours

SHAPING	Turn dough onto lightly floured work surface. Knead for 1 minute to
20 minutes	press out bubbles.
	The rolls will be cut one by one from a length of dough (36 inches) rather than made from individual pieces.

Divide the ball into 2 pieces. Return one piece to bowl for shaping later. With rolling pin and fingers, roll and shape piece into a length about 3 feet long and 4 inches wide. The dough should be about $1/4$ inch thick. Don't rush the rolling! If the dough resists, start the second piece and return to the first in 3 or 4 minutes. Keep a light sprinkle of flour on the work surface so the dough can move freely. From time to time, gently lift the dough to be certain it is not sticking. If it does, work flour under the sticky area.

When the dough has been rolled out, place 1 tablespoon of chocolate bits in a line 1 inch above the bottom edge. Leave a $1/2$-inch margin on both sides. Gently roll the dough so that two turns of dough surround the chocolate. Cut off a 6-inch length with a knife or dough scraper. Pinch seam and ends tightly to close. Place on the baking sheet, seam down. The dough will have lengthened another inch or so during rolling and may appear bumpy over the chocolate bits. Bits will melt and the shape of the *petits pains* will be uniform.

Repeat cutting and shaping *petits pains* from length of dough. When finished with the first piece, repeat with second ball of dough. If rolls stretch, try not to increase width of dough during rolling but pull and roll lengthwise.

THIRD RISING
45 minutes

Cover *petits pains* with wax paper and allow to rest at room temperature (70°–75°) until double in size.

BAKING
375°
25 minutes

Twenty minutes before bake period, preheat oven.

Uncover *petits pains* and place baking sheet on middle shelf of oven. Look in on *petits pains* after 20 minutes. If those on the outer perimeter are browning too fast while those inside are not, gently shift them around.

Petits pains are done when brown and firm to the touch.

FINAL STEP

Place on metal rack to cool. Delicious when a bit warm. Can be reheated with great results. Carry a pair to a football game in a warm inside pocket and be the envy of your neighbors. Freezes well.

RECIPE FROM ANGOULÊME

Searching for a loaf of bread while lost in a sea of grapes stretching from horizon to horizon can be aggravating, especially so in the spring of the year when one cannot even have the satisfaction of seeing a ripening cluster. In June, the grapes are the size of tiny beads and the new green leaves scarcely cast a shadow.

We had left Bordeaux en route to the aristocratic and feudal city of Angoulême to see what good breads had developed in this, one of France's most celebrated wine regions. The *Guide Michelin* showed a network of small roads leading to Saint Emilion, one of the lesser of several wine areas in the Bordeaux region, which together produce some 3,000 different wines. Wine from Saint Emilion had often graced our dinner table and we seized the opportunity to visit the source.

The fields had been laid out in strange shapes centuries before, and now narrow macadam roads and lanes followed where history and civilization had led. It had not occurred to me how similar all grapevines and all fields of grapes would be, and that I might get lost in such a civilized place. Our constantly changing position in relation to the sun convinced me that I was going in circles, but each time I tried to break out of the pattern, the car took special delight in returning me to the same spot a half hour later. Had the car been equipped with a smoke signal, I would have fired it.

A turn to the right instead of the left—and there stood the old town of Saint Emilion, an oasis in the midst of millions of vines.

With the car parked, Marje, at my request, checked the wine merchants of Saint Emilion, while I stalked up and down the steep streets in search of a *boulangerie*. She was more successful than I, and came back to report on the ancient Clos des Cordeliers, a ruined monastery that had been purchased by a vineyard, which had converted the few remaining intact buildings into tasting and storage rooms. The church proper was only a shell, with ivy climbing to the sky and softening the stark walls of the ruined cloister. The wine was good, the shade cool, but I was in the pursuit of bread and Angoulême, squeezed between ancient ramparts, as the late-afternoon goal.

It would have been pleasant, though unrealistic, to expect to drive up to Angoulême's most historic edifice, the Cathedral of Saint Pierre, park there, and wander quietly through the twelfth-century treasure, where seventy-five personages are immortalized in the niches of its remarkable facade. Not a chance! Our twentieth-century auto, small though it was, and the narrow twelfth-century streets were incompatible. Almost before I realized it, we had been carried with the traffic through the town to the very edge of the old city. I was almost past the tree-lined Place Victor Hugo and had started down the hill out of town when I caught a quick glance of a *boulangerie*, its windows filled with a handsome display of a kind of bread I had not seen. (I was to learn that it was the delicious *brioche vendéenne*.) I could not stop. Impatient horns and growling diesel trucks shoved us out of the city. Pity.

Early in the morning we drove back to the city from a suburban motel to find and hold a parking spot on the Place Victor Hugo only to discover that, overnight, the weekly outdoor market had set up shop. It was not the traditional display of goods and produce stacked on the ground or on weather-beaten tables protected only with a piece of flapping canvas. These were expensive enclosed trailers, shiny with stainless steel and glass and equipped with the latest in display cases, lights, and refrigeration. Drop the sides, and they were ready for business in all kinds of weather. These merchants traveled a regular circuit of other towns and small cities to set up for market days, and then back to Angoulême a week hence. Not all were so well equipped, however. There was a scattering of farm women on chairs they had brought themselves, keeping watch over the merchandise—the garden's choice in neat stacks, while in open boxes at their feet, were live chickens, kittens, ducks, geese, rabbits, puppies, and guinea hens.

There was a steady stream of shoppers crossing the street between the open-air market and the *boulangerie* of Monsieur Yves Ordonneau, 11 Place Victor Hugo. The flow of people in and out of his attractive shop was constant and heavy, and once inside one had to step out of the traffic pattern or be moved through the *boulangerie* without so much as a "bonjour!"

We had not been directed to Monsieur Ordonneau, except by chance, but it was evident from his clientele and displays of handsome loaves that we had chanced upon an outstanding *boulanger*. While the round *boules* of *pain de campagne*, dark-crusted and burned in places, were among his most striking loaves, his specialty, to the delight of his customers, was the *brioche vendéenne*, the spectacular stollen-type loaf we had seen but fleetingly the afternoon before.

Madame Ordonneau was a handsome young woman—jet black hair drawn back into a bun, sparkling white teeth. She and her husband were in their early thirties; enthusiastic about their shop and their way of life. In his white smock, Yves looked more like one of television's good-looking young medics than Angoulême's best baker.

The Ordonneaus were delighted we had found their *boulangerie*, and that we had made a special effort to retrace our steps after having seen the window display in a glance from a fast-moving auto.

In the Ordonneaus' *boulangerie,* this stollen brioche is their most treasured recipe.

In the excitement of getting there I had mistakenly worn my dark sunglasses into the shop, a forgetful thing that annoys me especially when my other glasses are at a distance. With dozens of customers coming and going, I was trying to carry on an English-French conversation as I thumbed a French-English dictionary, while at the same time looking for a place in the crowded room to put down my glasses, take photographs, flip on the tape recorder, make notes in my steno book, and with some decorum present a copy of my cookbook to the Ordonneaus. It was bedlam, or so it seemed, but the young couple was not in the least flustered. Each bread in the display case that I admired they insisted we take as a gift. These I added to the stock of things perched precariously on the narrow ledge by the cash register. The most bewildered person in the shop, however, was the bakery equipment salesman who came into the *boulangerie* with us, an order book in one hand and a catalog in the other, and found himself completely ignored by the Ordonneaus for more than an hour.

It was manifest that *brioche vendéenne* was their treasure. Would they allow me to use it in my book? His deep brown eyes sought his wife's. She smiled: "*Oui*, we would be pleased to know that our *boulangerie* is known in America."

The salesman looked relieved when finally I began to assemble our gear and gifts for departure.

Yves grasped my hand.

"*Monsieur*, the brotherhood of *boulangers* is everywhere. Please come back."

BRIOCHE VENDÉENNE ❧ VENDÉENNE BRIOCHE

[FOUR 1¹/₂-POUND LOAVES]

There is a score of ways to fashion brioche in France but two in particular seem the best for the fine dough made with this recipe from the Ordonneau boulangerie. One is a three-strand braid; the other, a stollen to which raisins are added. The latter also gets a sprinkling of confectioners' sugar after it is baked.

This is a large recipe that will produce about 6 pounds of dough, enough for two braids and two stollens. The recipe can be halved.

There are several unusual steps in the preparation of this dough, which is rich with eggs, sugar, and butter. There are two kneading periods—one before the addition of butter; the other follows. The butter phase is a sticky one (have a dough scraper handy), but the dough, with the help of a little more flour, will accept the butter, and then becomes a delight to handle.

The dough is allowed a minimum of ten hours to mature through three risings—four, two, and four hours, respectively. Be relaxed about the first two periods, for they can go beyond an hour or more, if convenient, but be there for the third, when it goes into the oven after you have judged its volume has increased 2¹/₂ times. It will brown quickly because of the rich dough and the brushed egg. The result will be a deep brown, almost black on some surfaces, but the overall effect is one of richness and goodness.

INGREDIENTS 2 packages dry yeast
1 cup warm water (100°–115°)
10 eggs
1 tablespoon salt
2$^1/_2$ cups sugar
9 cups all-purpose flour, approximately
$^3/_4$ pound (3 sticks) butter, room temperature
1 cup raisins (if desired)

Glaze:
1 egg
1 tablespoon milk
1 tablespoon confectioners' sugar, to sprinkle

BAKING SHEET One large baking sheet, greased or Teflon. Two small sheets if you are using two oven shelves.

PREPARATION In a small bowl, dissolve the yeast in warm water. Set aside. Crack eggs
15 minutes in large bowl and beat lightly to blend. Add the yeast mixture, salt, and sugar. Stir well. Blend in 4 cups of flour, one at a time. Beat briskly until mixture is smooth—about 100 strokes with a wooden spoon. Add more flour, $^1/_2$ cup at a time, mixing first with the spoon and then with the hand until the mass has lost its stickiness. About 8 cups of flour in all.

FIRST KNEADING Turn onto floured work surface and knead with the 1-2-3 motion of
8 minutes push-turn-fold, push-turn-fold, etc. Because there is as yet no fat in the dough, it will be sticky and may cling to hands and work surface. If so, clean surface with dough scraper and sprinkle with flour.

BLENDING Put the dough aside. Soften and cream the butter in a small bowl with
5 minutes a fork or rubber scraper. Pat the dough flat and over it spread half the butter. Fold dough over the butter and work the butter into it. Again, pat the dough flat; spread the balance of the butter and repeat. Until the butter works its way through the dough, it will be sticky. Toss heavy sprinkles of flour under the dough. Continue kneading. Presently the dough will lose its stickiness and become soft and elastic.

SECOND Knead dough, adding small sprinkles of flour if it continues to stick.
KNEADING
6 minutes

FIRST RISING Place dough in a large bowl. Place damp cloth (perhaps a dish towel)
4 hours on surface of dough. Be certain it is well wrung out. Put bowl in a place where it will be undisturbed for a long period of time. It is not necessary to keep it at more than room temperature (70°–75°). Dough will more than double in volume.

PUNCH DOWN
3 minutes

Remove cloth, punch down dough with extended fingers. Turn dough over.

SECOND RISING
2 hours

Moisten cloth again and re-cover dough. Leave undisturbed. Dough will rise to double its volume.

SHAPING
20 minutes

Ten minutes beforehand, plump raisins in a small bowl of water. Drain and pat dry. If you choose to make two braids and two stollen-type brioche, divide dough in half. Knead raisins into one portion. Again divide the dough. Shape into balls (a total of 4) and allow to rest while preparing baking sheets.

Braid: Divide one ball of dough into three equal parts and roll into plump strands about 14 inches long. If the dough resists or draws back, go on to another braid and return to the first a few moments later. Line the 3 strands parallel and touching. Braid from the middle to one end. Turn the strands around and complete the braid. Pinch the ends tightly together. Place on baking sheet. Repeat for other braid.

Stollen: Pat one ball of raisin-dough into an oblong shape, about 12 inches long and 1 inch thick. Fold slightly less than half of the dough onto the bottom portion. Press the top piece firmly into the piece beneath it so the dough will not spring open as it rises. The back of the piece will be straight, while the front will be a gentle arc from one end to the other. Place on a baking sheet. Repeat for other stollen.

THIRD RISING
4 hours

Place bake sheet (or sheets) in an undisturbed place at room temperature (about 70°–75°). Cover with wax paper. Dough should increase in volume about 2$1/2$ times.

BAKING
370°
25–40 minutes

While the oven heats, beat egg and 1 tablespoon milk. Brush all loaves. If oven is small, you may wish to bake on two shelves; if so, midway through bake period, shift breads from one shelf to another.

Although this is not a hot oven, the rich dough and egg wash will brown easily, so watch carefully after 30 minutes. If loaves are browning too rapidly, cover with aluminum foil or brown sack paper. Turn one loaf over. If it is nicely browned and sounds hard and hollow when tapped with a finger, loaves are done.

FINAL STEP

Remove from oven and place on metal rack to cool. When cool (or after freezing and thawing), sprinkle stollen-brioche liberally with confectioners' sugar. This bread freezes nicely for 1 or 2 months. So versatile it can be served any time—even toasted for breakfast. But it is meant for greater things—brunch or a fancy luncheon or to be served with a glass of wine.

RECIPES FROM BAYONNE

In the southwesternmost corner of France, where the Atlantic end of the magnificent Pyrenees is anchored in both that country and Spain, it comes as a pleasant surprise, like meeting an old friend in an unexpected place, to discover that a basketful of native American foods has been a part of the French-Basque cuisine for almost 400 years. Corn and pumpkin interested me most because they were made into breads, but the list included tomatoes, peppers, and, of course, turkey. A little later, along came the potato.

Christopher Columbus brought back corn to the Old World as a curiosity and shortly thereafter several of his Basque crew gave it to stay-at-home relatives in the Nive valley. It became so important in Basque culture that, in the largest festival of the year, the Corn Spirit parades as a white horse while the Wheat Spirit must be content as a dog. Corn took precedence even over hunting—dogs' tails were docked in order not to break the fragile young stalks. Corn replaced millet in the diet of the peasants, while pumpkin enjoyed more imaginative treatment in the hands of Basque cooks than it ever received at home and was used resourcefully in a wide variety of pies, *gratins,* cakes, and breads.

The day we were in Bayonne was neither a feast day nor a holiday, so the breads in the *boulangers'* windows were fairly ordinary—no special loaves of corn or pumpkin. But in Bayonne, which gave its name to a city in New Jersey and to the bayonet, a weapon developed by the city's iron workers, it is easy to turn to the Musée Basque, one of the finest ethnological museums of France. Not only did I see old kitchens of the several Basque regions, but I found a fine Basque cookbook—*La Cuisine Rustique: Pays Basque,* the rural cooking of the Basque country.

Here are several recipes adapted to the American kitchen. In a sense, some of them are coming home after an absence of several hundred years.

GÂTEAU AU MAÏS ❖ CORN CAKE

[ONE SMALL LOAF]

This is a delightful small bread that is leavened only with the air beaten into the egg whites. I bake it in a small 5-inch Charlotte tin and it forms a dainty loaf that, unmolded, looks like a tiny golden crown.

Like other Basque dessert breads, this gâteau *is sweet, but not cloyingly so. And like other dessert breads, it is excellent with fresh fruit. I had it first with fresh pineapple slices. Superb.*

Serves 6 to 8.

INGREDIENTS ¹/₂ cup sugar
¹/₄ teaspoon salt
1 cup yellow cornmeal
3 eggs, room temperature
¹/₂ cup (1 stick) butter or margarine, melted

BAKING PAN One small (7¹/₂ × 3¹/₂) loaf pan, greased or Teflon. Equally good is one round (5¹/₂-inch diameter) Charlotte pan.

PREPARATION
20 minutes
Preheat oven to 375°.

    Blend sugar, salt, and ¹/₂ cup cornmeal in a large bowl. Separate eggs, and drop yolks into center of dry mixture. Put whites aside in beater bowl. Melt butter and slowly blend it into the corn, drop by drop, as for mayonnaise. Add balance of cornmeal. Beat the egg whites stiffly and fold into corn-butter mixture, which will become a thin batter.

FORMING
3 minutes
Butter pan. Cut a piece of wax paper to cover the bottom. Butter paper and place in pan. Pour in batter.

BAKING
375°
45 minutes
Place pan on center shelf of preheated oven. Check *gâteau* after 30 minutes. It should be raised and browning. Fifteen minutes later, take from oven and pierce with a metal skewer or wooden toothpick. If it comes out clean, *gâteau* is baked.

FINAL STEP Unmold onto metal rack to cool. Slice thinly to serve. It should freeze well, but we have never had a slice left over to try.

Corn Cake, baked in a Charlotte tin, makes a good companion for fresh fruit.

BISCUITS AU MAÏS ❧ CORN BISCUITS

[FOUR DOZEN]

This is a true dessert bread—a light golden disk, a bit on the sweet side, perhaps, but a choice complement to a dish of strawberries or half of a grapefruit. It gets its rich look from eggs, yellow cornmeal, and butter. Although it is unleavened, it achieves a pleasant plumpness in the oven.

Be forewarned of an aftertaste that calls for one more . . . and one more . . . and one more . . .!

INGREDIENTS
¹/₂ cup (1 stick) butter, room temperature
¹/₂ cup sugar
1 cup yellow cornmeal
2 eggs, room temperature
1 teaspoon salt
1¹/₂ cups all-purpose flour, approximately

BAKING SHEET One large greased or Teflon baking sheet.

PREPARATION
15 minutes
In a large bowl, stir the butter into a soft mass with a wooden spoon or rubber scraper. Slowly add sugar, and blend together. About

Circles of dough become delicious Corn Biscuits.

75 strokes. Add cornmeal, eggs, and salt. Beat until smooth. Add 1¼ cups flour. The mixture will be soft and moist but can be rolled flat with a rolling pin to a thickness of about ¼ inch.

If too sticky to work, add ¼ cup more flour, blend with hands and flatten again with pin.

SHAPING
5 minutes
Use a 1½-inch-round cookie cutter to cut about 48 pieces. Reassemble scraps, roll again, and cut. Place close together on baking sheet but do not let them touch.

BAKING
375°
22 minutes
Preheat oven. Place baking sheet on center shelf. Near the end of the bake period, open the oven, and turn the baking sheet around. If those on the outer perimeter are browning too fast, either remove them if they are done (brown on the bottom) or move them to the center while pushing the lighter biscuits to the outside.

FINAL STEP
Remove from the oven and cool on metal rack. Delicious served warm and equally good frozen and warmed for a later service.

Corn Biscuits, specialties of the Basque country.

TALOA ✤ CORN SANDWICH MUFFINS

[EIGHT LARGE OR SIXTEEN SMALL MUFFINS]

A taloa *is deceptive. It looks like an English muffin, but it is essentially corn. While this recipe is made with half cornmeal and half all-purpose flour, the Basques, on occasion, will vary this to the extreme—3 cups cornmeal to 1 cup flour. The more cornmeal, the less the* taloa *will rise, as the corn contributes nothing to the leavening effect of the yeast.*

Slice open the taloa *for a sandwich, or toast one or both halves for a different kind of breakfast bread. The Basques also scrape out most of the inside dough, mix it with softened cream cheese, return it to the* taloa, *and it becomes a* marrakukua.

The sprinkle of poppy seeds is not authentic, but I thought it needed a contrasting touch. Or try sesame seeds.

Taloas, Basque corn muffins sprinkled with poppy seeds—delicious for breakfast.

INGREDIENTS   2 cups all-purpose flour, approximately
1 package dry yeast
2 teaspoons salt
1¹/₂ cups warm water (105°–115°)
2 cups cornmeal (yellow for golden color)
1 egg white, to glaze
1 tablespoon poppy seeds, to sprinkle

BAKING SHEET One or two baking sheets, dusted with cornmeal if not Teflon-coated.

PREPARATION
12 minutes
In a large bowl, stir together 1 cup all-purpose flour, the yeast, salt, and water. Let stand for 3 minutes to allow yeast to dissolve. Pour in cornmeal and blend with 25 strong strokes of wooden spoon or rubber scraper. Add remaining all-purpose flour, 1/4 cup at a time, first with the spoon and then with hands to make an elastic ball of dough that cleans the sides of the bowl.

KNEADING
6 minutes
Turn out on floured work surface and knead with a push-turn-fold motion until the dough is smooth, soft, and does not stick. Avoid making the dough dense with the addition of too much flour.

FIRST RISING
1 hour
Place dough in greased bowl, cover with plastic wrap, and leave at room temperature (70°–75°) until doubled in volume, about 1 hour.

SHAPING
5 minutes
Turn out dough and knead for a moment to expel bubbles. Divide dough into pieces—8 (for large muffins) or 16 (for small muffins).

Pat flat with palm of hand and roll into a circular disk with a pin. Larger muffins will be about 6 inches in diameter and 1/2 inch thick, smaller ones will be about 4 inches by 1/2 inch. When shaped, place on baking sheet.

SECOND RISING
50 minutes
Cover with wax paper and allow to rise.

BAKING
450°
20 minutes
Preheat oven 20 minutes before baking.

Brush tops of *taloas* with egg white and sprinkle liberally with poppy seeds.

Place on middle shelf of oven (if 1 baking sheet) or middle and bottom shelves (if 2 baking sheets), but switch pans after 12 minutes. If oven will take only one sheet, allow reserved muffins to rise additional time. *Taloas* on occasion may inflate to make the whole muffin a convenient pocket for a filling.

Taloas have no shortening and will not keep soft for more than a day or two. So use now—or freeze.

MÉTURE AU POTIRON BASQUAIS ❧ BASQUE PUMPKIN BREAD

[ONE ROUND LOAF]

Like the delicate corn gâteau, this Basque pumpkin bread is leavened only with beaten egg whites. The rum may be omitted, but somehow this authentic old recipe seems even more so with a tablespoon of the liquor that for centuries was an essential cargo on ships sailing between the New and Old Worlds.

It is a rich bread, rather dense and on the sweet side. Serve with a dry wine or fresh fruit.

INGREDIENTS
1 cup pureed pumpkin
1 cup milk
1 tablespoon butter
$1/4$ cup sugar
2 cups yellow or white cornmeal
$1/2$ teaspoon salt
3 eggs, room temperature
1 tablespoon light or dark rum, optional

Cornmeal and pumpkin, typical New World ingredients, find their way into this authentic Basque Pumpkin Bread.

BAKING PAN One round cake pan (7 inches in diameter and 4 inches high) or Charlotte mold. Buttered, with circle of wax paper (buttered) on bottom.

PREPARATION Preheat oven to 375°.
18 minutes   Pour pumpkin into medium bowl. Heat milk, butter, and sugar in saucepan over low flame, stirring constantly to soften and melt butter. Pour into bowl with pumpkin, and add corn meal, $1/2$ cup at a time, stirring to blend thoroughly. Add salt.

Separate eggs, dropping yolks into center of the corn mixture. Blend. In a mixing bowl, beat egg whites until stiff and fold into batter with a rubber scraper. Add rum, if desired, and mix.

FORMING Pour batter into prepared pan.
3 minutes

BAKING Place in oven on middle shelf. Test *méture* with a knife blade at the
375° end of 1 hour. If it comes out clean, bread is baked. If moist particles
1 hour stick to blade, return *méture* to oven for an additional 10 minutes. Test again.

FINAL STEP Allow *méture* to cool for 20 minutes before unmolding. Slice into thin servings. Enjoy as finger food or with a fork. It is best eaten warm.

RECIPES FROM CAMBO-LES-BAINS

Mention the word *Basque* and my blood immediately moves a bit faster and my mind slips into a higher gear and I dream of faraway and exciting places. It began more than a decade ago in Idaho when I traveled with Basque sheepherders as they took their bands of several thousand sheep out of the Sawtooth Mountains and loaded them aboard double-deck railroad cars bound for winter pastures in California's Imperial Valley. In the mountains, the bread was baked in a big iron pot set in campfire embers alongside a rushing mountain stream, and it was some of the best I had ever eaten.

It had been baked by the sheepherders, who, with their dogs, lived alone with the sheep for the spring and summer months in the high mountain pastures. They spoke only Euskera, the language of the Basques, and, as they were on a three-year work permit, they had little opportunity to learn English with only animals as companions. My interpreter was of Basque descent, the Idaho Secretary of State, and a rancher of considerable stature in the West. My friend said legend had it that Euskera was the pure language of Eden, the tongue in which Adam wooed Eve. It is not a beautiful language. It is spoken loudly, in short sentences, and in a clipped manner. "The Devil tried to speak our language and broke his teeth," my friend said, laughing.

When at long last one arrives in Basque country in the south of France, there is a comfortable feeling of having been there before. It is a composite of all the beautiful green-clad mountains you have ever seen.

But there are other indications that you have arrived, whether on the French or Spanish side of the Pyrenees. (The Basques consider themselves one people and tend to ignore national boundaries, a disregard that over the centuries has given fits to the authorities.) You are there when the next two men you meet are wearing the jaunty and practical beret, the black headcovering they wear formally to a wedding or a funeral or with equal aplomb to shovel manure or land a tuna. A Basque pulls his beret straight forward forming a visor to shade his eyes from the brilliant sun.

Another indicator is Basque names. Out in the country, they fashion the family name, in a flowing script, of wrought iron, about six inches high and two to three feet long. This is mounted on the stucco wall near the front door for everyone to see.

We had just passed Etchehandia and Errecartia and Aski Zau and now were in front of Ohartzabalea and Harrizabalete. It was in the steep field alongside the home of Izar Jai that the elder son and heir, with consummate skill, was guiding a tractor pulling a haying machine, while in the even steeper field immediately above, his parents were plowing behind a yoke of plodding oxen.

Also, there is *le gâteau basque*, the famous egg-and-butter-rich specialty of the region. Each *boulanger* has the usual variety of French breads, including a better-than-ordinary croissant (its tips almost touch so that it resembles a crab rather than a crescent), but in the forefront of all window displays are *les gâteaux basques*—rich, brown, and round. Street signs proclaim their regional glory as do postcards and posters in the shows.

My favorite *gâteau basque* recipe did not come from a *boulanger*, but as a gift from a shopkeeper in Cambo-les-Bains, where we headquartered in a lovely château, the Arrobia, that had once been the summer home of a wealthy Basque family, high on the plateau overlooking the quiet Nive River. Below us was the old town, where we sat one evening at one end of the local *fronton* court dodging young *pelote* players while waiting for our cassoulet to be served in the Chez Tante Ursule behind us.

The Arrobia, with its wide overhanging roof, was so spacious that we seldom saw any of the other dozen guests. It was so quiet at night that the only noise came from the frogs jumping into the pool in the center of the château's rose gardens. After a few days in Cambo, it was not difficult to understand how the Pyrenees around us and the mild climate had made it a delightful summer and winter spa honored at the turn of the century by dramatist Edmond Rostand's move there. Arnaga, his villa on the outskirts of Cambo, is a major attraction.

Madame Irrintzina, who owned a fabric shop not far from the hotel, was my benefactor as well as my teacher. Not only did I get the best of the several *gâteaux* recipes from her, but she gave me a lesson in pronouncing her name!

"Most Basque words are unpronounceable," she said. "The only way an outsider can even come close is to yodel. Yes, yodel. The TZ of my name starts in the head and moves to the chest. Like this." She opened her mouth and the two notes shot across the shop.

"Here, hold your finger on my throat and you can feel it develop."

It seemed more like a gulp, but again the clear notes rang out.

"You will find the recipe easier than the language," she laughed.

I did.

I made every effort to meet Monsieur Burrenne, the *boulanger* near the hotel whose croissants we celebrated each morning over coffee. The salesgirl at the counter said Madame Burrenne had chosen that day to have her first child and the new father was too excited to come to work.

I am happy for the baby but I do regret that its arrival in Cambo coincided with mine. Nevertheless, I came away from Cambo not only with four different recipes for *gâteau basque* but also the recipe for the crab-shaped croissants.

Gâteau Basque ⚜ Basque Cake

[ONE 9-INCH CAKE]

Gâteau basque *is the pride of every* boulanger *in the Pyrenees. It is fun to make and delicious to taste. While it is not a bread, a cake, or a pie, it combines some of the best features of all. It is, well,* gâteau basque! *A fine dessert.*

The Basque fill the gâteau *with either a pastry cream or preserved black cherries (Bing). Black cherry preserves is a specialty item not found everywhere in the U.S., so one must fall back on the tart red ones, Montmorency. My own preference is a layer of pastry cream spread with Smucker's Cherry Preserves. Outstanding.*

INGREDIENTS *Dough:*

2 cups all-purpose flour, approximately

2 egg yolks, room temperature

1 egg, room temperature

$^1/_4$ teaspoon salt

2 teaspoons grated lemon or orange peel

1 tablespoon light rum, if desired

$^1/_2$ pound (2 sticks) butter, softened

Filling:

$^1/_2$ cup all-purpose flour

2 cups milk

4 egg yolks

$^1/_2$ cup sugar

$^1/_2$ teaspoon salt

$^1/_2$ teaspoon vanilla

2 tablespoons light rum, if desired

1 12-ounce can cherry preserves

1 egg, beaten, to glaze

PIE PAN One 9-inch pie pan.

PREPARATION *Dough:* Place 2 cups of all-purpose flour in a medium bowl and fashion
15 minutes a well in the bottom. Drop in the egg yolks, egg, salt, grated peel, and
rum, if desired. Stir ingredients to mix while slowly pulling in flour
from sides of the bowl. Cut softened butter into 1-inch chunks and
drop into bowl. Work butter into the flour, first with scraper or
wooden spoon and then with hands. Add liberal sprinkles of flour, if
necessary, to make a firm dough. (Size of eggs will influence amount
of moisture in mix.) Do not work or knead dough more than necessary
to make a smooth ball.

REST Place dough in bowl, cover with plastic wrap, and put aside to rest for
1 hour 1 hour at room temperature (70°–75°). However, if the dough is soft,
place in the refrigerator.

PREPARATION *Filling:* Spoon flour into a saucepan and slowly add $^1/_2$ cup milk to make
12 minutes thin paste with no lumps. Stir in balance of milk, egg yolks, sugar,
salt, vanilla, and, if desired, rum. Place over low heat until pastry
cream thickens to hold shape. Stir constantly so mixture does not
burn or scorch. Set aside.

Cherries: While cherry preserves can be used from the jar, I prefer to
heat them in a small saucepan and strain them through a sieve to
separate fruit and syrup. Some products are too juicy and would
dilute the filling if used as is.

Not a bread, not a cake, not a pie, but a delicious *mélange* of all three, *Gâteau Basque* is the pride of Pyrenees *boulangers*.

FORMING
20 minutes

Preheat oven to 380°.

Divide dough into 2 pieces—one slightly larger than the other. Roll the larger piece between sheets of wax paper, loosening both sheets occasionally while rolling, to allow dough to spread. When rolled, dough should be slightly less than ¼ inch thick and 1 inch larger in diameter than pie tin. Peel off top paper. Use lower sheet to help pick up dough and invert over pan. Carefully peel off paper and with fingers carefully pat dough into place over bottom and up sides. Trim dough along outside edge of rim.

Spoon pastry cream into the shell. A deep pan will take more filling than a shallow one. Fill ¾ full. Spread the cherries over the surface and sprinkle amply with cherry syrup.

Roll remaining piece of dough between pieces of wax paper as before. Roll a thin circle ½ inch greater in diameter than top of pie pan. As with bottom piece, invert over pan. Trim. Crimp or pinch edges of top and bottom pieces together.

With a razor, cut a series of artistic whirls to allow steam to escape.

Brush with egg glaze.

BAKING
380°
40 minutes

Place on the low shelf of the oven. It will be done when crust is a golden brown.

FINAL STEP

Remove *gâteau* from oven with care. It will not become firm until it has cooled. Slice in narrow wedges to serve.

CROISSANTS CAMBO ✤ UNLAYERED CROISSANTS

[ABOUT THREE DOZEN]

While the flaky croissant, with layers and layers of buttery dough, is considered by most croissant fanciers to be the only croissant, it is not. Perhaps not as spectacular because it doesn't shower golden flakes, the unlayered croissant, like its flaky cousin, traces its antecedents back to Budapest in 1886 where the bakers were granted the privilege of making this special crescent-shaped bread for having sounded the alarm against the attacking Turks.

The unlayered croissant is easy to make. The butter becomes part of the dough early in preparation rather than folded in later.

The shaping of both is identical. The Cambo version is a little different in that the points of the croissant almost touch so that it looks like a small crab. A fine and unusual surprise to serve at breakfast or brunch.

INGREDIENTS
1 package dry yeast
2 tablespoons warm water (105°–115°)
4 cups all-purpose flour, approximately
$^1/_2$ teaspoon salt
$^1/_3$ cup non-fat dry milk
1 cup warm water (105°–115°)
$^1/_2$ pound (2 sticks) butter or margarine, room temperature

Glaze:
1 egg
1 pinch salt

BAKING SHEET One greased or Teflon baking sheet.

PREPARATION
20 minutes
Dissolve yeast in 2 tablespoons water in a small bowl or cup. In a large bowl, blend 2 cups of flour, salt, and dry milk. Pour in yeast mixture and 1 cup water. Stir this batter 30 strokes; drop in butter divided into several pieces. Blend the butter into the mixture. Add additional flour, $^1/_2$ cup at a time, stirring first with rubber scraper or wooden spoon and then working dough with the hands.

When dough is a shaggy mass, lift from the bowl after scraping particles from the sides.

KNEADING
5 minutes
Turn dough onto floured work surface and knead rhythmically until the dough is smooth, elastic, and has lost its stickiness. The dough should be firm, however, and should not slump when left in a ball for a moment or two on the work surface.

FIRST RISING
1$^1/_2$ hours
Place dough in bowl, cover with plastic wrap, and leave at room temperature (70°–75°) until double in volume, about 1$^1/_2$ hours.

SHAPING
30 minutes

Remove plastic wrap and punch down dough. Let rest on work surface for 2 or 3 minutes.

Punch dough flat and then begin to roll it lengthwise with a rolling pin into a rectangle 36 × 12 inches—and no more than ¹/8 inch thick. (A yardstick is handy for this operation.) Keep a light sprinkle of flour under the dough so it will be free to push out. With fingers and rolling pin, shape the desired rectangle. Don't rush it. Let the dough relax occasionally.

Allow the dough to relax in its final position for 3 minutes before cutting with a pastry wheel or sharp knife. With the yardstick as a guide, trim off uneven edges and reserve scraps.

The croissant pieces will be triangles—6 inches from tip to the base, which will be 4 inches across. Cut rectangle lengthwise into 2 pieces, each 6 inches wide.

If only 1 baking sheet can be utilized at a time, carefully cover one long strip with wax paper, fold, and reserve in the refrigerator until later.

With yardstick, mark series of 6-inch-by-4-inch triangles on remaining piece and carefully cut with pastry wheel. Lift triangles and place to one side.

Place triangle on work surface with the 4-inch base at 6 o'clock and apex at 12 o'clock. With rolling pin, roll the piece *one time* from bottom to top. This lengthens it and keeps it thin.

With the fingers, roll up the piece of dough from the base to the point, keeping the dough under slight tension. When it is lifted to the baking sheet, be certain the tip is under the body of the croissant so that it will not unroll in the oven. Finally, pull the ends down and together until they almost touch.

Leave 1 inch between pieces on the sheet.

SECOND RISING
1 hour

Cover with wax paper and leave for 30 minutes at room temperature (70°–75°). After ¹/2 hour, remove wax paper and brush the croissants with the egg-salt glaze. Leave uncovered.

BAKING
380°
25 minutes

Preheat oven 20 minutes before baking.

Brush croissants a second time with egg glaze and place baking sheet on middle shelf of oven. Halfway through the baking period, check croissants to be certain they are browning uniformly on the baking sheet. Croissants are done when a light golden brown. Bottom crust will be a deeper brown and feel solid under the fingers.

FINAL STEP

Place on metal rack to cool. If other croissants remain to be shaped and baked, clean baking sheet, remove reserved dough from the refrigerator and repeat process. Roll the dough trimmed from the rectangle into a smaller piece and shape into additional croissants.

RECIPE FROM CARCASSONNE

In the many years devoted to collecting recipes, I have been refused by only two persons. One was the cook in a country inn in Kentucky and the other was the widow of a *boulanger* in the walled Cité of Carcassonne who said her departed spouse had left her the recipe as an important part of the estate and she would not part with it.

"Je regrette mais c'est impossible," she said.

The centuries-old Cité, across the river from the newer and less appealing lower city, La Ville Basse, is the most complete ancient fortified city to be found anywhere. Its double lines of walls, its fifty towers, drawbridges and moats, a castle and a basilica, all this is home to 800 permanent residents, most of whom are there to take care of the needs of the thousands of visitors who are urged to leave their cars outside and make their entry through the gates on foot. Those who have hotel accommodations inside usually elect to drive because of the luggage. A stop-and-go light controls a single lane of auto traffic through the Narbonnaise gate and up the steep stone-paved street. It is a mad dash to the top, where cars are collecting for the journey down when the light changes.

After the hectic entrance, one must retrace this path on foot to find the *boulangerie-pâtisserie* of Madame A. Bacharan in a new-by-Carcassonne standards edifice built in 1810. A big loaf of fresh-baked country bread hangs by the open door and the window is filled with breads, cakes, and candies. In the morning, there is a steady procession up the hill of children who buy a *brioche chocolat* or a croissant to carry to school. In the afternoon, the procession is reversed and downhill come the children to Madame Bacharan's for ice-cream cones. Mingling with the children are the regular patrons and tourists who have come to buy her delicious breads, including the *spécialité de la maison.*

The pride of the small shop is *Galette de Dame Carcas,* a round loaf, no more than an inch thick, and pierced a dozen times before brushing with egg and then baking. There was a stack of eight or ten of these dark brown crusted loaves in the window under a large sign calling attention to Madame Bacharan's treasure. Another stack was on the counter where Madame stood tending trade.

Dame Carcas, after whom the loaf was named, tricked Charlemagne when he lay siege to La Cité by pretending there was ample food behind the stone walls when in fact the people were starving. Her stratagem: a pig was stuffed with the last handfuls of wheat from the granary and thrown off the high walls to burst into pieces on the ground in front of the attacking Franks. They were so astounded with the fat animal that they dropped the siege. For that clever deception, she has a bread named after her.

When I asked Madame Bacharan about the *galette,* she gave me a broad smile as she broke off a piece of a loaf and handed it to me. She watched as I savored the soft, rich bite that had a faint aroma of a special spice I could not identify.

When I asked her if I might have the recipe, a frown quickly replaced the smile.

Madame Bacharan with the prize possession of her little *boulangerie-pâtisserie,* the Twelfth-Night Cake of Dame Carcas.

"*Non, Monsieur,* I cannot part with the recipe. My dear husband who baked for so many years and who made it so famous would not want it out of the shop."

She crossed herself, and to be certain I understood about the late Monsieur Bacharan, she closed her eyes, dropped her head against her clasped hands and murmured, "*Il est mort il y a trois ans.*"

Obviously, I cannot reveal Madame Bacharan's secret because I don't have it, but in my research on the *galette,* I discovered that it is the symbolic bread eaten most often in celebration of Twelfth Night. I uncovered a number of recipes that I baked in my kitchen and one of these so closely parallels the Carcassonne loaf that I am certain Monsieur Bacharan, wherever he is, must have a forgiving smile at this moment.

GALETTE DE DAME CARCAS ⚜
TWELFTH-NIGHT CAKE OF DAME CARCAS

[ONE OR TWO LOAVES OR CAKES]

While the Galette de Dame Carcas *celebrates the ending of the Carcassonne siege by the clever ploy of one woman, to most French the* galette *is the bread or cake baked during the Twelfth Night celebration between Christmas and Epiphany. In provinces north of the Loire, notably in the Paris region, it is made with flaky pastry. In the south of France, including Carcassonne, the* galette *is made with yeast dough, as is this one. Delicious served at brunch, luncheon, or tea.*

INGREDIENTS	Finely grated *zeste* or peel of 2 oranges
	1 tablespoon orange juice
	2 teaspoons dry yeast
	1 tablespoon warm water (105°–115°)
	2½ cups all-purpose flour, approximately
	½ cup sugar
	½ teaspoon salt
	6 egg yolks, room temperature
	4 ounces (1 stick) butter, room temperature

Glaze:
1 egg
1 tablespoon milk

BAKING SHEET One baking sheet, ungreased.

PREPARATION Beforehand, finely grate the peel of 2 oranges and place in cup. Add 1 tablespoon orange juice. Set aside.

15 minutes   Dissolve 2 teaspoons of dry yeast in 1 tablespoon warm water (105°–115°) poured in a cup or small bowl. In a medium bowl, pour 1 cup flour and blend with sugar and salt. Form a well in the flour and pour in yeast mixture. Separate 6 egg yolks and drop one at a time into the bowl. Stir to pull in flour from the sides to blend with yeast and each yolk as it is added. The batter will be heavy. Divide the stick of butter into small pieces and drop into the batter. Blend into the mixture with 20 strong strokes of wooden spoon or rubber scraper. Add orange peel and juice. Add additional flour to form a ball that can be lifted from the bowl.

KNEADING The dough will be buttery and will not stick to the hands or work
5 minutes   surface. Dust the surface with sprinkles of flour to control excess butterfat coming to the surface. Do not make the dough so dense or hard

that it loses its elasticity. It must be soft to the touch, yet maintain its shape when left standing on the work surface for 2 or 3 minutes.

REST
30 minutes
Leave the ball of dough on the work surface and cover with the inverted mixing bowl.

SHAPING
5 minutes
The recipe will make one round *galette*—about 9 inches in diameter and 1¹/₂ inches thick—to serve to a dozen persons with tea or coffee. It can also be made into two small disks—6 inches by 1¹/₂ inches.

Press the dough into a circle, flatten the dough with the hands to about 1 inch in thickness, and place on the baking sheet.

RISING
45 minutes
Cover the *galette* (1 or more) with wax paper and leave undisturbed at room temperature (70°–75°).

BAKING
400°
25 minutes
Preheat oven 20 minutes before baking.

Remove wax paper. Brush the *galette* with the egg-milk glaze and, with a wooden or metal pick or skewer, pierce dough completely through a half dozen times. Place on middle shelf of oven.

The *galette* will be a bright golden brown when baked. Turn *galette* over and tap bottom crust to be certain it is hard and sounds hollow when tapped with a forefinger.

FINAL STEP
Place *galette* on metal rack to cool. Delicious served warm or cool. It is even better after it has aged overnight.

RECIPES FROM LIMOUX

Consider now the pepper cakes of Limoux.

While that line has the pleasant lilt of an old French nursery rhyme (but is not), the Limoux pepper cake is one of the unusual and good breads of France. It is not a cake, but a tiny twisted golden wreath of yeast-raised dough, speckled with pepper, and formed around the finger. It is most often served as an hors d'oeuvre or snack with drinks or coffee or tea.

Pepper (and cheese) bread is a frequent product of my own kitchen, so the mention of a small "cake" made with fresh ground pepper caught my attention in a French food atlas. It was the *spécialité* of Limoux, a small city only a few kilometers south of where we were staying in the fortified citadel of Carcassonne. The decision to drive to Limoux was not a difficult one because the cold stones of the old fortress walls were getting colder by the hour in a week when the entire European continent was gripped in an unseasonable cold snap. One more deep-freeze château-turned-museum-art gallery would be too much, Marje's muffled voice came out from under the blankets.

The sun was brilliant, the fields reflected the midday warmth as we sped south through rolling hills carpeted with tens of thousands of grapevines. (Wherever do they get the hands necessary to pick such an immense harvest?)

Unlike most French towns and cities in this historic part of France, with streets laid down originally by cattle and goats, Limoux's long and straight rue Jean-Faaves through a prosperous business section is a surprise. There were a half dozen *boulangeries* along the street and I chose the *boulangerie* of Roger Rebolledo because of the sparkling expanse of glass protecting an impressive assortment of breads. Madame Rebolledo was arranging a huge stack of small circular breads on a large tray as we came into the store.

"We have read about the town's pepper cakes," I told her after we had introduced ourselves. "Could you show us one?"

Madame Rebolledo laughed and pushed the big tray on which she had been working toward me.

"Here are a hundred! We call them *gâteaux au poivre*," she said. "I will call my husband and he will tell you about them."

I bit into one of them. It was crisp; there was an assertiveness about the pepper, not overwhelming, but more than just a hint.

Monsieur Rebolledo was a smiling man with the arms and shoulders of a gymnast.

"Be careful with the yeast—not too much or the *gâteaux* will be too fat," and he puffed out his cheeks to underscore his point. "They must be petite and delicate. Allow them no time to rise before you put them in the oven. Slip them in immediately, and leave them just long enough to be a shade beyond golden.

"And always use fresh ground pepper!"

Boulanger Roger Rebolledo of Limoux holds a tray of his famous pepper cakes.

While he talked, M. Rebolledo effortlessly twisted two tiny strands of dough—pushing forward with one hand and pulling back with the other. *Voilà!* He cut the twisted rope of dough into several lengths. One at a time he formed them into rings around an index finger held to the table. Overlapped ends were pressed together. With a few rapid motions, he soon had a large baking sheet completely covered with the *gâteaux*.

"You see, *Monsieur,* nothing to it."

Pepper cakes with a gluten diet loaf and a *flûte*.

GÂTEAUX AU POIVRE ❖ PEPPER CAKES

[FOUR DOZEN LITTLE CAKES]

Since pepper is the most important single ingredient in these small gâteaux, *grind it fresh, if you can. If a grinder is not a part of your* batterie de cuisine, *buy a fresh container of ground pepper at a large market where there is a fast turnover on the spice shelves.*

Don't hurry the dough. When it wants to pull back, walk away from it for a moment or two until it relaxes. Start again. This should not be rushed.

Ideally, the individual strands of dough should be slender, about the girth of a lead pencil. If a strand becomes too long and unmanageable as you roll it out, cut it in two.

I often start with 6 or 8 pieces of dough and may subdivide these into more than 14 or 16 pieces as I cut them back to convenient lengths.

Don't expect perfection the first time. Not until the third batch did I succeed in making a truly delicate, pencil-thin strand. And it was about the fourth batch before I succeeded in making a perfect round-the-finger wreath. M. Rebolledo said he had been doing it for more than two decades.

INGREDIENTS	$2^{1}/_{2}$ cups all-purpose flour, approximately
	$^{2}/_{3}$ cup warm water (105°–115°)
	1 teaspoon dry yeast (not packet, *teaspoon*)
	2 teaspoons pepper, freshly ground preferred
	1 teaspoon salt
	12 tablespoons ($1^{1}/_{2}$ sticks) butter, room temperature
	Glaze:
	1 egg or egg yolk
	1 teaspoon water

BAKING SHEET One baking sheet, greased or Teflon.

PREPARATION
15 minutes
In a large bowl, pour $1^{1}/_{2}$ cups of flour and make a well to hold water and yeast. Pour both into well, stir together and, when dissolved, add pepper and salt. Mix with flour until it forms a shaggy mass. Drop in butter divided into a dozen or so bits to make mixing easier. With scraper or wooden spoon, work butter into the flour until it is wholly absorbed. Add additional flour (about 1 cup) until dough forms a smooth, buttery mass.

KNEADING
5 minutes

The dough will be easy to knead because of its high butter content—but if it seems too moist or sticky, toss down several liberal sprinkles of flour and work them in. Knead for about 5 minutes.

SHAPING
20 minutes

Preheat oven to 425°.

This dough goes directly into the oven after shaping, so whatever leavening effect there is takes place in the oven. M. Rebolledo warned against a vigorous rising, which might tear the delicate wreaths apart.

The dough will weigh about 1¹/₂ pounds. Divide it into 6 or 8 pieces and begin rolling them into long strands the thickness of a lead pencil. First roll each piece into a rough cylinder. Lay both hands on the center of the roll and move the dough back and forth across the work surface—slowly spreading the hands apart and forcing the roll longer and thinner. Don't *force* the dough to spread, however, because it may tear apart. However, be firm when you push *down* on the roll with your hands. You cannot collapse it.

When one strand seems to be resisting move on to the next. Return to the first and continue the motion. When the strand gets so long that the ends are getting tangled (more than 18 inches) cut in two.

Twist two slender strands together. The double strand will try to unwind when you lay it down, so pinch the ends to the work surface until they relax somewhat in the twisted position. Go on to the next pair.

When the strands have been paired, hold the tip of the index finger against the work surface. The dough is wrapped around the finger to form the small wreaths. Allow enough additional length so that the ends can be pinched together (about 5 inches overall) and cut with a knife. Make certain the strands don't untwist before over-lapping and pinching together.

Place on baking sheet ¹/₂ inch apart. Repeat for all the double strands. When all *gâteaux* have been made, brush with egg-water glaze. For an extra peppery taste, sprinkle a bit of ground pepper over the egg-water coating.

BAKING
425°
22 minutes

Place sheet directly into the hot oven. No rest period or rising. Look at the cakes after 15 minutes. If those along the outside edges of the sheet are browning too fast, push them to center and move center cakes to the outside.

Cakes will be baked dry with little moisture left in them.

FINAL STEP

Remove from oven. Place on metal rack to cool. They will remain fresh for several weeks if kept in a covered container. They will freeze nicely for many weeks.

Pain de Régime Gluten ❧ Gluten Diet Bread

[ONE MEDIUM LOAF OR BRAID]

The taste of gluten bread is unusual, but the high price of gluten flour is too steep for it ever to become anything other than a pain de régime, *a diet bread. The price tag on a pound of gluten flour is* ten times *that of a pound of all-purpose flour. Obviously, it is an expensive process that washes wheat flour down to a single element, gluten, which is dried and ground into flour.*

Yet, it has a haunting, wheaty taste that will mystify a first-time taster. The dough has a lovely tawny color when being worked. While it is more firm than most doughs, it rises well into a handsome brown loaf.

France is big on pains de régime, *diet breads, and this loaf I found in a Limoux bakery down the street from M. Rebolledo, who makes the fine pepper cakes.*

INGREDIENTS	3 cups gluten flour, approximately
	$^1/_2$ cup all-purpose flour
	$1^1/_2$ teaspoons salt
	1 package dry yeast
	$^1/_2$ cups warm water (105°–115°)
	2 teaspoons shortening
BAKING PAN	One medium-size ($8^1/_2 \times 4^1/_2$) loaf pan, greased or Teflon.
BAKING SHEET	For braid: one baking sheet, greased or Teflon.
PREPARATION 15 minutes	In large bowl, place 1 cup gluten flour, $^1/_2$ cup all-purpose flour, and salt. Stir to blend. Fashion a well in center and sprinkle in yeast. Carefully pour water into well and stir to dissolve yeast particles. Let stand for 2 minutes. Pull in dry ingredients with wooden spoon or scraper and beat vigorously 75 strokes. Add shortening and stir to blend. Gradually add additional gluten flour, $^1/_4$ cup at a time, until the dough loses its wetness and can be worked without sticking to the hands.
KNEADING 5 minutes	Turn the dough onto a work surface lightly dusted with gluten flour. Knead with a strong 1-2-3 rhythm of push-turn-fold. The dough will be elastic, even rubbery. It is not a rewarding dough to make because it never gets the soft, warm feel of other doughs. It continually resists and pushes back.
FIRST RISING 1 hour	Place the dough in a greased bowl, cover with plastic wrap, and leave at room temperature (70°–75°) until dough has doubled in volume.
SHAPING 15 minutes	Punch dough down and turn onto work surface. Knead for 30 seconds to work out bubbles. For a pan loaf, press the ball of dough into a flat oval, the length of the baking pan. Fold in half, pinch seam together, tuck ends, and place in pan seam down.

Many French bakers braid their gluten loaves. Divide dough into 3 pieces. Roll into balls and let rest for 3 minutes. Each piece of gluten dough will resist your attempts to roll it into a 12- to 14-inch strand. Be patient. Don't force it, or the dough may tear. Allow 10 minutes or more for the rolling-out process—moving from one strand to another. Place the strands parallel. Braid from the middle, pinch ends of strands together. Turn and braid the other end from the middle; pinch ends to seal dough.

SECOND RISING
1 hour

Place pan or sheet in undisturbed place at room temperature (70°–75°). Cover dough with wax paper. Leave until dough in pan has risen 1 inch above edge, or braid has doubled in volume.

BAKING
390°
40 minutes

Twenty minutes before baking, preheat oven. Place bread in oven. Because the gluten dough browns rapidly, cover with foil or a piece of brown sack paper after 20 minutes. Turn one loaf over and tap with forefinger. If it sounds hard and hollow, bread is done.

FINAL STEP

Place on metal rack to cool. If the bread is on the diet of just one person in the family, you may wish to slice off a supply for 2 or 3 days and freeze the balance.

RECIPES FROM MONACO

To write that Monsieur Albert Phillips at 6 Rue Grimaldi is *boulanger* by appointment to Their Serene Highnesses, Prince Rainier III and Princess Grace, is overstating it a bit. His flaky croissants and crusty French and Italian loaves regularly are delivered up the hill to the royal palace, but so are the bakery products of several of the other eight *boulangers* in the sovereign principality of Monaco, whose densely clustered hills and headland look southward over the Mediterranean Sea. The palace plays no favorites among the bakers.

Monaco is clean, beautiful, friendly, and expensive (but not more so than the big cities of her big neighbors, France and Italy). It is not very large—about 450 acres, smaller than many Nebraska wheat fields. It is also a busy place—busy with hosting, entertaining, feeding, and lodging three million guests a year. All of this is done by its 24,000 residents, of whom only Prince Rainier, his family, and 3,475 others can claim Monégasque descent. The Prince is no Rainier-come-lately to the throne. His family, the Grimaldis, began their reign 679 years ago.

Almost everything in Monaco is geared to the visitor and a good place to begin is at the center of the Monégasque universe, the gaming tables at Place du Casino. From here, life radiates out to the beautiful Monte Carlo beach, the pools, at Stade Nautique Rainier III, the Hotel de Paris (where the great Escoffier helped set up the kitchen with a brigade of sixty-five cooks), a wax museum, a zoo, the outstanding Musée Océanographique (established by Prince Albert I, a fervent ichthyologist), and, of course, the palace on the hill, which looks just as the palace of any tiny Mediterranean principality should look. Finally, one cannot walk or drive without crossing or following many of the streets (most seemed to be named for Grimaldi kin) down which, once a year, Grand Prix race cars scream and roar to tear apart Monaco's gentle ambience.

While M. Phillips's place of business, L'Epi d'Or (the Golden Ear of Wheat), may not be listed by the Office National du Tourisme as one of the city's stellar attractions, it is, nevertheless, greatly admired by a large and steady clientele moving constantly through the large plate-glass doors with their handsome polished brass fittings, and by tourists drawn to the beautiful window displays of pastries and breads.

While the shop, at the corner of Rue Grimaldi and Rue Princess Caroline, is a thriving business with a half-dozen saleswomen, about half of the bakery's daily production of 1,500 croissants and 1,400 loaves goes each day to Monaco hotels and restaurants.

Five miles to the east lies Italy, whose influence on Monégasque baking is evident though subdued (as compared to the French). The morning I spent in the *boulangerie* with M. Phillips, his crew was baking a special order of Italian loaves for the *buffet exotique* that evening at the nearby Holiday Inn.

L'Epi d'Or is a three-story operation. The family's living quarters are on the second floor, the retail store, combined with a tea room for on-the-spot tasting of three-score kinds of *pâtisserie*, is on the ground floor, and, in the cellar, the *boulangerie*, which sent

The royal family of Monaco, in the *palais* up the hill, are patrons of M. Phillips' *boulangerie*.

up baskets of bread and a rainbow variety of cakes and petits fours to the shop overhead via a large but slow-moving dumbwaiter.

The elevator vexed the impatient M. Phillips, who, during the course of the morning, made several astonishing dashes up a short ladder, threw open a small metal door, crouched, and, with head down, shot out onto the sidewalk of Rue Princess Caroline. (This half-door was the only way into and out of the bakery.) He would continue his dash around the corner and into the formal Rue Grimaldi entryway, carrying whatever special order it was he would not trust to the mechanical contrivance.

M. Phillips, a spare man about five feet, six inches tall, whose furious exits no doubt help maintain a wiry figure, was born forty years ago near Toulon. His father, a professional golfer, was English; his mother, French. He apprenticed to a baker at thirteen, and ten years later bought the L'Epi d'Or, which had been in the Grimaldi location for 100 years. The big windowless cellar accommodates nine bakers, two of whom have the rank of *pâtissiers* and work in a section set aside for pastries. The other seven work in and around a huge three-tiered oil-fired oven that dominates the room.

To a home baker accustomed to mixing only warm water with yeast and flour to give a healthy boost to the resulting dough, the sight of an elaborate refrigerated water cooler alongside the big mixing bowls came as a shock. "No, it is not for drinking," M. Phillips assured me. "It is for the mixing!"

He believes, as do many bakers, that dough can get too warm during the machine mixing-kneading and that the way to counter this is to start with cold water which, in some instances, is down in the 40's. This is not guesswork on his part; he follows a precise formula based on the temperature of the room plus the temperature of the flour.

"This way we get the true flavor of the wheat as it would be if it were all done by hand, without the machines," he said.

Pain de Gruau ❧ Finest Wheaten Bread

[SIX 17-INCH LOAVES—OR TWO 1-POUND LOAVES AND ONE DOZEN ROLLS]

The French call it pain de gruau, *the finest wheaten bread. Here, it is baked in the classic shape of* l'épi, *the ear of wheat—its pointed pieces sprouting as if from a stalk. It is done to perfection by M. Phillips, whose* boulangerie *carries the name L' Épi d' Or, golden ear of grain.*

Pain de gruau *is made with bread flour, which in the U.S. is obtainable at mills supplying commercial bakers. Hard wheat, the source of this flour, is grown in the western United States and Canada, where sub-zero winter temperatures are the rule rather than the exception. It has always been at a premium in France, which gets a small supply from Africa, but the New World is the chief supplier of this finest of all flours for making bread.*

A French boulanger *is mindful of two or three things when he makes* pain de gruau. *To slow the development of the dough, the water is cooler by several degrees than that ordinarily used in most bread production; and, to avoid excessive fermentation, the first rising of the dough is about 3 or 4 hours, a short time commercially.*

Finally, loaves are formed in two stages, with a rest period in between to allow the dough to relax and to regain suppleness. Without this relaxation, the dough would tear when rolled or stretched into lengths.

This is an excellent table bread, whatever form it takes. Directions for shaping long hearth loaves and rolls follow these for épis.

INGREDIENTS
5^1/$_2$ cups hard-wheat bread flour, approximately
1 tablespoon salt
^{1}/$_4$ cup non-fat dry milk
1 package dry yeast
2^1/$_2$ cups water (70°–75°—about room temperature)
1 teaspoon malt syrup (or sugar)

BAKING SHEETS
One or two baking sheets, greased or Teflon. Also a length of canvas to contain long loaves while rising. The length of the largest baking sheet will determine the size of the *épis*. Most home ovens accept a 14 × 17-inch sheet, which dictates a 17-inch *épi*.

PREPARATION
15 minutes
In a large bowl, mix together 2 cups bread flour, the salt, dry milk, and yeast. Pour in water, blend to make a heavy batter. Add malt syrup (or sugar) and stir briskly to dissolve. Add additional flour, ^{1}/$_2$ cup at a time, stirring first with a heavy wooden spoon or rubber scraper until difficult to stir—then use hands to form a heavy mass that can be lifted from the bowl.

The dough will feel cooler than 70° because of its moistness.

KNEADING
10 minutes
Place the dough on the work surface that has been dusted with a sprinkle of flour. Knead with a rhythm of 1-2-3, push-turn-fold,

push-turn-fold. Break the rhythm occasionally by whacking the dough down against the work surface. This helps to develop the gluten so necessary to yeast-raised bread. Add sprinkles of flour if dough seems excessively moist or sticky.

This dough takes more kneading than dough made with all-purpose flour.

FIRST RISING
3–4 hours
Clean and grease bowl and return dough to it. Cover tightly with plastic wrap and leave undisturbed at room temperature (70°–75°), until dough has more than *tripled* in volume.

SHAPING #1
5 minutes
Punch dough down and turn onto work surface. Knead for 30 seconds. Divide the dough into 6 equal pieces.

REST
15 minutes
Set dough pieces aside to rest under wax paper for 15 minutes. This rest or relaxation is important to *pain de gruau.*

SHAPING #2
10 minutes
Carefully roll each piece into a 17-inch length. Place each on a canvas strip or *couche* (see page 14). Pull up folds of cloth on either side of the dough. Prop rolling pin, stick, or pan against one end. Place the second length of dough alongside and tightly against its mate from which it is separated by a fold of cloth. Repeat for all six pieces. Prop other end.

If the dough is sufficiently firm and does not slouch, the pieces may be placed directly on the baking sheets to rise. They may spread slightly, but this should not mar the effect of the scissor cuts to follow.

SECOND RISING
1 hour
Cover with wax paper or cloth and leave undisturbed to rise at room temperature (70°–75°), about 1 hour, or until double in bulk.

Preheat oven to 425° 20 minutes before the bake period.

CUTTING
5 minutes
Roll each loaf off the *couche* onto a length of board, cardboard, or another bake sheet and place on prepared baking sheet.

Place no more than 3 *épis* on one bake sheet. The points to be cut with scissors must not touch adjoining loaves. This may mean reserving other loaves in the cloth folds until the first bake is finished.

Use scissors with long blades.

In a 17-inch *épi*, there will be about 6 cuts, about $2^{1}/_{2}$ inches apart. Hold the scissors directly above the length of dough and cut at an angle of about 45°. Cut deep into the dough—$^{2}/_{3}$ through its diameter.

Make the first scissors-cut near the bottom end of the loaf as it rests in front of you. With the other hand, lift and turn the cut piece to the left. Make a second cut and turn this piece to the right—and so on up the length of the loaf, a total of 5 or 6 pointed pieces.

Repeat with other pieces.

Five minutes before baking, place broiler pan on bottom shelf of oven and pour in 1 cup of hot tap water to create steam.

M. Phillips cuts *pain de gruau* into the classic shape of an *épi,* an ear of wheat.

BAKING
425°
30–35 minutes
Place in the oven. *Epis* are baked when golden brown and crisp. Tap the bottom with a forefinger to determine if the crust is hard and sounds hollow.

FINAL STEP Place on rack to cool. Allow guests to break off their own pieces.

Pain de gruau may take several forms. Here are the instructions for shaping this batch of dough into long hearth loaves and a dozen rolls.

SHAPING #1
5 minutes
Following the *first rising,* turn dough onto work surface and divide into desired number of loaves and rolls.

For 2 loaves and a dozen rolls, divide dough into 3 equal pieces. Roll 2 pieces into large balls and set aside to rest for 15 minutes. This rest or relaxation is important to *pain de gruau.* Divide the remaining dough into 12 equal pieces and, under cupped palms, roll each into a tight ball by pressing hard against the work surface.

REST
15 minutes
Set aside under wax paper to rest 15 minutes.

SHAPING #2
18 minutes
Shape each large piece of dough under the palms—carefully rolling and stretching it until the roll is about 12 to 14 inches long—a short *baguette* or a long *bâtard*!

Place length of dough on canvas strip or *couche* (see *couches,* page 14). Pull up folds of cloth on either side of dough. Prop rolling pin, stick, or pan against one side. The second length of dough is placed alongside, tightly against its mate but separated with a fold of canvas. Prop the cloth against the other side and cover loaves with wax paper. Roll each small roll under the palm to lengthen it slightly. Place on the baking sheet, and cover with wax paper.

SECOND RISING
1 hour
Allow loaves and rolls to rise until double in bulk, about 1 hour.

BAKING
400°
20–35 minutes
Preheat oven 20 minutes before the bake period.

Five minutes beforehand, place broiler pan on bottom oven shelf and pour in 1 cup hot tap water—to create steam.

Lift each loaf off the *couche* with a length of board, cardboard, or another baking sheet and place on prepared baking sheet. With razor blade, cut 4 or 5 diagonal slashes down the length of each loaf. Carefully make 3 cuts across each of the small rolls. Place in oven.

Breads are baked when golden brown. Rolls will be baked in about 20 minutes; the loaves, about 30 to 35 minutes. Turn one loaf over and tap bottom crust with forefinger. If the crust sounds hard and hollow, the bread is done. If the bottom crust is soft, return loaf to oven for an additional 10 minutes.

FINAL STEP Place on metal rack to cool.

The Italian influence on neighboring southern France makes Panettone a popular bread in Monaco.

PANETTONE ⚜ ITALIAN PANETTONE

[FOUR MEDIUM HEARTH LOAVES]

Italy, not very far away from Monaco, makes a substantial contribution to the variety of breads available in the principality as well as to that part of France that fronts it.

While many of the fine Italian panettone *loaves are baked in tall cylindrical pans, this loaf is baked on a baking sheet or directly on the hearth without benefit of a mold. Five minutes after it has been in the oven, open the door and drop a tablespoon of butter on the center of the developing crust.* Voilà! Eccolo!

The original of this recipe was a classical example of starting with a cup of flour, some yeast and a little water and carrying it through several sponges to make more than 5 pounds of fine dough. This adaptation eliminates two of the sponges with no loss of flavor.

INGREDIENTS
Starter:
¼ cup warm water (105°–115°)
1 package dry yeast
1 teaspoon malt syrup
¾ cup all-purpose flour, approximately

Dough:
All of the starter
1¼ cups warm milk (105°–115°)
7 cups all-purpose flour, approximately
2 teaspoons salt
4 ounces (1 stick) butter, room temperature
4 egg yolks, room temperature
2 eggs, room temperature
1 cup sugar
½ cup candied mixed fruit or citron
2 tablespoons pine nuts
1 tablespoon anise seeds, ground
⅔ cup raisins
4 tablespoons butter, room temperature, for crusts

BAKING SHEET   One or two greased or Teflon baking sheets, according to need.

PREPARATION   *Starter:* Pour warm water and yeast into a medium-size bowl. Stir to
5 minutes   dissolve and let rest for 3 minutes. Add malt syrup, which is heavy,
6 hours   sticky stuff, so stir to dissolve in the liquid before adding flour. Add
or overnight   flour sufficient to make a soft ball, and knead briefly for 2 or 3 minutes. Cover bowl with plastic wrap and leave at room temperature (70°–75°) for a minimum of 6 hours or overnight.

15 minutes   *Dough:* Place the starter into a large bowl and pour over it the warm milk (105°–115°).

Stir in 2 cups of flour, the salt, and butter cut into pieces. In a separate bowl, beat together egg yolks, eggs, and sugar until light yellow and frothy, about 3 minutes. Slowly pour this into the flour mixture, blending it well.

With wooden spoon or rubber scraper, stir in additional flour, ½ cup at a time, until the batter is thick and can be worked with the hands into a shaggy mass. Lift out of the bowl.

KNEADING   Dust the work surface with liberal sprinkles of flour and begin to knead
6 minutes   the dough with the help of a dough scraper, if dough remains sticky. Use rhythmic push-turn-fold motion, occasionally varying this by banging the dough down hard against the countertop or table. Dough will become soft, elastic, and nice to work.

FRUIT-NUTS
5 minutes

When dough is smooth, put aside for a few minutes while the fruit and nuts are assembled. Chop mixed fruit (or citron) and pine nuts into smaller pieces. Mix with ground anise seeds and raisins.

Punch dough into a flat oval and spread half of fruit-nut mixture over the top. Fold into dough and knead until they disappear, then repeat with balance of mixture. Knead the dough thoroughly so the fruit and nuts are well distributed.

FIRST RISING
2 hours

Return dough to washed and greased bowl, cover tightly with plastic wrap, and set aside undisturbed for about 2 hours at room temperature (70°–75°) to triple in volume.

SHAPING
5 minutes

Remove plastic wrap and punch down dough with fingers. Lift dough to flour-dusted work surface and divide into 4 pieces (for medium-size loaves). Shape each into a ball with cupped hands. Place on one or two baking sheets, as needed. Flatten tops of loaves slightly.

SECOND RISING
1^1/$_2$ hours

Arrange lengths of wax paper over the dough so the surface does not dry out. Leave at room temperature (70°–75°) until loaves have about doubled in bulk.

BAKING
375°
40 minutes

Preheat oven 20 minutes before it is time to bake the *panettone* loaves.

Before placing in oven, cut an X with a razor blade on top of each ball. The X should be about ^{1}/$_2$ inch deep and extend to a point halfway down the sides. (Butter comes later.)

Place baking sheets on top and middle shelves if baking with both trays, otherwise use middle shelf.

Five minutes after the bread has been placed in the oven, open door, pull the shelf forward, and quickly drop 1 tablespoon of butter in the center of each loaf where the X crosses. Close oven door.

Midway in the bake period, shift baking sheets from top to bottom and bottom to top.

Loaves are done when deep brown and sound hollow and hard when bottom crust is tapped with the forefinger.

FINAL STEP

Place on metal rack to cool. This is a lovely, light bread that is excellent for any festive occasion. Serve it for a brunch, a breakfast, or a tea. Freezes well, but should be used within 6 weeks for full measure of freshness.

PAIN ITALIEN ❧ ITALIAN BREAD

[TWO HUSKY 2-POUND LOAVES]

Pain italien is close kin to French bread but there is a difference. Monsieur Phillips, less than an hour away from the Italian border, has been influenced over the years by a knowledgeable clientele on what is and what is not *pain italien*. He uses two ingredients that surprised me—oil and dry milk. No sugar, of course, but a small helping of malt syrup.

The best results with this recipe can be obtained with bread flour with its high gluten content that allows the maximum expansion of the dough in rising and in the oven.

Bakers in Northern Italy have a unique way of dividing a loaf of bread while it is rising and baking. A piece of string is wrapped around the ball of dough as it is put on the baking sheet to rise. As the bread expands, the string holds a crease. Expanding more in the oven, the crust breaks along the line to produce a different-looking loaf. Delicious served with any meal, but especially with Italian food.

INGREDIENTS	1 tablespoon salt
	1 tablespoon malt syrup (or sugar)
	$1/3$ cup non-fat dry milk
	$2^{1}/_{2}$ cups cool water (70°–75°)
	2 packages dry yeast
	$1/_{2}$ cup cool water (70°–75°)
	6 cups hard-wheat bread flour, approximately
	1 tablespoon vegetable oil

BAKING SHEETS One large or two small baking sheets, greased or Teflon. These loaves are quite large—8 inches across. Two would crowd the average baking sheet.

PREPARATION This is a good recipe in which to let the electric mixer work for about 10 minutes in the early stages of developing the dough as a soft batter.
10 minutes In a small bowl, mix the salt, malt syrup, milk, and $2^{1}/_{2}$ cups of water. Stir to dissolve the malt, which is heavy and thick. Set aside.

In another small bowl, dissolve the yeast in $1/_{2}$ cup of water. Stir and let stand for 3 to 4 minutes to dissolve.

In the mixer bowl, place 4 cups of flour and form a well in the center. Pour in the malt-milk mixture, stir to form a batter, and then add yeast and oil.

MIXER Let the mixer take over at medium speed for 10 minutes. Scrape down
10 minutes the sides of the bowl during the process, if necessary. If by hand, beat with a large wooden spoon for an equivalent length of time.

Pain Italien takes several forms in M. Phillips' *boulangerie,* one tied with a string before baking.

5 minutes   Stop mixer. Add additional flour, $1/2$ cup at a time, stirring first with a spoon and then working the flour into the dough by hand. When dough is firm, take out of the bowl.

KNEADING This is a wonderful dough to knead—elastic, soft, warm to the touch.
8 minutes It seems to invite kneading. Nevertheless, break the kneading pattern of push-turn-fold once in a while by throwing the dough down hard against the work surface. Do this a half dozen times and then return to push-turn-fold. The dough hook of an electric mixer is good for this, but this much dough has a tendency to climb into the spring mechanism holding the dough hook. Hold the dough down with a rubber scraper. If you use a dough hook, knead dough for about 5 minutes.

FIRST RISING Return dough to the large washed and greased bowl, cover with plastic
2 hours wrap, and leave at room temperature (70°–75°) until dough has *tripled* in volume. In my large bowl, this means that the dough is pressing up against the plastic wrap.

PUNCH DOWN Turn back the plastic wrap, punch, and deflate dough with extended
2 minutes fingers. Turn dough over. Re-cover bowl.

SECOND RISING Allow the dough to rise for 30 minutes.
30 minutes

SHAPING The *boule* or ball is the favored form of *pain italien* in M. Phillips's
boulangerie. But it can also be made into *bâtards* and the longer
baguettes.

20 minutes   Turn the dough onto the floured work surface and knead briefly
to press out the bubbles. Divide the dough, which will weigh about
4 pounds, into 2 pieces or as many as you wish. Form each into a ball
and allow to rest for 20 minutes.

15 minutes   For a *boule,* shape dough into a ball, gently pulling the surface of
the dough taut with cupped hands. Place on the baking sheet and
press dough into a flat loaf—about 8 inches in diameter by $1/2$ inches
thick.

If desired, tie a length of string around one of the loaves as it is
placed on the baking sheet. Secure by tying.

THIRD RISING Cover the loaves with a cloth (I use a piece of army blanket), so that
1 hour some air reaches the dough to form a light crust. Wax paper held on
water glasses can also be used. Leave at room temperature (70°–75°).
To form long loaves see *couches,* page 14.

BAKING Preheat oven 20 minutes before the bake period.
425°   Cut a tic-tac-toe design on one loaf, but not on the loaf tied with
40–50 minutes a string.

This is a dry oven—no water in a pan—but brush loaves with
water before placing baking sheets in the oven.

If two shelves are used, rotate baking sheets 2 or 3 times after
loaves begin to brown, about 20 minutes.

Loaves are done when they are a golden brown and when bottom
crust is hard and hollow-sounding to the tap of the forefinger.

FINAL STEP Place loaves on metal rack to cool.

PAIN DE MIE DE MONACO ✤ SANDWICH BREAD

[TWO MEDIUM LOAVES]

Pain de mie *is known also in France as* pain anglais—*a tribute of sorts to generations of English travelers who wanted the kind of white thin-crusted bread they got at home in Britain. In the beginning, it was reserved for the English, but gradually it came to be used (and appreciated) for croutons, breadcrumbs, sandwiches, canapés served as* hors d'oeuvres, *and for toast served with tea.*

Monsieur Phillips said, sadly, that if he didn't make pain de mie *for visitors to Monaco they would simply cut the beautiful thick crusts off his regular French loaves. It was clear that he was appalled by the thought.*

In the U.S. a similar bread is the Pullman loaf.

The loaf below can also be made with raisins added.

INGREDIENTS
6^1/$_2$ cups all-purpose flour, approximately
2^1/$_3$ cups milk, warmed (105°–115°)
4 teaspoons salt
2 teaspoons sugar
1 package dry yeast
4 ounces (1 stick) butter, room temperature
^{1}/$_4$ cup raisins, optional, for 1 loaf

BAKING PANS
Two medium-size (8^1/$_2$ × 4^1/$_2$) loaf pans or special *pain de mie* or Pullman pans with a sliding lid on top to keep the loaf's rectangular shape. A lid can be devised for the ordinary loaf pan by placing a board wrapped in aluminum foil or a small baking sheet over the top of the pan or pans and weighing it down with 4 or 5 pounds of stone, brick, doorstop, metal bar, or the like.

Whichever is used, it is convenient to pencil two marks on the inside of each pan. The first mark is ^{1}/$_3$ from the bottom—the height of the dough initially. The second mark is ^{3}/$_4$ up the side. When the dough rises to the second mark, it then goes directly into the oven. The dough will rise in the oven to completely fill the pan and press against the lid.

PREPARATION
15 minutes
In a large bowl, place 3 cups of flour and form a well in the center. Pour in the milk and pull in some of the flour from the sides to make a light batter. Stir in the salt, sugar, and yeast. Blend carefully to dissolve the yeast. Let stand for 3 to 4 minutes before continuing. Pull in additional flour from the sides to make a heavy batter. Cut butter into small pieces and work them into the dough.

Add additional flour ^{1}/$_2$ cup at a time, and work it into the dough with the hands. It may be sticky because of the butter, which will be absorbed by the flour.

Weight on top of aluminum-covered board will help shape dough into a delicious rectangular sandwich loaf.

KNEADING
8 minutes

Turn dough onto floured work surface and knead with a firm push-turn-fold motion. Use dough scraper to lift and throw down the dough against the table if stickiness persists. Add sprinkles of flour, if needed.

FIRST RISING
3¹/₂ hours
30 minutes

Place dough in a large bowl, cover with plastic wrap, and leave at room temperature (70°–75°) until dough has more than doubled in volume. Turn back covering after 3¹/₂ hours, punch down dough, re-cover, and leave for another half hour.

SHAPING
10 minutes

Turn dough onto work surface and divide into two pieces.
    If raisins are to be added to one loaf, press the dough into a flat oval, and spread raisins on the top. Fold dough over them and knead.
        All surfaces of the pans—sides, bottom, and top—are to be greased.
        With hands, press each piece of dough into a rectangle as long as the pan and twice as wide. Fold dough, pinch seam, roll the dough forward so the seam is down. Place in the pan. It should come ¹/₃ of the way up the pan. If there is too much dough, take some out. With the knuckles, pat the dough flat and into the corners of the pan.
        Repeat for second pan.

SECOND RISING
1–1¹/₂ hours

Cover the pans with clear plastic wrap so the dough can be watched coming up the sides of the pans to the three-quarter mark. Leave at room temperature (70°–75°) to observe.

BAKING
400°
50 minutes

Preheat oven ¹/₂ hour before anticipated time of baking. The oven must be ready so loaves can go directly into it when it is time.

When the dough reaches the three-quarter mark, place the prepared cover on the pans. Move to the middle shelf of the oven. Place weights on covers.

A half hour into the bake period, the loaves will be formed and the covers can be removed to allow the moisture and steam to escape. Turn one loaf from pan to test for doneness. If crust is solid to the touch, bread is baked.

FINAL STEP

Turn out loaves to cool on metal rack. This bread should be allowed to mature for 24 to 36 hours to develop full flavor. *Très bon!*

RECIPES FROM SISTERON

Happily, the light at the end of the tunnel was Sisteron, the fortified fifth-century city that is the northernmost outpost of Provence. It is a legendary part of France that includes not only Grasse, the city of perfume, and the fourteenth-century papal city of Avignon, but the Côte d'Azur, where travel writers for years have sought gaudy adjectives to describe a sea and sky common to St. Tropez, Cannes, Nice, and Antibes. Provence is more than just a place. It is a state of mind like Hawaii or Tahiti or Bali. It is also a country of good cooking, laced with garlic, where olive oil replaces butter. Its breads are delicious and, near the eastern border, influenced by the Italian kitchen.

We had driven up and down mountains and across valleys in the rain all afternoon, moving south on N 75 (Route Napoleon) when, ahead, half hidden in the swirls of mist, loomed yet another giant rock outcropping. "We must be near Sisteron because the *Michelin* map says we are," my wife said. But there was nothing to indicate that a city of 6,500 was nestled somewhere nearby. Then up high I caught a glimpse of a flagpole near the top of the great rock. And when it seemed I had nowhere else to drive but into the black stone wall, the road curved gracefully to the left and disappeared into the mouth of a tunnel. We followed. When we emerged, the mist had cleared and we were in Sisteron, the heart of the Alpes de Haute Provence. From here, it would be all downhill to the Mediterranean.

The small city has been described by a native son and author as "twenty narrow streets sheer as staircases . . . all jumbled together like the streets of an Arab village." It had gained a certain prominence in 1815 by surrendering to Napoleon, who had just escaped from Elba. On a height dominating the city is the Citadelle, the fortified mountain position under which our tunnel had just taken us.

We had been told along the route that here we would find the unusual shape that Provence *boulangers* give some of their loaves. The breads were called *fougasses.* While my French-English dictionary defined a *fougasse* as a land mine, the *fougasse* I sought was a flattened loaf cut through at several places with a knife or pastry blade (*coupe-pâte*) and stretched by hand to separate the pieces into ladders and fans and other delightful shapes.

The car was parked in the shadow of one of the stone watchtowers that faced the Grand Hôtel du Cours, which was immediately across the street from what had been the inner line of defense centuries before. Now the empty towers were occupied by sparrows in the lower levels and swallows higher up.

The following morning was bright and clear and I followed the narrow, winding street that dropped away sharply behind an old church to surface two blocks away alongside the *boulangerie* of Monsieur Claude Vevey at 5 Place de l'Horloge, so named for its clock tower built in 1806.

M. Vevey, I had been told at the hotel, made the finest *fougasse* and *pain seigle,* a round rye loaf, in the region. He was busy at the oven, but his pretty wife brought two shapes, the ladder and a tree, out into the sunlight so I could get a picture of them. She said her husband was very proud of his breads, especially the *fougasse.*

Madame Vevey holds *fougasses* her husband has made in tree and ladder shapes, favorites in their Provençal bakery.

FOUGASSE ❧ LADDER BREAD

[NUMBER VARIES]

A fougasse is a flat piece of pain ordinaire *dough cut through and pulled into one of several unusual shapes. Actually, there is no limit to the number that can be shaped once the home baker has overcome a reluctance to cut away with knife and scraper.*

The most common forms are ladders and trees. Mine seem always to be ladders which is why, around our house, it is called ladder bread. The dough is rolled flat into a ¹/₂-inch-thick rectangle, cut, and then pulled from opposite ends to open up the cuts. It has an informal look about it that makes it a happy choice and a conversation piece for a barbecue, a spaghetti dinner, or whatever. To serve, just break off a limb or a rung as wanted.

INGREDIENTS One batch, about 3 pounds, of *pain ordinaire* dough (page 163).

BAKING SHEET One baking sheet, greased or Teflon.

PRIOR STEPS Here are the steps and times for the dough before the loaves are shaped:

Prepare Dough	18 minutes
First Rising	2 hours

SHAPING
15 minutes

Remove plastic wrap and punch down dough. Turn it onto a lightly floured work surface and knead briefly to press out the bubbles. The dough will be light, elastic, and a pleasure to work.

This 3-pound batch of dough will make two large *fougasses*—a ladder and a tree. Divide the dough into two pieces. Roll into balls and set aside for 3 to 4 minutes to relax the dough.

With a rolling pin and the hands, roll and stretch one piece of dough into a long, narrow rectangle. If the dough is obstinate and pulls back, don't fight it—leave it for 5 minutes (while beginning the other piece). When the piece is rolled out to a thickness of between 1/2 and 3/4 inch, make 4 or 5 diagonal cuts through the dough, at equal distances apart, down the length of the piece. A dough scraper or putty knife can be pressed down through the dough or it can be cut with a sharp knife, a razor blade, or pastry wheel. I prefer the dough scraper. Holding the ends, pull the dough until the cuts have opened to form a ladder.

A stylized tree within a circle begins with an oblong piece of dough rolled flat. Three diagonal cuts slanting downward are made on one side of an imaginary center line. Matching cuts are made on the other side of the line. Open the cuts by pulling gently. Do not cut through or tear the encircling piece of dough.

SECOND RISING
60 minutes

Cover the loaves with wax paper and leave undisturbed at room temperature (70°–75°) for 1 hour.

BAKING
450°
400°
45 minutes

Twenty minutes before baking, preheat oven to 450°. Five minutes before baking, pour 1 cup water in broiler pan placed on lower shelf. Be careful of the burst of steam.

Place baking sheet on the middle shelf. Oven will be moist with steam generated by the high heat. Reduce oven heat to 400°. Halfway through the bake period, shift baking sheet so *fougasses* are exposed equally to the oven's temperature variations.

When baked, loaves will be golden brown with crispy crust both top and bottom. Turn over one loaf and tap with forefinger. If it is hard and sounds hollow, bread is done.

FINAL STEP Remove from oven. Place on metal rack to cool before slicing or breaking off pieces.

PAIN DE SEIGLE SISTERON ⚜ SISTERON RYE BREAD

[TWO LOAVES]

Most of the best-liked rye breads begin with a bubbling batter of all-rye starter left to ferment for a day or two, or even longer. This rye, however, begins with a 1-pound piece of dough, called the chef, *saved from a previous bake of white bread.*

The chef *provides some of the fermented taste and aroma desired in most rye breads; it contains some of the leavening, and supplies all of the necessary white flour required for a not-too-dense rye loaf.*

The slice is moist, yet it is not as compact as other French rye breads. It has no sugar, no shortening except what might have been in the chef.

The Sisteron bread is a round ball with a circle scribed around the top of the loaf with a razor blade, allowing the dough to expand in the oven to show an attractive band of light crust.

INGREDIENTS *Chef:*
1 pound of dough saved from an earlier bake of white bread.

Dough:
2 cups warm water (105°–115°)
1 tablespoon salt
1 package dry yeast
4 cups rye flour
$^1/_4$ cup all-purpose flour, approximately

Dough from a previous bake adds flavor and aroma to this unusual sourdough-type rye from Provence.

BAKING SHEET One greased or Teflon baking sheet.

PREPARATION *Chef:* A piece of white dough can be saved, covered, in the refrigerator for up to a week or 10 days. No problem.

12 minutes *Dough:* Place chef in a large bowl and pour the warm water over it. Dissolve the salt and yeast in the water surrounding the chef. Add 2 cups rye flour and break up piece of dough with 25 strong strokes of wooden spoon or rubber scraper. Stir in the balance of rye flour, $1/2$ cup at a time. It will be a sticky mass, so sprinkle with white flour and turn out on work surface.

KNEADING Use pastry or dough scraper or putty knife to fold and push dough
5 minutes until it loses some of its stickiness. Sprinkle liberally with white flour as you knead with the hands. Keep work surface scraped clean of coating of rye dough. Late in the kneading, the dough will respond and can be worked freely without sticking. Patience.

FIRST RISING Place dough in large bowl, cover with plastic wrap, and leave at room
1 hour temperature (70°–75°) until it has doubled in volume.

SHAPING Dough will be light and puffy when turned from the bowl onto the
5 minutes work surface. Unlike white dough, which is very cohesive, this will have a tendency to break into pieces as you begin to work out the gas bubbles.

Divide the dough into 2 pieces and round each into a ball with cupped hands, pulling down gently as the dough is turned to keep the surface taut. Flatten the tops of the balls slightly and place on baking sheet.

SECOND RISING Place wax paper over the loaves and leave at room temperature
45 minutes (70°–75°) until they have risen almost double in volume—about 45 minutes.

BAKING Preheat oven 20 minutes before baking.
380° Uncover loaves. Just before placing in oven, make a precise circle
45 minutes with a razor blade on top of each loaf. Start the cut about $1/2$ inch deep, keep the blade still, and turn the bread (and baking sheet) under it. A lazy Susan would be ideal for this chore.

Place in the middle shelf of the oven. Midway during bake period, shift baking sheet end for end.

Bread is done when light brown and the bottom crust sounds hard and hollow when tapped with a forefinger.

FINAL STEP Remove from oven and place on metal rack to cool. If the crust is too hard for your taste, place in plastic bag overnight. Freezes very well.

RECIPE FROM BEAUCAIRE

Had we known about the unusual loaf of bread that for generations has been the *spécialité* of the *boulangers* of the small city of Beaucaire in the south of France, we certainly would have driven over one afternoon from Avignon, only 35 kilometers away. It was not until I had returned to my Indiana kitchen that I came across no less than three references to *le pain de Beaucaire.* All seemed to reproach me for not having found it when I was there.

But through a delightful correspondence with M. Fernand Moureau, *ancien boulanger,* a retired baker who was born in a Beaucaire bake shop seventy-eight years before, I have corrected that oversight. The sprightly M. Moureau took me in hand, via an exchange of letters, and taught me the unusual techniques employed by the bakers of Beaucaire to make this loaf.

Merci, M. Moureau.

PAIN DE BEAUCAIRE ❧ BEAUCAIRE BREAD

[SIX TO EIGHT SMALL LOAVES]

This bread has gained considerable fame throughout France, not for its ingredients, but for the unusual treatment of the dough after kneading.

The esteemed Professor Raymond Calvel, of the French baking school in Paris, says this process produces one of the best breads of France.

The dough is rolled into a rectangle, then cut into two long strips, one of which is placed on top of the other. The double strip is then cut into small rectangles, each of which will be a loaf. The loaves rise, but just as they go into the oven, they are placed on their sides to bake!

The ancien boulanger, *M. Moureau, is fearful that the chemical treatment of today's flour will change the nature of the starter and dough, and in his letters urged that an unbleached flour be used.*

INGREDIENTS   *Starter:*
1 cup unbleached or all-purpose flour
1 package dry yeast
1 cup warm water (105°–115°)

Dough:
All of the starter
$1^1/_2$ cups warm water (105°–115°)
1 tablespoon salt
5 cups unbleached or all-purpose flour, approximately
1 tablespoon melted butter or margarine, to brush

Beaucaire loaves are baked on their sides.

BAKING SHEET One baking sheet sprinkled with cornmeal.

PREPARATIONS
10 minutes
overnight
Starter: Twelve hours before baking (or longer for stronger fermentation), mix flour, yeast, and water in a small bowl. Cover with plastic wrap and leave at room temperature (70°–75°) overnight.

20 minutes *Dough:* Pour all of the starter into a large bowl and add water and salt. Stir with wooden spoon or rubber scraper. Add flour, 1 cup at a time, and mix first with the spoon or scraper and then as the dough becomes shaggy work it with the hands.

KNEADING
15 minutes
This is a longer than usual kneading period, so have a fellow kneader standing by or simply walk away from it from time to time when it gets to be tiring. Turn dough onto work surface and knead with a rhythmic push-turn-fold movement.

This should be a firm dough, more so than other white doughs, so allow it to take up as much flour as it will absorb in the first 5 minutes.

REST
15 minutes
Allow the dough to rest on the work surface under an inverted bowl.

SHAPING
15 minutes
The traditional *Beaucaire* loaf is large, but I have scaled it down in size to be more manageable for the home baker.

With a rolling pin (and stretching gently with the hands), work the dough into a rectangle about 18 inches long by 10 inches wide.

The dough will be about $^1/_2$ inch thick. Allow the dough to rest before cutting the sheet lengthwise into two pieces with a pastry wheel or razor blade. The dough at this point has not set and may pull if cut with a less-than-sharp knife.

Brush water over the surface of one piece. (The *ancien boulanger* scorns this step, but my *Beaucaires* are more successful when brushed.) Place the dry strip on top of the first.

RISING
2 hours

Choose a place to leave the dough to rise at room temperature (70°–75°) for 2 hours—table or countertop or large bread or cutting board. Sprinkle surface with cornmeal so the dough won't stick and can move as it expands. Position dough and cover with wax paper during rising.

BAKING
400°
30–35 minutes

Place empty baking sheet in oven to preheat 20 minutes before bake period. The sheet must be hot when the breads are placed on it.

The dough will be puffy. With a yardstick, mark the strip into pieces $2^1/_2$ to 3 inches wide. The dough will not collapse if it is cut carefully with a sharp knife—gently move the blade back and forth rather than forcing it through the dough, which may pinch the cut ends together. The cut surface will show an open network of bubbles.

Remove the hot baking sheet from the oven and place on a protective pad near the cut breads. Dust sheet with cornmeal.

With the help of a spatula or dough scraper, carefully lift each piece and set it on its cut edge on the baking sheet. If the demarcation line between the top and bottom layers of dough has sealed and is not pronounced, dip a sharp knife blade in water and make a $^1/_2$-inch cut down the line where they were joined. During ovenproof, the loaf will open up along this line.

Place in oven. Halfway through the bake period, shift baking sheet fore to aft so the breads are equally exposed to the oven heat. Ten minutes before the breads are done, take sheet from the oven and brush loaves with melted butter. Return to oven.

Loaves are done when crusts are light brown and sound hard when tapped with a forefinger.

FINAL STEP

Remove from the oven and place on a metal rack to cool. These are delicious eaten any time, but the sooner the better because they will dry out in a day or so. Slice for great toast. Split open, they are fine for sandwiches.

RECIPES FROM GRENOBLE

For many months, I had been looking forward to visiting Record II because I could not believe the superlatives showered by knowledgeable friends on the French bread baked in this huge supermarket on the outskirts of Grenoble.

But unlike a U. S. shopping center, which is usually a cluster of individual shops and stores, Record II is one store behind a line of forty smartly uniformed young women seated at as many checkout counters. And while it has some of everything from rugs and tires to dresses, it is big on food and, in the French style, has a complete section each for fish, pork, beef, sausage, lamb, fowl, tripe, horse, and on and on. Customers bring their empty wine bottles to the store where they fill them at a line of spigots projecting from a tiled wall. Red wine or white.

You expect new and exciting things in Grenoble, the site of the 1968 Winter Olympics and one of the most vibrant of French cities. With one of the country's highest population growth rates, this southeastern city on the Isere River has multiplied fivefold in the past century and spread to the plains across from its ancient foothold at the base of the mountains. It has a lot going for it including the Universities of Grenoble I, II, and III, a nuclear research station, a clutch of museums, and a *téléferique* to the top of the mountains overlooking the city.

The busiest corner in Record II was the bakery. Three saleswomen stood in front of open wire racks on which breads hot from the ovens were stacked on end to cool. Each compartment had its sign—*baguette, couronne* (crown), *campagne* (country loaf),

The bakery is a 3-star attraction at Record II, a big supermarket near Grenoble.

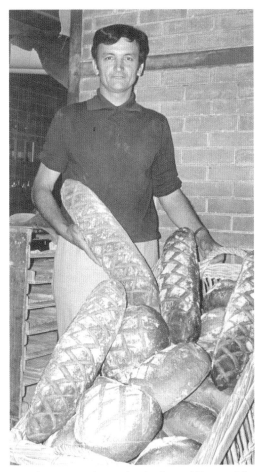

M. Pierre Morel, master baker of Record II, with some of his country loaves.

seigle (rye), and *complet* (whole wheat). The size and prices of the loaves varied from 200 grams (½ pound) for the traditional baguette (18¢) to 1 kilo (2¼ pounds) for the husky country loaf ($1.20).

A lady in line volunteered to my wife that she was an expatriate New Yorker who, with her French husband-chef, had owned a Manhattan restaurant until last year when the scene got too rough and they returned to Grenoble.

"We think this has to be the best bread in France—there's just no doubt about it," she said. "And it certainly is better than anything we ever served in New York."

The bakery itself was an integral part of Record II and separated from the customers only by a big window. I stood watching with a half-dozen waiting customers as a baker loaded a large brick oven with the *campagne,* about 600 of which they produce on an important market day such as a Saturday. The oven was fired with wood, preferably from fruit trees, which the French consider unexcelled as a source of heat for country bread. The dough was made with *levain,* an important distinction to the French, for it meant it was prepared in the old-fashioned way with a leavening of active dough saved from the day before, and slow-baked until the loaves were deep-crusted and deep brown, often to the point of being scorched. The other oven (an electric six-tiered metal monster) was used for those breads that were leavened with yeast. Here, some 2,000 *baguettes* alone were produced each day.

The bakery had been an inspiration. When Record II opened five years earlier, the owners wanted a three-star attraction that would be a magnet for the store. French bread baked in the old way would do it, they reasoned, but could it be done in quantity? Yes, said Monsieur Pierre Morel, one of the city's most respected *boulangers,* and he would do it. He did, and the bakery has been an unparalleled success.

Sixteen kilometers to the south, high above the French presidential Château de Vizille, I dropped back a century as I sat listening to the soft, hesitant voice of ninety-nine-year-old Madame Doz, who was seated near a kitchen table at which for most of her life she had made the same kind of bread I had seen at Record II less than an hour before. Her wood-fired oven, no longer used, was in a shed behind the house, and a brown hen, nesting in one of the old cloth-lined wicker baskets used to form the loaves, clucked her disapproval when Madame Doz and I came through the door. The oven's interior chamber, which held the fire and was where the bread was baked, was about eight feet long by four feet wide, ample space, said Madame Doz, for a two weeks' supply of bread for the family to be baked at one time. When the oven was hot enough, the burning embers and ashes were pulled out with a long-handled scraper and dropped into a small pit below. There was no flue so the door was left open to allow the smoke to escape. When the fire was pulled, the door was closed to retain the heat.

"Had we lived down in the valley," she continued, "we probably would have gone into Vizille to do our baking in the community oven, or we might even have bought our bread; but we were people up high on the mountain and went down below only when we needed to. We farmed sixty acres here. We grew everything we needed. Each year we harvested about seven tons of wheat, which we carted down to the town to be milled. But that's all changed now with good roads. We even buy our bread in Vizille."

Just outside the kitchen door, water from a spring higher up the mountain tumbled into a long stone trough in which, for years, milk cans had cooled and horses and cattle drank. As we started to leave, I held a drinking glass brought from the car under the clear, cold stream. I offered it to Madame Doz.

There was a twinkle in her eye when she spoke—

"Young man, in this house we drink only wine."

Madame Doz, a charming lady of 99, recalls local history for the author.

Pain Ordinaire Carême ⚜ A Daily Loaf

[FOUR 10-OUNCE BAGUETTES, BOULES, OR COURONNES]

Fresh bread each day for the master—wherever he is in the world—is the promise of this 175-year-old recipe by Carême, the great French cook and author (1784–1833). The man who has been called the cook of kings and the king of cooks wrote:

> *"Cooks who travel with their gastronomically minded masters can, from now on, by following this method, procure fresh bread each day."*

Almost identical to Carême's simple recipe is the dough made at Record II by M. Morel for baguettes, ficelles, *and* couronnes.

M. Morel parts with M. Carême only when it is time to put the bread in the oven. M. Carême wants the loaves to go directly into the oven the moment they are formed, while M. Morel allows his to rise for one hour, and then into the oven.

The loaf is made with hard-wheat bread flour to give the dough the ability to withstand the expansion it undergoes by more than three times its original volume. Baking at high heat provides the oven-spring that makes possible the formation of the larger cellular structure, the distinguishing characteristic of pain ordinaire.

INGREDIENTS
2 packages dry yeast
2 1/2 cups cool water (70°–75°)
6 cups hard-wheat bread flour, approximately
2 teaspoons salt
2 teaspoons water

BAKING SHEET One baking sheet, greased or Teflon, or long *baguette* pans, greased, if available.

PREPARATION Let an electric mixer take over the early part of the preparation by beating the batter for a full 10 minutes. Do not overload a light mixer with a thick batter.

If mixing by hand, stir vigorously for an equal length of time.

10 minutes — In a mixing bowl, sprinkle yeast over the water, and stir by hand to dissolve. Let it become creamy, about 3 minutes. Add flour (about 4 cups for a heavy machine, such as a Kitchen Aid) to make a batter in which the beaters run without undue strain. Batter will become smooth and pull away from the sides as the gluten develops. It may also try to climb up the beaters and into the motor! Push it down with a rubber scraper.

When about finished, dissolve salt in 2 teaspoons of water and add to the batter. Blend for 30 seconds.

KNEADING MIXER
5 minutes — If the machine has a dough hook, continue with it and add additional flour, 1/4 cup at a time, until the dough has formed under the hook

and is cleaning the sides of the bowl. If it is sticky and clings to the bowl, add sprinkles of flour. Knead for 5 minutes.

BY HAND
8 minutes

If kneading by hand, add additional flour to the beaten batter, 1/2 cup at a time, stirring first with a utensil and then working by hand. When the dough is a shaggy but solid ball, turn onto the work surface and begin kneading with an aggressive push-turn-fold motion. If the dough is sticky, toss down sprinkles of flour. Break the kneading rhythm occasionally by throwing the dough down hard against the table top—an excellent way to help along the development of the dough.

FIRST RISING
2 hours

Place the dough in a large greased bowl, cover with plastic wrap, and leave at room temperature (70°–75°) for 2 hours. The dough will more than treble in volume—and may even be pushing against the plastic covering.

PUNCH DOWN
3 minutes

Turn back plastic wrap and turn dough onto the work surface to knead briefly, 2 or 3 minutes. Return to the bowl and recover.

SECOND RISING
1 1/2 hours

Dough will again rise to more than treble its volume in about 1 1/2 hours.

SHAPING
10 minutes

Turn the dough, which will be light and puffy, onto the work surface. Punch it down. Don't be surprised if it pushes back for it is quite resilient. Divide into as many pieces as you wish loaves. One-fourth (10 ounces) of this recipe will make a *baguette* 22 inches long and 3 to 4 inches in diameter. Allow pieces of dough to rest for 5 minutes before shaping.

For *boules* or round loaves, shape the pieces into balls. Place in a cloth-lined basket (*banneton*) or position directly on baking sheet. For *baguettes,* roll dough 16 to 22 inches in length and 3 to 4 inches in diameter. Place in pan or baking sheet or in the folds of a long cloth (*couche*).

The *couronne* or crown can be made in several ways. One is to flatten the piece of dough, press a hole through the center with the thumb, and enlarge the hole with the fingers. Another is to roll a long strand of dough 18 to 24 inches and curl into a circle—overlapping and pinching together the ends. Yet a third is to take 2 or 3 shorter lengths of dough and join them together in a circle, not overlapping top and bottom, but the ends pressed together side by side in a uniform pattern.

THIRD RISING
1 hour

Cover the loaves with a cloth, preferably of wool, to allow air to reach the loaves and to form a light crust. Leave at room temperature until the dough has risen to more than double its volume.

BAKING
450°
25–30 minutes

This is a *very hot* oven. Preheat 20 minutes before baking. Place a broiler pan on the bottom shelf to hold a cup of water to be added later.

Five minutes before baking, pour 1 cup of water into the hot pan. Be careful of the burst of steam. It can burn. Carefully move loaves in baskets and in *couches* to the baking sheet. Make diagonal cuts down the length of long loaves and tic-tac-toe designs on *boules*.

Place on the middle shelf of the oven.

Loaves are done when a golden brown. Turn one loaf over and if the bottom crust sounds hard and hollow when tapped, the loaf is done.

FINAL STEP

Place on rack to cool. One of the exciting sounds in the kitchen is the crackle of French bread as it cools. Crackle away! Spread with butter and enjoy with any dish.

PAIN DE CAMPAGNE MADAME DOZ ✤
MADAME DOZ' PEASANT LOAF

[TWO 2-POUND HEARTH LOAVES]

The peasant bread baked by Madame Doz in the big wood-fired oven back of the farmhouse and by Monsieur Pierre Morel at Record II was made with levain, *a portion of dough left from the previous bake. The Doz family kept its* levain *for one and sometimes two weeks in a corner of the dough tray under the top of the big walnut table in the kitchen. At Record II, the turnover is faster and* levain *moves ahead from one batch of dough to the beginning of the next in a matter of hours.*

While it is difficult to duplicate the Doz flour milled in the valley below from wheat grown on a few mountainous acres, the mixture in this recipe of unbleached flour, stone-ground whole wheat, and wheat germ—through three leavenings—produces a husky and delicious bread. It has the same quality and character as the Record II loaves.

For more than a century, the Doz family has used this dough tray and walnut table.

M. Morel uses a tiny pinch of ascorbic acid in his dough. It helps the cellular formation of the loaves, he says. It is the only chemical additive allowed the French boulanger.

A levain *can be kept by the home baker in the refrigerator for a period of days, as Madame Doz did in her cool mountain kitchen, but it must be dough without sugar or shortening or it may spoil. Keep the* levain *in a container that will allow the dough to expand during its first hours in the refrigerator.*

INGREDIENTS   *Starter:*
1 package dry yeast
²/₃ cup water, cool (70°–75°)
¹/₃ cup buttermilk, room temperature
1 teaspoon vinegar
1¹/₂ cups unbleached or all-purpose flour

Levain:
All of the starter
1 cup water, cool (70°–75°)
2 cups whole wheat flour, stone ground or plain
¹/₂ cup wheat germ
1 cup unbleached or all-purpose flour, approximately

Dough:
All of the levain
2 cups water, cool (70°–75°)
1 small pinch ascorbic acid, optional
4¹/₂ cups unbleached or all-purpose flour, approximately
4 teaspoons salt
4 teaspoons water

BAKING SHEET   One baking sheet, greased or Teflon, for round *boules;* or pans for
AND PANS   *baguettes* or *ficelles*, greased.

PREPARATION   *Starter:* In a large bowl, dissolve yeast in water. Add buttermilk when
8 minutes   yeast is frothy (but not before because fat will coat yeast particles)
12–24 hours   and add the vinegar. Stir in flour to make a heavy batter. Cover tightly
with plastic wrap and let stand at room temperature (70°–75°) for
a minimum of 12 hours or until it rises and falls. It can be held for
24 hours if more convenient.

Levain: A true *levain* is taken from the dough of the previous bake,
but for a beginning batch the process starts here.

5 minutes   Uncover the bowl containing the starter. Stir in the water, whole
6–12 hours   wheat flour and wheat germ.

The *levain* is to be a soft ball of dough, not a batter, so add sufficient white flour, about 1 cup, to make it a solid mass. Turn onto the floured work surface and knead the *levain* for 3 to 4 minutes before returning it to the bowl. Re-cover and leave at room temperature (70°–75°) for a minimum of 6 hours. It can be left longer if convenient. Ball of dough will rise and spread under the plastic wrap and then take on the appearance of a heavy batter.

15 minutes *Dough:* Two things are different in this recipe. The white flour is made into a soft dough and then blended with the ball of *levain*. The salt is not added until late in the kneading. Don't forget it. Set it out now as a reminder.

Uncover *levain*, stir it down with a rubber scraper or by hand, and lift onto the work surface. Round into a ball and set aside.

In the bowl pour water, the optional ascorbic acid, and $1^1/_2$ cups of unbleached or all-purpose flour. Stir to blend into a thick batter. Add flour, about $^1/_2$ cup, to make a soft ball of dough that can be lifted from the bowl. Place it on the work surface and knead until it is smooth, adding sprinkles of flour if it is sticky.

Press the *levain* into a flat oval and cover it with the ball of white dough. Fold the two together and continue the folding and kneading process until the two are completely blended. The combined doughs should be elastic yet firm, so add at least 1 additional cup of white flour as the kneading begins. A test is to shape the dough into a ball and see how well it retains its shape when you remove your hands. If the dough slouches badly, it needs considerably more flour. If it holds its shape, yet is elastic and responds to the fingers by pushing back—there may be enough flour. Another test: Slap the ball of dough with the outstretched hand. Leave the hand on the dough while counting to 15. If your hand comes away without dough sticking to it, the dough probably has enough flour.

KNEADING The combined doughs will blend into a light brown ball, sprinkled
7 minutes with tiny darker brown flakes. Use a forceful push-turn-fold motion—aggressively throwing the ball of dough down hard against the table top from time to time.

SALT Stop the kneading for a moment to dissolve the salt into the 4 teaspoons of water. Press the dough flat with a depression in the center to hold the salt solution. Fold the dough over the liquid and return to kneading.

KNEADING The dough may become slick and squishy until the liquid is absorbed;
3 minutes if so, sprinkle with flour. Knead for an additional 3 minutes.

FIRST RISING
2 hours

Place the dough in the washed and greased bowl and leave at room temperature (70°–75°) until it has more than doubled in volume. It may press against the plastic wrap covering the bowl.

SHAPING
10 minutes

Remove plastic wrap and punch down dough with the extended fingers. Turn onto work surface and divide into as many pieces as you wish loaves. The dough will weigh about 4 pounds.

Depending on whether the dough is shaped as round hearth loaves or as *baguettes* or *ficelles,* it may be placed to rise directly on the baking sheet or sheets or in pans or in *bannetons,* or *sur couche.*

SECOND RISING
1¹/₂ hours

Cover with a cloth and leave at room temperature (70°–75°) to rise to triple its original bulk, about 1¹/₂ hours.

BAKING
450°
35–40 minutes

Place broiler pan on lower oven shelf and preheat oven 20 minutes before baking. Five minutes before baking, pour 1 cup of water into the pan. There will be a burst of steam as the water hits the hot pan, so be careful. Use a long-handled container to pour the water.

Uncover loaves. Those in *bannetons* are turned over on the baking sheet. Those in the cloth folds (*couches*) are rolled onto a length of cardboard. Lift and roll off onto the baking sheet. Those already in pans or on a baking sheet leave as is, of course.

Cut the tops with a razor blade (see *coups de lame,* page 16).

Place loaves on the middle shelf of the oven, or, if the top shelf is also to be used, be aware that bread bakes faster there and must be interchanged with breads on the middle shelf halfway through the bake period.

Loaves are done when a golden brown and crusty. Turn over one loaf and tap bottom crust with a forefinger. If it sounds hard and hollow, the bread is baked.

FINAL STEP

Place loaves on metal rack to cool, or stack on end so air can move around them. The loaves will crackle loudly as the crusts cool and crack. Try to wait until almost cool before breaking or slicing to serve.

PETITES GALETTES SALÉES ❖ LITTLE SALTED BISCUITS

[ABOUT FORTY-FIVE PIECES]

These are delicious, butter-rich flat biscuits cut from a thin sheet of unleavened dough. They have a slightly salty taste that makes them ideal for entertaining—served alone or with spreads. The salt is in them—not sprinkled on.

While I cut mine into 2-inch squares with a pastry cutter, you can have any size or shape you desire.

INGREDIENTS $^1/_2$ cup (1 stick) butter, room temperature
$^1/_2$ cup hot water (125°)
$2^1/_4$ cups all-purpose flour, approximately
$^1/_4$ cup non-fat dry milk
4 teaspoons sugar
2 teaspoons salt

BAKING SHEET One baking sheet, which does not need to be greased because of the high butter content of the *galettes*.

PREPARATION
15 minutes
Cut butter into several pieces and drop into a medium-size bowl. Pour in hot water, which will further soften butter. Let stand for 5 minutes or until liquid is warm but not hot. Stir in $^3/_4$ cup of flour, non-fat dry milk, sugar, and salt. This will be a soft batter. Stir to blend thoroughly. Add rest of flour, $^1/_4$ cup at a time, to form a ball of dough.

KNEADING
3 minutes
Turn dough onto dusted work surface and knead until the dough is smooth. It may need additional sprinkles of flour to give body to the dough. There is no leavening in this dough, so it is not necessary to develop gluten as for a yeast-raised product. The kneading is to blend ingredients and make a smooth dough.

REST
1 hour
Place dough in bowl, cover with plastic wrap, and put aside at room temperature (70°–75°) for one hour.

SHAPING
10 minutes
Preheat oven to 400°.

Turn dough onto work surface and roll into a rectangle about 10 inches by 18 inches—and no more than $^1/_8$ inch thick. Don't rush. Pull gently with the hands to help form rectangle. I keep a yardstick handy to measure the area, mark off 2-inch squares, and guide the pastry wheel.

A pastry wheel or a pastry jagger, especially the latter, which is a wheel that cuts with a scalloped edge like pinking shears, makes a handsome *galette* and does not tear or pull the dough as a knife might do.

Before moving *galettes*, prick each with the sharp tines of a fork 3 or 4 times.

Lift *galettes* carefully and place on baking sheet. If sheet won't hold them all, cover balance with wax paper and leave on work surface.

BAKING
400°
15–20 minutes
Place in preheated oven, but stand by as these bake rapidly. Look at *galettes* after 8 minutes. *Galettes* should be light brown with somewhat darker edges and brown on the bottom. Don't be afraid to shuffle them around to achieve uniform baking. If some are fatter than others and feel soft when pressed on top, return to the oven. But watch them!

FINAL STEP
As they are removed from the oven, place on metal rack to cool. Delicious warm. They will stay fresh for days in a closed container, and freeze well.

Dough for Little Salted Biscuits is cut with a pastry jagger.

Biscuits cool on a rack. Ready to serve with drinks!

RECIPES FROM THE RHÔNE VALLEY

When a cookbook author quests for new recipes, he leaves to others the crimson sunsets and azure skies. On a beautiful June day (I do remember that), I drove the 152 kilometers from Nice to Toulon—east to west through the whole of the French Riviera—and a week later was hard pressed to recall ever having been there, though I vividly remember stopping in traffic and seeing an especially handsome loaf of bread displayed in a window of a *boulanger* in St. Tropez (or was it St. Raphael?). Parking was impossible so I never got back to ask for the recipe, but my mind would not let it alone. For long stretches of lovely coast (according to Marje), I hypothesized as to how the *boulanger* made that bread.

In all fairness, I must confess that on that drive I was also preoccupied with thoughts of two friends. Richard Olney we would see yet that afternoon in the small village of Solliès-Toucas, on the hills inland from the sea. I was anxious to congratulate him on a new book on French cooking that had been given a national award in the U.S. for the best of all cookbooks of the year.

The other friend, Wendell Phillippi, a newspaper editor in Indiana, was responsible for our having chosen this particular route up the Rhône Valley. He had armed me with World War II battle maps and charts and insisted we had to see where he fought the Germans in World War II. More importantly, we must visit the Count and Countess in whose *château* he maintained an observation post for a number of days under a heavy German artillery barrage.

The cookbook author had moved to the south of France after a sojourn in Paris, where he had been writing for several French wine and food magazines and, in the doing, had built a considerable reputation. He would be the first to say that it had been quite a change from the meat-and-potatoes fare of an Iowa farm, where he was one of eight children.

Olney moved his typewriter, oils, and canvases south to an abandoned house to an old olive grove on the edge of Solliès-Toucas and wrote two exceptionally fine books on French cooking.

He had no phone so we could not tell him that we would arrive shortly. Earlier, we had written from the U.S. only that we would be there sometime in the summer. First, we had to find the olive grove. A straggly line of hiking grade-school children was enthusiastic, interested, curious (about Americans), but highly uninformative. After circling the town twice, I stopped the car in front of an open shed pushed back into the rock. An old man rested in its deep shade.

Were we close? I wanted to know. You can't be much closer, the old man said, and pointed to steps cut into the hill behind.

"You can't get lost. He's the only person up there," said the old man, waving his hand toward the hill.

"I would add mountain climbing to Richard's other skills," my wife said, as we scrambled up the rock-littered goat path. Years before, four men had pushed and tugged six hours up this path to deliver a cookstove, while Olney rushed the white wine to keep their spirits up.

Standing in his red jogging suit at the end of a path worn through a jungle of herbs was Olney, who had been drawn to the commotion the two of us were creating in our ascent.

"This calls for a celebration," he said, plunging a bottle of champagne into a bucket of ice the moment we reached the house.

It was the magnificent fireplace dominating the kitchen-living area that I wanted to see above all else in the house. I had written to him several years before to ask for design details of the fireplace, which had been pictured in his first book. It was in the chimney of the fireplace that he often would suspend a marinated, rolled boar's belly or other delicacies to be smoked for several days in the mild heat of smoldering olive wood and bundles of rosemary.

Richard's approach to food was straightforward. "Good and honest cooking and good and honest French cooking are the same thing. The principles of good cooking do not change as one crosses frontiers or oceans. The success of preparation depends on nothing more than a knowledge of those principles plus personal sensibility."

He was blunt about most French bread. He didn't like it.

"In this village, there is no good bread baked unless I bake it myself."

In his excellent *French Menu Cookbook*, he gives a recipe for his version of a country loaf.

There was no activity on the hearth or in the chimney this hot day, so I had to forego a lesson in smoking meat. I did get instruction on the fine points of trussing a boar's belly in the unlikely event I should ever acquire one for my own chimney.

We said goodbye to Olney, slid back down the steep path, thanked the old man (still resting in the shade) for his directions, and headed the car up the Rhône Valley.

When my Indiana friend was here, he was part of the 36th Infantry Division pursuing (and defeating) the German 17th Army. When we turned north at Aix-en-Provence, we were pursuing and hoping to capture one or two special recipes, and looking forward to meeting the Count and Countess Charles d'Andigne. The Count did not have a role in my friend's adventures at Château Condillac since early in the war he had been shipped to the coal mines for helping the French Resistance cause.

Driving the wide *autoroute* A7, it was not possible to relate to the war my friend had fought thirty years before. Along the Atlantic coast and in the Marne and Meuse names such as Dieppe, Saint-Lô, Arromanches, Soissons, Verdun, and Château-Thierry came alive, but here fighting had moved too fast to give towns and villages more than a momentary brush with war. It was hell, certainly, but it didn't stay around to make a name for itself.

The way up to the *château* began near the river and progressed through the foothills on successively narrower roads to finally turn through a gate in a high stone wall onto a courtyard, beyond which spread a breathtaking view of the distant Hautes Alpes. (It was from that direction that a couple of German artillery shells came to break up the dinner party the Countess was giving for my friend and his fellow officers in celebration of the liberation of the *château* and of Paris that same day!)

There was a gentle rain when I pulled our car up to the elegantly carved front door. The crushed stone surface of the courtyard had been freshly raked and the stone furrows ran straight and true from one wall to the other. Our car crunched over the perfect pattern.

When we were seated with the Count and Countess in the lovely eleventh-century drawing room with its great vaulted ceiling, we talked of many things—how the Americans kept her from the *château* until my friend ordered the guards to let her in and of how the war has receded in memory to the point that once-vivid incidents have now become blurred and seem to have happened to someone else. Finally, we talked about a famous bread, *pogne de Romans* (more about this delicate and delicious loaf under Romans-sur-Isère).

"When you make it," said the Countess, "remember that orange flower water is the special ingredient that is a delicate flavoring and use it lightly."

I had been on the trail of *pogne de Romans* for some time and, before going up the hill to the *château*, I had wandered through the old walled city of Montélimar, which had been a stopover point for Napoleon on his way to Elba on April 24, 1814.

Montélimar is famous for its nougat confections, but its *boulangeries* and *pâtisseries* throughout the city have taken Romans' famous bread as their own. Each shop proclaimed that its *pogne* was better than the one farther on. Each proclaimed that its *pogne* was made with the freshest butter. Despite this enthusiasm, I decided that I would have my *pogne* in Romans.

But it was in Montélimar, in a small *boulangerie* near the north gate to the city, I found *les muffins* and *les buns*.

LE MUFFIN DE MONTÉLIMAR ❧ THE MUFFIN OF MONTÉLIMAR

[EIGHTEEN PIECES]

This is not your ordinary muffin! The yeast-leavened batter is allowed to rise for 1 hour, sugar and butter are blended in, and the muffin tins filled two-thirds full. They go directly into a hot oven (425°), where they rise to small golden peaks. Near the end of their oven sojourn, they are turned upside down in their tins and returned for browning.

This is a very special muffin. It is le muffin de Montélimar!

INGREDIENTS 1 package dry yeast
1¹/₂ cups warm water (105°–115°)
¹/₂ cup non-fat dry milk
2¹/₂ cups all-purpose flour
1 egg, room temperature
¹/₂ teaspoon salt
¹/₄ cup sugar
2 ounces (¹/₂ stick) butter, melted

MUFFIN TINS Muffin tins with total of 18 to 20 cups, buttered or Teflon.

PREPARATION
10 minutes

Mix yeast in warm water to dissolve in large bowl. Stir in milk. Add flour, 1/2 cup at a time. The batter will be thick, smooth. Break and drop in the egg. Blend only enough to mix all ingredients thoroughly. Salt, sugar, and butter will be added later.

RISING
1 hour

Cover bowl tightly with plastic wrap and put aside at room temperature (70°–75°) to allow the batter to ferment and rise.

FORMING
5 minutes

Preheat oven to 425° before filling muffin tins.

Turn back plastic wrap and add salt and sugar. Stir down to blend before adding melted butter. When the butter has been absorbed, use a large spoon to fill muffin cups 2/3 full with batter, which will be stringy and elastic. It may be helpful to push the batter out of the spoon and into the cup with a rubber scraper.

If all the batter is not used, pour remainder into a plastic container sufficiently large to allow it to expand a little and place in the refrigerator for a later bake.

BAKING
425°
25 minutes
10 minutes

Place muffin tins on the middle shelf of the oven. When the muffins have risen into small peaks and are light golden brown—about 25 minutes—remove tins from oven, loosen muffins and turn each upside down in its cup. Return to the oven to brown for an additional 10 minutes.

FINAL STEP

Place on rack to cool somewhat, but serve warm—they are delicious! Store unused batter, as suggested above, rather than attempting to freeze and store muffins. They are better right from the oven.

Yeast-raised muffins, an unusual recipe from the Rhône Valley.

LE BUN DE MONTÉLIMAR ✤ THE BUN OF MONTÉLIMAR

[EIGHT PIECES]

Like le muffin, le bun de Montélimar *is different. Don't expect it to embrace a hamburger. It is not a common kind of bun. It is a small bread, studded with currants or raisins, that should be welcome on every breakfast table—family and/or company. It reminds me of England's famous Bath bun—without the mace.*

INGREDIENTS
1 cup currants or raisins
1 package dry yeast
$^1/_2$ cup warm water (105°–115°)
3–3$^1/_2$ cups all-purpose flour, approximately
$^1/_4$ cup non-fat dry milk
1 teaspoon salt
1 pinch ginger
$^1/_2$ cup sugar
4 ounces (1 stick) butter, room temperature
1 egg

Glaze:
1 tablespoon milk
1 egg

BAKING SHEET One baking sheet, greased or Teflon.

PREPARATION
12 minutes
Plump currants in water in a small bowl for about $^1/_2$ hour, rinse, and pat dry on paper towels. Reserve.

In a large bowl, sprinkle yeast over warm water, stir to dissolve, and let it stand until creamy, about 4 minutes. Add 1 cup of flour, the dry milk, salt, ginger, and sugar. Stir briskly to blend. Beat in the soft butter and when it is blended into the batter, break in the egg. The batter will be thick. Sprinkle in the currants and continue to add flour until the dough is soft and velvety.

KNEADING
3–4 minutes
Dough should be soft and delicate, just beyond the sticky stage. Toss down sprinkles of flour on the work surface during kneading. A dough scraper or putty knife is a big help in working and turning this soft dough.

FIRST RISING
45 minutes
Return the dough to the washed and greased bowl, cover with plastic wrap, and leave at room temperature (70°–75°) for about 45 minutes.

SHAPING
8 minutes
Turn dough onto work surface. Knead briefly to press out bubbles and divide dough into 8 equal pieces. Roll each under a cupped hand

to form a uniform ball. Place on the baking sheet. Press top of each bun down slightly to flatten.

SECOND RISING
40 minutes

Cover buns with plastic wrap and leave undisturbed at room temperature (70°–75°).

BAKING
400°
30 minutes

Preheat oven 20 minutes before baking buns.

　　　Brush each with egg-milk glaze and place sheet on middle shelf of oven. Halfway through the bake period, turn baking sheet end for end—and brush each bun again.

　　　Five minutes before removing buns, brush with egg-milk mixture for a third time.

　　　Les buns are done when they are a rich golden brown on top and have a deep brown crust on bottom.

FINAL STEP

Place on metal rack to cool. Delicious when served warm. In my house, none have ever been left to freeze, but they should do fine.

Le Bun de Montélimar, yeast-raised, studded with currants—serve warm for breakfast.

SCHNECKES ✣ CURRANT ROLLS

[TWO DOZEN]

A schnecke is much prettier than its name. It is a not-too-sweet version of a cinnamon roll, without the cinnamon. Ideal for breakfast or brunch. On a baking sheet, the schnecke spirals up toward the center to reveal a light yellow interior dotted with small black currants.

Schneckes are made with the qualité supérieure *dough that is the basic dough for* petits pains au lait, *milk rolls, with the addition of currants (or raisins), sugar, and melted butter and egg-milk glaze to brush.*

INGREDIENTS 1 batch *petits pains au lait* dough (page 97)
3 tablespoons butter, melted, to brush
1 cup granulated sugar, to sprinkle
1 cup currants (or raisins)

Glaze:
1 egg, lightly beaten
1 tablespoon milk

(Brown sugar may be substituted for white, and chopped walnuts may be mixed with currants or raisins.)

BAKING SHEET One baking sheet, greased or Teflon.

PRIOR STEPS Here are the steps and times for the dough (page 97) before rolls are shaped:

Prepare Dough	12 minutes
Kneading	7 minutes
First Rising	4 hours or overnight
Second Rising	1^1/$_2$ hours

SHAPING
25 minutes Divide dough into 2 pieces. With rolling pin, shape one piece into a rectangle 8 inches wide and about 18 to 20 inches in length. Dough should be about ^{1}/$_4$ inch thick. Allow the rectangle to rest for 1 or 2 minutes so it will not draw back when rolled. Brush with half the melted butter. Sprinkle ^{1}/$_3$ cup granulated sugar over surface. Sprinkle ^{1}/$_2$ cup currants over sugared dough. Carefully roll dough (from the short end) to make a roll (like a jelly roll) 2^1/$_2$ to 3 inches thick. With sharp knife, cut slices the width of the index finger (about ^{3}/$_4$ inch) and place on baking sheet so pieces barely touch. (They will expand to fill all open spaces.) Repeat with second piece of dough.

THIRD RISING
1 hour

Cover with wax paper and allow to rise at room temperature (70°–75°) for about 1 hour. Dough will be light, puffy, and pushing into neighboring pieces.

BAKING
375°
25–30 minutes

Preheat oven to 375°. Remove paper. Brush with beaten egg-milk mixture. Sprinkle with remaining granulated sugar. Place in moderate oven and bake until *schneckes* are light brown and the centers have spiraled upward. Pull one or two loose and turn over to make certain bottoms are brown and done. If deeper brown crust is desired, return to oven for an additional 10 minutes.

FINAL STEP

Take *schneckes* from pan, break apart, and place on metal rack to cool (if left on baking sheet, they will get soggy). Serve warm, or freeze.

Schneckes are perfect, not-too-sweet companions with tea or coffee.

RECIPES FROM ROMANS-SUR-ISÈRE

To this traveler, three things stood out above all others in the small city of Romans-sur-Isère. Almost a hundred years before Columbus sailed for the New World, the citizens of Romans commissioned a clock to be installed in a stone tower, at the bottom of which were the dungeons of the old fortified city. The unusual thing about the clock was a *jacquemart,* or life-size mannequin, standing on a platform above the clock that struck the big bell with a mighty hammer to sound the hours. The figure is unchanged over the years, but it has shed its dress many times to conform to shifting political trends. He has been a citizen of the town, a Polish lancer, a guardsman, and a troubadour. Today, he is painted into the colorful military uniform of an early eighteenth-century *gendarme.*

The *jacquemart* and the twelfth-century Saint Barnard Church, on the edge of the Isère River, dominate the skyline of this city of some 30,000, and are two of its most celebrated attractions.

The third is a bread, *pogne de Romans,* a round loaf whose photograph on a postcard is easily the best seller in town. The shiny brown *pogne,* its smooth, brown top crust split by the oven's heat to show a deep crevice, is surrounded on the card with smaller pictures of the church, the *jacquemart,* and other scenes. The legend leaves no doubt about priorities: *"Romans et ses pognes fameuses."*

Others have tried to capitalize on the *pogne* mystique and we found it in *boulangeries* in towns for miles around. Credit was always given, however. It was never *pogne de Grenoble* or *pogne de Montélimar.* Always *pogne de Romans.* If there was a quibble, it was not about its origins, but over whose *pognes* contained the most and the freshest butter.

There was a street fair in full swing along the Isère when we crossed the bridge into the old part of the city. This lower section was not a happy place, for it had the forlorn and deserted look of better days centuries ago.

I had been told that the best *boulangers* in Romans could be found in the blocks surrounding the *jacquemart.* The *gendarme* had just finished hammering out 2 o'clock when we came out of the old district into the deep shade of trees surrounding the square. Marje walked in one direction and I another looking for *pognes* in window displays. Marje said 4 rue Jacquemart looked promising.

The sign read: "Boulangerie-Coquet-Pognes." It was a narrow shop that ran through to another entrance in Place Earnest Gailly to allow customers to come into the shop from either direction. The bakery was small, no more than 10 by 20 feet, and matched in size the family's kitchen across the hall from where Madame Coquet could keep an eye on both the trade and a baby. The oven, narrow and high, had been custom-tailored to fit into the small room.

M. Georges Coquet was about thirty-five years old and had a wide smile, a row of perfect teeth, the shoulders of a football tackle, and moved with the grace of an athlete. M. Coquet was the *boulanger,* the *pâtissier,* the everything in this one-man (and wife) enterprise. Since he could not afford the luxury of putting off all the things a baker usually does in his pre-dawn work day, M. Coquet had to do most of his preparation the afternoon before. This meant he mixed and kneaded the dough and formed it into a dozen kinds of breads, including the *pogne*, but instead of allowing the breads to rise and putting them forthwith into the ovens, he stacked the loaded trays and pans in a large refrigerator where they would be held until the following morning. He would then fire up his ovens, take the raised loaves from the refrigerator, and have warm, fresh-made breads for his morning customers.

"Without the *réfrigérateur* it would be impossible for me to get it all done. I think, too, the extra time gives the breads more flavor. This way the loaves rise very slowly so they will be perfect for the oven by tomorrow morning when I take them out."

While the *pogne de Romans* is his most famous product, M. Coquet has created with his talented hands a braided adaptation of the *ficelle* or string, which is the long, thin loaf found everywhere in France. While this is not a new recipe, M. Coquet is the only *boulanger* I have seen work with such ease in transforming the single long strand of dough into a braided roll, *une tresse*.

When I asked him to show me, he first tried with a piece of cord but it proved unmanageable. He made a small batch of dough on the table and this he rolled into a string for the demonstration.

I have included it here not as a new bread, but as a unique form, the *ficelle de Romans*.

POGNE DE ROMANS ❧ ROMANS LOAF

[TWO ROUND LOAVES]

The uncommon ingredient in pogne de Romans *is eau de fleur d'oranger, orange flower water, a distillation from the blossom of the bitter orange tree. It is used in France and elsewhere on the Continent and in the Mideast to flavor beverages, pastries, and candies. Confectioners in large U.S. cities can recommend sources since it is an ingredient of subtle fragrance used frequently by them. Many fine specialty food shops carry it and I have suggested an excellent source in Sources of Supply on page 22.*

Orange extract may be substituted for orange flower water, but it will not be quite the same loaf of bread.

The pogne *is a rich bread—butter, eggs, and sugar. A small glass of rum or brandy, says Monsieur Coquet, is a necessary touch.*

A ball of starter is allowed to grow and gain strength before it is blended into the main body of the rich dough.

INGREDIENTS   *Starter:*
2 packages dry yeast
$^1/_2$ cup warm water (105°–115°)
1 cup unbleached or all-purpose flour, approximately

Dough:

6 cups unbleached or all-purpose flour, approximately

6 eggs, room temperature

$^1/_4$ cup rum or brandy (or water, if preferred)

1 cup sugar

2 tablespoons water, approximately

2 teaspoons salt

$^1/_4$ cup orange flower water (or 4 teaspoons orange extract)

8 ounces ($^1/_2$ pound) butter or margarine, room temperature

Glaze:

1 egg

1 tablespoon milk

BAKING SHEET One large baking sheet or two small ones. Cut disks of brown sack paper to fit under each *pogne* as it is placed on the baking sheet. Butter papers before using.

PREPARATION

10 minutes *Starter:* In a small bowl, dissolve yeast in warm water (105°–115°). Add approximately 1 cup unbleached or all-purpose flour to make a solid mass of dough that can be lifted from the bowl and kneaded for 2 to 3 minutes on the floured work surface. Add sprinkles of flour if sticky.

1$^1/_2$ hours Return the ball of starter dough to the small bowl (washed and greased), cover with plastic wrap, and set aside at room temperature (70°–75°) for about 1$^1/_2$ hours to develop and double in bulk.

Dough: The dough can be made ready any time during the period the starter is rising, and kept in a bowl covered with plastic wrap.

15 minutes In a large bowl, pour 1$^1/_2$ cups unbleached or all-purpose flour and form a well by pushing the flour to the sides of the container. Break in 4 eggs, one at a time, pulling just enough flour in from the sides after each egg to form a thick but fluid batter. Add rum or brandy (or water, if preferred) and blend into the egg-flour mixture. Pour in sugar. If the mixture is thick and cannot be stirred, add 2 or more tablespoons of water to thin.

This blending-mixing chore is a good one to turn over to the electric mixer. Beat for about 2 to 3 minutes at medium speed. Batter will be smooth and a light golden yellow. Add salt and orange flower water and stir in.

Break the butter out of its angular shape (quarters or a half-block) by mashing with a dough scraper or putty knife. When it is soft and plastic, drop about a quarter of it in the batter and blend together. When the batter has absorbed the butter, add another portion. Repeat for the balance.

When all of the butter has been stirred in, break in the 2 remaining eggs, one at a time, and blend well at medium speed.

When the mixture is smooth, add rest of flour, $1/2$ cup at a time, to make a ball of dough that can be lifted from the bowl and placed on the floured work surface.

FIRST KNEADING
4 minutes

Knead the dough with a strong push-turn-fold motion, adding sprinkles of flour if the dough is sticky. Dough will be soft, elastic, and easy to work because of the high fat content.

REST
until starter is ready

Form the dough into a ball and return to the large bowl to rest until the starter has developed. Cover with plastic wrap.

BLENDING-KNEADING
8 minutes

When the starter has developed, it is added to the larger ball of yellow dough. Place the large ball on the work surface and flatten. Spread the starter dough over it. Fold over the yellow dough to envelop the white starter dough and work and knead together. When the white dough has been completely absorbed into the yellow dough, and no streaks of color remain, the dough has been sufficiently kneaded.

FIRST RISING
$2^1/2$ hours

Place the dough in the clean bowl, cover with plastic wrap, and leave at room temperature (70°–75°) until nearly doubled in volume, about $2^1/2$ hours.

SHAPING
15 minutes

Prepare the paper disks on which the *pognes* will rest during second rising and in the oven.

The famous *pognes* of Romans-sur-Isère rising on their paper disks.

Turn dough onto work surface. Knead for 2 minutes and divide into 2 pieces. Form each into a ball. Flatten the ball so the *pogne* is about 8 inches in diameter. Press a thumb down hard in the center. With the fingers, open a hole; with both hands enlarge the hole to about 4 inches across. Work with the dough gently to smooth the surface of the *pogne*. Place *pogne* on the buttered paper disk on the baking sheet. Repeat for second piece.

SECOND RISING
2¹/₂–3 hours

Place baking sheet and *pognes* in an undisturbed place at room temperature (70°–75°) for 2¹/₂ to 3 hours. Cover with a cloth or wax paper during the first hour, but then uncover, and brush with glaze. Leave uncovered for remainder of time.

BAKING
360°
40 minutes

Preheat oven 20 minutes before baking *pognes*.

Brush the pieces again with glaze. With a razor blade, make 3 connecting cuts on top of each *pogne* to form a triangle. Each line will be curved to allow the ends of the cuts to overlap. If delicate points pull away when cut, carefully rearrange with tip of razor blade.

Place on the middle shelf of the oven.

Pognes are done when crusts are a deep glistening brown.

FINAL STEP

Place on metal rack to cool. When the *pognes* are cool, place in plastic bags and allow to age a day before serving.

M. Coquet proudly displays one of his largest *pognes*.

Petits Pains au Beurre ✤ Small Butter Loaves

[SIXTEEN SMALL LOAVES]

Petits pains au beurre *(butter) are some of the best small breads in France and small wonder—milk, butter, and cream. They are a dairy farmer's dream and a home baker's delight.*

These can quickly become petits pains aux oeufs *(eggs) by substituting 4 egg yolks for the* 2/3 *cup of cream. The yolks, of course, give them a fine golden color, and the taste is equally good.*

INGREDIENTS
Starter:
1¹/₃ cups milk, scalded and cooled (105°–115°)
2 cups all-purpose flour
2 packages dry yeast

Dough:
All of the starter
²/₃ cup light cream (or egg yolks, see above), room temperature
1 teaspoon salt
4 ounces (1 stick) butter, room temperature
3 cups all-purpose flour, approximately

BAKING SHEET One large or two small baking sheets, greased or Teflon.

PREPARATION
10 minutes
1¹/₂–8 hours
Starter: Heat milk and let it cool to warm (105°–115°). Pour milk into a bowl and stir in flour and yeast to make a thick batter. Cover with plastic wrap and leave at room temperature (70°–75°) until it ferments and bubbles, about 1¹/₂ hours. If more convenient, the starter may be left overnight to develop even more flavor.

8 minutes
Dough: Turn back plastic wrap on the starter and blend in cream (or egg yolks). Add salt. Add just enough flour to make the batter thick again—and stir in butter broken into small pieces. When butter has been absorbed by the batter, add flour, ¹/₂ cup at a time, working the dough with the hands. When the mass is shaggy, lift from bowl.

KNEADING
7 minutes
Place the dough on the work surface and knead with a strong push-turn-fold motion. If the dough is sticky, throw down light sprinkles of flour. This is a fine, delicate dough that is a pleasure to handle because of its high butterfat content. Occasionally bang the dough down hard against the work surface—to relieve the tedium of kneading, but also to hasten the development of the gluten content of the dough.

FIRST RISING
3 hours
Return dough to washed and greased bowl, cover with plastic wrap, and leave undisturbed at room temperature (70°–75°) until dough has doubled in volume.

SHAPING
20 minutes
Turn ball of dough onto work surface and knead briefly to press out the bubbles.

Perhaps the easiest way to make all *petits pains* of uniform size is to press the dough into a flat oval—cut into 4 pie-shaped pieces. Make a flat oval of each of these smaller pieces and cut into quarters—a total of 16. (If you wanted 32, for example, cut each into 2 pieces, and so on.) This is a surprisingly accurate way to do it.

Roll each of the 16 pieces into a tight ball under cupped hands and set aside. Start with the first ball and roll into a cylinder as long as the hand is wide. With the side of the palm, hit the dough lengthwise down the middle, fold over, and continue rolling. *Petits pains* should be about 6 to 7 inches long. Place seam down on baking sheet. Allow $1^1/_2$ inches between them.

SECOND RISING
35 minutes
A cloth placed over the *petits pains* is best because it allows a thin crust to form during the rising. I use a piece of woolen blanket. An alternative is to cover the small breads with wax paper during the first 20 minutes, and then uncover. Let rise at room temperature (70°–75°).

BAKING
410°
30–35 minutes
Preheat oven 20 minutes before baking (a longer period wastes fuel!). Uncover *petits pains* and, with a razor blade or very sharp knife, make a $^1/_4$-inch-deep cut down the length of each small piece.

If both top and middle shelves are to be used, remember the top rack is considerably hotter, so midway in the bake period, move the lower baking sheet up and the upper sheet down.

Petits pains are done when they are a lovely brown and are firm when pressed with the finger.

FINAL STEP
Place on a metal rack to cool. These are so good that I have eaten them not only during the main course but also as dessert. Exceptional.

LA FICELLE DE ROMANS ❧ SMALL BRAIDED BREADS OF ROMANS

[NUMBER VARIES]

The small braided ficelle *or string is a form used by other French* boulangers, *but none can execute it better than M. Coquet of Romans.*

The braid or tresse *is common in baking, but M. Coquet's braid binds often troublesome ends into the body of the braid, so that the more it expands, the tighter the entire braid is locked together. In other kinds of braids, ends often pull loose to ruin an otherwise handsome bread.*

Practice your way through one or two batches of dough to perfect a braid to your liking. The first half dozen may not be prizewinners. Unbraid and do them over, if you wish. The trick, if there is one, is to visualize the two sides of the loop and the loose end as three parallel strands waiting to be woven.

INGREDIENTS   Approximately 2¹/₂ pounds of dough for *petits pains au beurre* or *aux oeufs* (page 185), *pain ordinaire* (page 163) or *pain de campagne* (page 74).

Glaze:
1 egg yolk
1 tablespoon milk

BAKING SHEET   One baking sheet, greased or Teflon.

PRIOR STEPS   Here are the steps and times for the dough for *petits pains au beurre* or *aux oeufs* (page 185) before the braids are shaped.

Prepare Starter	10 minutes
Fermentation	1¹/₂–8 hours
Prepare Dough	8 minutes
Kneading	7 minutes
First Rising	3 hours

SHAPING
25 minutes   Remove plastic wrap and punch down dough. Turn onto lightly dusted work surface and knead for a moment or two to press out bubbles. The dough will be light and elastic.

The *petits pains au beurre* or *aux oeufs* recipe will make between 2¹/₂ to 3 pounds of dough. Divide into 4-ounce pieces and shape into balls about the size of a medium orange. Set aside. Each will make a braided *petit pain* about 6 inches long.

To make a braid, roll the ball of dough under the palms into a long, slender 24-inch strand, about ¹/₂ inch in diameter. The dough will be more responsive if, once or twice during the rolling, you flatten the dough along its length with a smack of the side of a clenched fist. Fold the flattened dough along its length and continue forming the strand under the palms.

For the first few braids, place a yardstick on the table so that you can uniformly judge two critical lengths—24 inches overall and 16 inches where the loop is joined.

With the length of dough stretched in front of you, loop one end over the length of dough at about 16 inches or $^2/_3$ of the length. Leave 1 inch of dough to overlap. Pinch at the juncture to secure. Gently turn the loop and long tail toward you, with the top of the loop at 12 o'clock.

Lift the loose end and drop it into the loop. Pull it through to the left. Twist the loop counterclockwise, lift the end, and drop it through the loop. Twist the loop clockwise, lift the end, and drop through the loop. This will be enough for a 6-inch braid. The number of turns on the loop will vary according to the length of the strand. The nub at the top should always be protruding out, whereas the bottom nub may be under, depending on the number of turns of the loop.

Place the braid on the baking sheet and repeat the braiding of the other pieces.

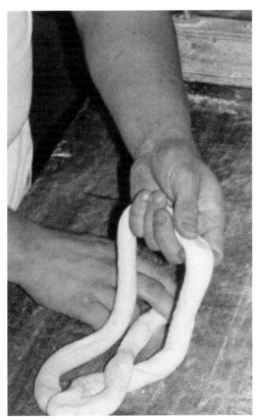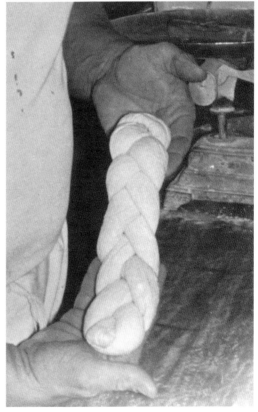

With left hand, M. Coquet twists loop to accept strand of dough in braiding *La Ficelle de Romans.*

SECOND RISING
40 minutes

A cloth over the *petits pains* is best because it allows a thin crust to form during rising. The small breads may also be covered with wax paper during the first 20 minutes, and then left uncovered. This is at room temperature (70°–75°).

BAKING
400°
25 minutes

Preheat oven 20 minutes before baking.

Brush braids with egg yolk–milk glaze.

Place in the oven. The *petits pains* are done when a lovely dark brown and firm to the finger, about 25 minutes. Halfway through the bake period, turn the bake sheet around.

FINAL STEP

Place on a metal rack to cool. As you look at your first attempt remember that the third, fifth, or seventh time may produce prettier braids, but not necessarily more delicious.

RECIPES FROM GANNAT

Gannat was our destination. For years I had been baking a lovely, rich, golden and moist loaf made with butter, eggs, diced Swiss cheese, and brandy. I knew it only as *Gannat*, after the town where it is a regional favorite. The recipe had been given to me by a friend who knew nothing of its origins, so I was pleased to be going there to discover how closely my recipe matched the Gannat original.

Deciding on a hotel in Gannat was not difficult. There was only one, The Agriculture, and it carried a rating in the *Michelin Guide* of "good, average." While there was no choice, I would feel more comfortable if a resident would confirm that The Agriculture was indeed good, average.

I addressed my question to a short, rotund man sweeping the sidewalk in front of his shop. It brought an immediate response, and in English.

"It is a good small hotel. Commercial, yes, but an English couple, friends of ours, who were there last week, found it quite suitable. The food, especially the fish, is very good. A good cellar. The chef, Roger Lallemand, is known throughout the region as one of our best and he has written a fine book about our cuisine."

He hesitated. "But he has gone to Paris to work and he will not be there to welcome you.

Marjorie Clayton and M. Malleret, authority on Gannatois cuisine, in his bookstore.

It was such a rush of welcome information that I went further to ask if he could suggest a *boulanger* in the town with whom I might talk. I was a cookbook author, I explained, and wanted to know how the true Gannat loaf was made.

"Ah, I am Louis Malleret," he said. "Let me put down the broom and we will talk about this interesting subject in my shop." He took one last swipe at the sidewalk.

The store was a book-lined sanctuary where he sold not only books, but newspapers, magazines, and stationery supplies. The interior was dark, with only one small bulb overhead, but it had a warm, comfortable feeling that matched M. Malleret's equally warm personality.

M. Malleret had been a chef in Gannat and in the Ritz Hotel in London until a back injury forced him to leave the hotel and establish his bookstore. He was secretary of the société Culturelle of the Gannatois region and editor of its publications. For me, he was a find.

"The Gannat loaf you speak of is called the *gâteau de Gannat*. It has a long history that goes back to the sixteenth century. Only quite recently, my friend and I researched Gannatois rural cuisine and discovered what we think is the earliest recipe for the *gâteau*. My friend Monsieur Brun and I remember his grandmother preparing it in the same manner, so we feel we have a direct connection going back for more than three hundred years."

But today, M. Malleret said unhappily, the *gâteau de Gannat* is not made the way it should be made. He shook his head sadly.

"To be authentic—and to have that special flavor—it must be made with *fromage blanc*, white cheese, which I think you call farmer's cheese. Today, however, the bakers make it with Swiss or Gruyère. But it is not the same!"

Fromage blanc can be made at home, he said, and it is nothing more than clabbered milk left for two or three days to ripen.

M. Malleret had not mentioned adding a jigger of brandy when he had listed the ingredients for the old recipe. Why?

"*Mon Dieu!*" M. Malleret fairly exploded, the glasses quivering on the tip of his nose. "Brandy is fine for the *boulanger*, but not for his bread."

"I must be truthful to say that I have not yet tried the old recipe," M. Malleret said. "We found it only a short while ago. Please write and let us know if it is as good as both my friend and I recall it was in the kitchen of his *grandmère*."

So, this is a report to M. Malleret and his friend that the *recette ancienne* is a treasure, and that the old way, while the cheese-making takes more time, is better to my taste than one prepared with the other cheeses and laced with brandy.

This is also a report to my Gannatois friends that other *recettes anciennes* they gave have blossomed in my kitchen. They are treasures and should be urged upon the new generation of Gannat *boulangers*.

GÂTEAU DE GANNAT ❧ GANNAT CLABBER BREAD

[THREE 2-POUND LOAVES]

"A noble old dish," M. Mallaret called it, and since the sixteenth century it has been a favorite of the Gannatois region, where it is known either as gâteau de Gannat *or* pompe au fromage.

It is a lovely brown loaf, light in weight and open in texture, that rises high to be served on all occasions, especially the festive ones. This authentic gâteau de Gannat *differs from those found in the* boulangeries *because it foregoes the commercial cheeses and is made without brandy. Also, there is no sugar.*

Its most curious ingredient is fromage blanc, *clabber made in the kitchen from whole milk treated with rennet. Whipped cottage cheese may be substituted, but the clabber is easy to make and the whey, the clear liquid that drains from the clabber, is vitamin-packed. It can be used in place of milk or water in other bread recipes.*

This is a large recipe. The three 2-pound loaves make it worthwhile to spend time making the clabber or whipping the cottage cheese. The rennet (junket) *tablets may be obtained on the ice cream and custard mix shelves of most supermarkets.*

INGREDIENTS *Clabber:*
2 quarts whole milk, room temperature
1/4 rennet tablet

(1 pound large-curd cottage cheese may be substituted for clabber.)

Dough:
8 cups all-purpose flour, approximately
1 package dry yeast
1 tablespoon salt
10 eggs, room temperature
2 cups clabber or whipped cottage cheese
1/4 pound (1 stick) butter or margarine, room temperature

Glaze:
1 egg
1 tablespoon milk

ROUNDS PANS OR BAKING SHEET This loaf can be baked in round cake pans (1-inch sides) or placed on a baking sheet. Results are equally good. Grease pans if not Teflon.

PREPARATION
10 minutes
12 hours
Clabber: At least 24 hours before preparing dough, pour milk, warmed to 70°, in medium-size crock. Crush 1/4 rennet tablet, dissolve in spoonful of milk, and stir into the bowl of milk. Cover with plastic wrap or cloth and leave for at least 12 hours at room temperature. When milk has curdled, pour curds into cheesecloth and suspend

A Gannatois regional favorite, this loaf is made with cottage cheese or clabber.

over a bowl to drain. I use a large square of cheesecloth, double thickness, placed over a large bowl while I fill it with curds. I tie the corners together, lift the bag from the bowl, and fasten it to a shelf brace and allow it to drain for 6 hours.

Empty clabber into a bowl and keep refrigerated until ready to proceed with *gâteau.* Bottle and refrigerate whey for use in other breads.

For more flavorful curds, leave the clabber for 24 to 36 hours before draining.

Cottage cheese: As a substitute for clabber, cream 1 pound of large-curd cottage cheese in blender, or mash and whip with fork.

15 minutes | *Dough:* In large bowl, stir together 2 cups of all-purpose flour, the yeast, and salt. Form a well in bottom of bowl and break eggs into this. Stir with wooden spoon or rubber scraper and gradually draw flour from the sides. Pour in clabber and work this into egg-flour mixture. Cut butter into chunks and drop into bowl. Add additional flour, 1 cup at a time, blending in the pieces of butter, first with spoon and then with the hands. Dough will become smooth because of the *fromage blanc* and butter.

KNEADING
7 minutes | Turn dough onto dusted work surface and knead with forceful 1-2-3 motion of push-turn-fold. Occasionally, crash dough down against work surface to relieve kneading rhythm. Add sprinkles of flour to absorb butterfat on surface of dough and on work surface. Dough will be firm but elastic and will not stick.

FIRST RISING
1¹/₂–3 hours | Don't rush the dough, said M. Malleret. Let it mature and grow in good flavor, he urged.

Place in cleaned and greased bowl and cover with plastic wrap. Leave at room temperature (70°–75°) for at least 1¹/₂ hours, preferably longer, until double in bulk.

SHAPING
15 minutes | Punch down dough and divide into 3 pieces. Press into balls and allow to relax for 5 minutes. In the meantime, prepare pans or baking sheet.

For pans: Place dough in center of each pan and with palm of hands and fingers press dough flat and into the sides. It may pull away; if it does, go back to it a few moments later and repeat.

For baking sheet: Round the pieces of dough between cupped hands, place on the sheet and flatten dough to half its original rounded height.

SECOND RISING
1¹/₂ hours | Cover pans or sheet with wax paper and leave at room temperature (70°–75°) until dough has doubled in volume.

BAKING Twenty minutes before baking, preheat oven.

400° Brush loaves with egg-milk glaze and place in oven. (If oven can
35 minutes only take 2 loaves, leave ⅓ of the dough at First Rising for an additional hour and then follow schedule.) Watch loaves. If they brown
too fast, cover with foil or brown sack paper for last 15 minutes of
bake period. Turn loaves over; if bottom crusts sound hard and hollow when tapped with forefinger, bread is done.

FINAL STEP Place on metal rack to cool. This loaf is a fine gift for the holidays.
Excellent toasted. (Dieters love it because a slice weighs less than
1 ounce—and no sugar.)

PIQUENCHAGNE ⚜ PEAR BREAD

[TWO MEDIUM PAN LOAVES OR CROWNS]

*Seldom is a fruitbread yeast-raised. Most are quick breads, leavened with baking powder
or baking soda. Not so this one. The odor lifts the kitchen—delicate, sweet, and defi-
nitely pear. Très bon.*

Nevertheless, I must confess that early on I had decided not *to include this bread,
but was persuaded otherwise by an orchardist, who said such a recipe would be a boon
to those raising pears or gifted with the fruit by pear-rich neighbors. I tried it and was
impressed.*

*While the old Gannatois recipe suggested fresh ripe pears, pared and sliced, it is
just as easy to simmer the bits for a few minutes and puree with a fork or, better still,
put through a food mill. The pepper on the pears is the undefinable something.*

Piquenchagne, before and after baking—an unusual pear-flavored bread with a hint
of pepper.

INGREDIENTS	*Pears:*
	2 medium-size fresh pears
	$^1/_2$ cup water
	$^1/_2$ teaspoon ground pepper

Dough:
1 package dry yeast
2 tablespoons honey
2 teaspoons salt
2 eggs, room temperature
4 to 5 cups all-purpose flour, approximately

Glaze:
1 tablespoon milk
1 egg

BAKING PANS OR BAKING SHEET Two medium-size ($8^1/_2 \times 4^1/_2$) loaf pans or a baking sheet, greased or Teflon. You may wish to shape the dough into *couronnes* or crowns, hence the baking sheet.

PREPARATION
25 minutes

Pears: Peel, core, and cut 2 pears into small pieces. Place in a saucepan with $^1/_2$ cup water and bring to simmer. Cook for 10 to 15 minutes or until fruit is tender. Remove from heat, pour off water, and allow to cool before mashing with a fork or putting through a food mill to puree. Stir in pepper.

15 minutes

Dough: Pour cooled pear puree into a large bowl, add yeast, honey, salt, and 2 eggs. Stir to blend. Add 2 cups flour and beat into mixture with 50 strokes. Stir in the additional flour until it is a stringy mass. Turn from bowl onto work surface.

KNEADING
5 minutes

Add liberal sprinkles of flour if dough sticks to the hands or work surface. Knead with a strong push-turn-fold motion. If it continues to be moist or sticky, add small amounts of flour. Dough will become smooth and soft to the touch.

FIRST RISING
1 hour

Place in a greased bowl and cover tightly with plastic wrap. Leave at room temperature (70°–75°) until dough doubles in volume.

SHAPING
8 minutes

Remove plastic cover and punch down dough. Knead for 30 seconds to press out bubbles. Divide dough into 2 equal pieces. Shape into balls and let rest on the work surface for 3 minutes. Form the loaf by pressing ball into an oval about the length of the prepared pan. Fold the oval in half, pinch the seam to seal, tuck under the ends, and place in the pan, seam down. Repeat for second loaf.

The old Gannatois loaf was a *couronne* or crown. To shape in this way, flatten one ball of dough by pressing it down, then pierce the center with one or two fingers. Slowly work this into a larger hole by carefully pulling against the sides of the hole with both hands, as the crown rests on the work surface. Let the crown rotate slowly as the hands gradually enlarge the hole to about 3 inches in diameter for a small crown or 5 inches for a large. Place on baking sheet. Repeat for second *couronne*.

SECOND RISING
45 minutes

Cover bread with wax paper. Leave at room temperature (70°–75°) until dough in pans has pushed about 1 inch above the edge of pans. Crowns will double in bulk. Preheat oven 20 minutes before ready to bake.

BAKING
350°
40 minutes

Brush loaves with milk-egg glaze. For an attractive decoration on the *couronne*, circle the top crust with a razor cut, 1/2 inch deep. Place in oven. Thirty minutes later, turn breads around to balance temperature variations in oven. The bread will be baked when both bottom and top crusts have browned nicely and the bottom sounds hard and hollow when tapped with a finger.

FINAL STEP

Remove from oven. Remove breads from pans and place on metal rack to cool. The same with *couronnes*. Delicious toasted. Freezes well. The neighbors who gave you the pears will love *their* loaf.

POMPE AUX GRATONS ❧ CRACKLING BREAD

[TWO MEDIUM OR THREE SMALL LOAVES]

There is no mistaking this fine loaf from the heart of rural France for the American crackling bread, which is made mostly with cornmeal. This is pompe aux gratons, deserving to be served at a special breakfast or brunch for a visiting prince, a nabob, or an old family friend. It is unusually rich, almost cake-like, and contains not only cracklings but butter and eggs.

About cracklings: These are the crisp bits left over after lard has been rendered over heat from fat cut from the hog carcass during butchering. The best cracklings are made from fatback, the solid sheet of fat over the hind quarters of the animal. There should be no meat scraps or pieces of skin included.

Five pounds of ground fatback can be slowly rendered in a large kettle over a low flame to produce light brown cracklings that come floating to the top of the hot fat. These are pressed through a sieve to get 2 cups, or about 1/2 pound, of quality cracklings. Allow at least 2 hours to reduce the fat to lard. Don't let it scorch! After lifting off the cracklings, pour the lard into containers and store in the refrigerator. A fine shortening for many recipes.

If you find cracklings in a specialty food store or in a supermarket, slaughterhouse, or frozen food plant, be certain they are top grade; not a mixture of meat pieces and hide impossible to chew.

INGREDIENTS
2 packages dry yeast
1^1/$_2$ cups warm water (105°–115°)
5 cups all-purpose flour, approximately
1 teaspoon salt
^{1}/$_3$ cup non-fat dry milk
4 eggs, room temperature
^{1}/$_4$ pound (1 stick) butter, room temperature
2 cups (^{1}/$_2$ pound) cracklings, see above

Glaze:
1 egg
1 tablespoon milk

BAKING PANS
Two medium-size (8^1/$_2$ × 4^1/$_2$) or three small (7^1/$_2$ × 3^1/$_2$) loaf pans, greased or Teflon.

PREPARATION
15 minutes
In a small bowl, dissolve yeast in warm water. Pour 2 cups flour into a large bowl and add salt and dry milk. With wooden spoon or rubber scraper, stir yeast mixture into dry ingredients to make a thin batter. Drop in eggs, one at a time, and stir to blend after each addition. Add 1 cup flour and blend. Cut butter into 6 or 8 pieces and drop into the batter. Beat the butter thoroughly into the batter and add additional flour, ^{1}/$_2$ cup at a time, to make a rough ball of dough that can be lifted from the bowl.

Punch the dough into a flat disk. Spread 1 cup of cracklings over the dough and fold in. Knead for a moment or two until the cracklings disappear. Push down dough and add remainder of cracklings. Fold in. If the cracklings have introduced additional moisture (fat), it may be necessary to knead ^{1}/$_4$ cup or more of flour into the dough to firm it again.

KNEADING
6 minutes
Knead the ball of dough on the lightly floured work surface with a 1-2-3 rhythm of push-turn-fold. Because of the high fat content of the combination of cracklings and butter, the dough will be soft, pliable, and not sticky.

FIRST RISING
1–1^1/$_4$ hours
Place dough in bowl, cover with plastic wrap, and leave at room temperature (70°–75°) to double in volume, about 1 hour.

SHAPING
10 minutes
Divide the dough into as many loaves as desired. Prepare pans. Shape each piece of dough into a ball and allow to rest 2 or 3 minutes before pressing into a circle, roughly the length of the loaf pan. Fold the dough in half, pinching the long seam closed. Tuck in the ends and place in the pan with the seam under. Repeat for other loaves.

Crackling Bread, a rural French version of an American favorite.

SECOND RISING
1 hour

Cover with wax paper and leave undisturbed at room temperature (70°–75°) to allow dough to rise to edge of the pans. (This rich dough is somewhat slower to rise than ordinary white dough.)

BAKING
380°
35–40 minutes

Preheat oven 20 minutes before baking.

Remove wax paper and brush dough with egg-milk glaze. If desired, cut a design on the crust before placing on the middle shelf of the oven.

Loaves will be light golden yellow when baked. Turn 1 loaf from the pan to determine if bottom crust is deep brown and sounds hard and hollow when tapped with forefinger. If the bottom crust is soft, return bread to oven for an additional 5 minutes.

FINAL STEP

Place loaves on a metal rack to cool. *Pompe aux gratons* is delicious cool or reheated. Marvelous aroma of a country kitchen.

A wedge of this cheese *galette* makes a fine accompaniment to coffee, tea, or wine.

GALETTE DE GANNAT ❖ GANNAT CHEESE BREAD

[TWO ROUND LOAVES]

This beautiful brown freckled bread from a 200-year-old Gannatois recipe fills the house with the delightful aroma of bread and cheese. A superb combination!

While the old recipe calls for no leavening, this yeast-raised adaptation produces a more open-textured and lighter bread than the original.

If you wish to make it the old way, leave out the yeast and 2 tablespoons of water. Put the dough aside to rest for 1 or 2 hours before shaping. It will not rise, of course, but the dough will mature nevertheless. In truth, many prefer the dense formation of the unleavened loaf.

While the original recipe calls for Gruyère cheese, which is expensive and some- times difficult to find, I substitute imported Swiss cheese with fine results. Excellent for breakfast, brunch, or a special luncheon or tea.

INGREDIENTS 1 package dry yeast
2 tablespoons warm water (105°–115°)
4$^{1}/_{2}$ cups all-purpose flour, approximately
1 teaspoon salt
6 eggs, room temperature
$^{1}/_{2}$ pound (2 sticks) butter or margarine, room temperature
$^{1}/_{2}$ pound grated Gruyère or Swiss cheese

BAKING SHEET One baking sheet, greased or Teflon.

PREPARATION
15 minutes
In a cup, dissolve yeast in 2 tablespoons of warm water and set aside.

In a large bowl, stir together 1 cup of flour and 1 teaspoon salt. With wooden spoon or rubber scraper, form a well in flour and pour in yeast mixture. Break eggs, one at a time, and drop in bowl. Pull flour in from the sides to mix with yeast and eggs. When all eggs have been added and blended well, the dough will be a heavy batter. Cut the butter into small chunks and drop into the bowl. Stir to blend the butter into the mixture. When butter has been worked into the batter, add additional flour, ¹/₂ cup at a time, stirring first with the spoon and then by hand. The dough will be rich in butterfat and will not be sticky. Add flour sufficient to make a ball of dough that is elastic yet does not slump when left to rest for a moment or two.

KNEADING
5 minutes
Turn the dough onto a floured work surface and knead with a strong push-turn-fold motion, adding sprinkles of flour if excessive butterfat works to the surface. Knead for 5 minutes.

3 minutes
Press the dough into a flat circle. Spread the grated cheese over the dough, and fold over the cheese. Knead for an additional 3 minutes to distribute cheese evenly throughout the dough.

FIRST RISING
1¹/₂ hours
Return the dough to the bowl, cover with plastic wrap, and leave at room temperature (70°–75°) until nearly doubled in volume.

SHAPING
5 minutes
Turn the dough from the bowl and divide into 2 pieces, each of which will weigh about 1¹/₄ pounds. With the hands, shape each into a round loaf or *galette*—10 inches in diameter and about ¹/₂ inch thick. Place on baking sheet.

SECOND RISING
¹/₂ hour
Cover *galette*s with wax paper. Leave at room temperature (70°–75°) for about ¹/₂ hour.

BAKING
375°
40 minutes
Turn on oven 20 minutes before bread is to be baked.

Place loaves in middle shelf of oven. Midway through the bake period, inspect *galettes* and turn baking sheet around.

Galettes are done when they are light brown and heavily freckled (thanks to the cheese bits). Carefully turn over 1 loaf with a spatula to be certain bottom crust is dark brown and feels solid to the touch of the forefinger.

FINAL STEP Place *galettes* on metal rack to cool. Cut warm *galettes* into wedges to serve. Can be frozen and reheated with excellent results.

RECIPES FROM ROCHEFORT-MONTAGNE

"Turn off the new road through Rochefort-Montagne (population 1,272) and drop down into the old town for an exceptionally fine loaf of local bread, *la tourte*," the owner of the Gannat hotel had said that morning over a breakfast cup of coffee.

We turned off the road, as advised, and, much to our surprise, into the welcoming arms of the parade committee of the town's annual *fête*. While it was not yet noon, the merry-go-round and Ferris wheel were whirling merrily and noisily, empty of passengers. The parade chairman ushered us off to a side street and then turned to a half dozen old war veterans standing with flags yet unfurled. He pushed them into marching order behind a chauffeured Rolls-Royce decorated with long garlands of flowers. A handsome young woman and an elderly man sat behind tinted glass in the discreet isolation of the back seat. The local aristocracy, my wife suggested.

As the car and the old men started slowly down the winding street, we walked in the other direction to the *boulangerie* to find *la tourte*.

The metal sign on the sidewalk read *"pain cuit au bois,"* bread baked in a wood-fired oven. The very best kind. The loaves, both white and rye, were huge, almost five pounds. While some customers were buying the entire loaf, most, like ourselves, were purchasing pie-shaped slices, by weight. It would be the pièce de résistance of our luncheon of sliced cold terrine of pork, several cheeses, and a bottle of wine—spread over the hood of our little car as soon as we could find a quiet spot along the highway.

It was evident the *boulanger* and his wife were too busy with holiday trade to spend time explaining how the unusual *tourte* was prepared. Later, I was to get the recipe with precise instructions from the president of the Syndicat des Boulangers in Limoges, Monsieur Charamnac. His handsome loaves have often been cover subjects for French gourmet magazines.

Allier-Magazine, a regional publication, described the *tourte*—"Patiently kneaded, baked as long as necessary, this bread is the first gastronomic treasure of rural France."

LA TOURTE ✤ ROUND COUNTRY LOAF

[THREE 1¹/₂-POUND LOAVES]

At one time on farms in the Bourbonnais region in the heart of France, cattle were fed tourteaux, *cakes of pressed sunflower and other oil-bearing seeds, in large wicker baskets. The mistress of the house would commandeer such a basket and line it with cloth to raise the big loaves of* pain de campagne *for her baking once a week. While the farmhouse* tourte *might measure 12 to 16 inches across, any 8- or 10-inch round or oblong basket lined with a piece of tightly woven cloth, heavily floured, will make an excellent* tourtière *to hold the dough.*

There are several unusual steps that give a tourte *a cell structure different from any other yeast-raised bread. First, the yeast is dissolved in* cold *water. The dough is kneaded for 15 minutes before the salt is added, and then for 3 minutes longer. The dough rests only 10 minutes before it is dropped into the baskets to rise for 5 hours.*

My kitchen notes read "husky, filling, and fulfilling." It is all of these, plus the additional dividend of a bread that keeps fresh for days.

INGREDIENTS	*Starter:* ¹/₂ cup bread or all-purpose flour ¹/₃ cup warm water (100°–120°) Pinch salt 1 teaspoon dry yeast (save balance of package for dough) *Dough:* All of the starter (about 7 ounces) 2¹/₃ cups cold water (about 50°) Remainder dry yeast package (about 2 teaspoons) 6¹/₂ cups bread or all-purpose flour, approximately 1 tablespoon salt 2 teaspoons water
BAKING SHEET AND BASKETS	One baking sheet, greased or Teflon. Three baskets lined with cloth. Any receptacle of similar shape, such as a bowl, may be substituted.
PREPARATION 5 minutes 12 hours	*Starter:* At least 12 hours beforehand, mix ¹/₂ cup flour and ¹/₃ cup warm water in a small bowl. Add salt and dry yeast. Cover with plastic wrap and put in warm place (80°–85°), where it will bubble happily.
5 minutes	*Dough:* On bake day, pour all of the starter into a large bowl and add *cold water.* Sprinkle in balance of yeast. Stir to dissolve. Add 3 cups of flour. Beat briskly until mixture is smooth—about 100 strokes with wooden spoon or rubber scraper. Add more flour, ¹/₂ cup at a time, stirring first with spoon and then with hand, until the dough is a rough mass and is no longer sticky.

KNEADING
15 minutes
Turn onto a lightly floured work surface and knead with the 1-2-3 motion of push-turn-fold, push-turn-fold. If the dough sticks, toss light sprinkles of flour over the work surface. Occasionally, raise the dough above the table and bang it down hard. Not only does this help create the gluten network in the dough, but it is also a relief from kneading. Knead for 15 minutes to develop a smooth, elastic dough.

SALT
2 minutes
Push the dough flat. Dissolve salt in water and pour into a depression in the dough. Fold dough over salt solution.

KNEADING
3 minutes
Continue kneading. Add sprinkle of flour if solution causes the dough to become slick.

REST
5 minutes
Divide dough into 3 balls and allow to rest while preparing the baskets. (See *Bannetons*, page 13.) Ideally, the heavy cloth (denim, muslin, or duck) should be tied to the bottom of the baskets so it does not come out when the dough is turned onto the baking sheet.

RISING
4–5 hours
Round each of the 3 pieces of dough into balls and place in prepared baskets with the seam or rough edges up. Set baskets in undisturbed place at room temperature (70°–75°). Cover with wax paper brushed with shortening, so the paper does not stick. Dough will more than double in volume.

BAKING
500°
45 minutes
Turn on oven 40 minutes before baking. The dough will require steam from a broiler pan placed on the lowest oven shelf. The pan can be placed in the oven earlier and 1 cup of water poured into it for a burst of steam just before loaves go into the oven. Steam may puff harmlessly from around the edges of the door.

Gently turn the loaves onto the baking sheet, the seam or rough edges under.

Place bread in oven. Midway through the bake period, shift loaves. If they are browning too fast, cover with foil or brown sack paper.

Turn 1 loaf over. If it is deep brown and gives a hard, hollow sound when tapped, the loaf is baked. If not, return to oven for an additional 5 minutes.

FINAL STEP
Remove from oven and place on metal rack to cool. While this loaf will remain moist and delicious for several days, freeze loaves that are to be kept for more than 5 or 6 days. Excellent with cheese, soups, and all meats. Toasting emphasizes its wheaty flavor.

Circular or criss-cross cuts add a distinctive look to this hearty rye *tourte*.

La Tourte de Seigle ⚜ Rye Country Loaf

[TWO LOAVES]

A fine companion loaf to the wheat flour tourte *is a rye* tourte *that was long the staple of farm kitchens in the Massif Central region of France, where poor soil could produce only rye in abundance.*

The few boulangers *who still bake this loaf say it has unequaled flavor, is easily digestible, and has the special property of keeping for two or three weeks—and all the better for it. It has since been rediscovered and business is booming among the* boulangeries *making* la tourte de seigle.

While few home bakers have the ideal tourte *oven—an old brick oven fired with apple wood—a preheated heavy baking sheet or baking stone in the oven will get* la tourte *off to a fine start.*

INGREDIENTS *Starter:*
1 cup rye flour
³/₄ cup warm water (105°–115°)
Pinch salt
1 teaspoon dry yeast

Dough:
All of the starter (about 1 cup)
1¹/₂ cups warm water (105°–115°)
2 teaspoons dry yeast
1 tablespoon salt
1¹/₂ cups all-purpose flour
3 cups rye flour, approximately

BAKING SHEET
AND BASKETS
One heavy baking sheet to be preheated and sprinkled with corn-meal. Two woven baskets, about 8 inches in diameter and about 3¹/₂ inches deep.

PREPARATION
6 minutes
Starter: The starter can be made two or three days in advance and allowed to mature.

In a large bowl, stir together flour, water, salt, and 1 teaspoon yeast (save the remaining 2 teaspoons in packet for dough). Cover with plastic wrap and leave undisturbed at room temperature (70°–75°) for 1, 2, or 3 days. The longer it develops, the more the bread will have the genuine *tourte* flavor.

12 minutes
Dough: Remove plastic wrap and stir down starter. Pour in water, yeast, and salt. Blend and allow yeast to dissolve for 3 or 4 minutes. Add all-purpose flour. Stir batter 25 strong strokes with wooden spoon or rub-ber scraper. Add rye flour, a cup at a time, until it is absorbed into the batter and becomes a mass. Continue to stir with spoon until dough has lost most of its stickiness and can be turned from the bowl.

KNEADING
6 minutes
Dust work surface with flour and begin kneading. It will probably be sticky, so work dough with pastry scraper for a minute or two. Add sprinkles of *all-purpose* flour to control stickiness. Knead with 1-2-3 rhythm of push-turn-fold movement. (Knead slowly, said the *boulanger*.)

Rye dough will not fight back as will white dough, yet it will be elastic, soft, and responsive to the touch. It simply does not have the resilience of doughs made wholly with wheat flours.

REST
15 minutes
Form the dough into a ball and allow to rest while the baskets or *bannetons* in which the dough will rise are prepared. Line each bas-ket with a tightly woven cloth that will not allow air to reach the

dough. Sprinkle flour liberally over the cloth. A bowl of similar dimensions may be substituted and lined with a cloth.

SHAPING
2 minutes
Punch down the dough and divide into 2 pieces. Fashion each piece into a round ball and drop into the prepared basket or bowl.

RISING
2–3 hours
Cover the baskets with a cloth (I use a piece of old woolen blanket) or wax paper. Leave undisturbed for 2 to 3 hours at room temperature (70°–75°) until the dough has more than doubled in volume and the expanding dough has torn rough crevices across the crusty surface.

BAKING
375°
1–1¹/₂ hours
Preheat oven 20 minutes before baking and place empty baking sheet on the middle shelf of the oven. Also have a water-filled spray atomizer at hand.

Uncover loaves. Remove hot baking sheet from the oven with care! Sprinkle heated sheet with cornmeal. Normally, the basket is overturned directly onto the baking sheet so that what was the top of the risen dough is now the bottom.

I like to preserve the rough texture of the dough as it is in the basket, so I will turn the dough into my hand and then onto the pan, right side up, as it were. Try it both ways to see which gives you the crust you like.

Place the *tourtes* in the oven and give the interior 2 or 3 sprays of water from the atomizer. Close door quickly to keep in the steam. After the bread has been in the oven for 45 minutes, turn baking sheet end for end to equalize oven temperature on loaves.

This is a heavy loaf and it is difficult to determine when it is completely baked. After 1 hour, turn a loaf over and check bottom crust. If it is a deep brown and sounds hollow when tapped with a forefinger, it is probably done. Also check with a metal skewer or cake-testing pin by inserting it down through the thickest part of the loaf. If it comes out clean, with no particles sticking to it, the loaf is baked.

FINAL STEP
Remove loaves from oven. The bread is better after it has aged a day or so—or even longer. The hard crust will become less so and the fine rye taste accentuated. Store bread in bread box or paper bag.

Also can be frozen for long periods. Excellent for a buffet—to serve with cheese, meats, and spreads.

RECIPES FROM WICHTRACH

The large picture window was the dominant feature of the white two-story building, one of a half-dozen houses along a short side street in the village of Wichtrach, in the canton of Bern, in Switzerland. A modest sign—*Bäckerei*—identified the place.

When I first looked, the man inside who was standing behind the window at a flour-dusted table had stopped what he was doing and was gazing entranced at something beyond me. Bread pans and hunks of dough were scattered on the workbench before him. His concentration was so complete that I turned to look.

He was looking at a spectacular mountain scene—*his* mountain scene—that at a glance encompassed all of the magical elements of Switzerland, a scene that through all of its seasonal variations held him forever enchanted, he told me later.

Immediately before him (and behind me) several brown milk cows confined in a small lot bobbed their heads in the deep grass. Each bob sounded a clear, bright note on a tulip-shaped brass bell strapped around each neck. A strand of electric fence kept them from wandering into several garden plots just beginning to flourish nearby. Behind the gardens, in a small orchard, apple and pear trees burst with white and pink blossoms.

But the breathtaking sight in the middle of this picture was the sharply towering peaks of the Bernese Alps that ringed the valley. It was early summer. The snow line had not yet retreated very far up the mountains, so the blanket of white contrasted dramatically with the light green of faraway meadows and the deeper green of the village cow pasture and orchard in the foreground. Above, a dozen swallows cut designs in the cloudless blue sky.

When I turned back to the window, the man was looking at me and smiling. He seemed delighted that I had shared one of his special moments with his mountains.

He was Rolf Thomas, who had come to Wichtrach a dozen years before. It had not always been a happy time for this gentle man with the engaging smile. Born in Germany four years before World War II, Rolf lost both parents in the latter days of the conflict. Times were desperate. A relative advised the boy that if he wanted to eat, he could become an apprentice to a chef, a baker, or someone whose business was food. In a small cellar bake shop, he found a man and wife who gave him lodging for his labors. Grateful to be eating, he nevertheless grew to dislike the windowless cellar for he never knew if it were day or night, clear or storming. He liked baking, however, and promised himself that someday he would have his own shop, one *above* ground.

When the war ended, Rolf emigrated to Switzerland, where he worked in the bakery of a large Lucerne hotel. While it was on the ground floor, the windows, primarily for light and ventilation, were six feet overhead. He still felt confined.

Working in the sales department of the same Lucerne hotel was a tall, blond, and pretty Swiss girl, who had only recently returned from a year's apprenticeship in a London hotel. She, too, wanted her own business, preferably somewhere in the Bern canton where she was born. When Verena and Rolf were married, they spent most of their honeymoon talking with flour and bakery equipment salesmen to find a small family-run bakery that might be for sale.

One salesman said he knew just the place. A hundred-year-old *Bäckerei* in Wichtrach, forty kilometers south of Bern, on Highway 6, leading south and east to the resort areas of Thun and Interlaken and to the great glacier at Grindelwald. The baker, the salesman said, had lived a full life and now wanted to sell.

"The window!" cried Rolf when they stopped their small car in front of the building. They turned to look at the view that would never grow old for either of them.

"We stood entranced, scarcely believing how fortunate we were in finding precisely what each had dreamed about," she said.

A dozen years later, my wife and I found ourselves in Wichtrach, on the same street and standing before the same window. We were there after fleeing Bern, the capital city of the Swiss federation, which had been chaotic with Pentecost holiday traffic fighting its way around and through an extensive street construction project.

A knowledgeable friend had guaranteed us "one of the greatest weekends" of our lives (weather permitting, he cautiously added) if we would only take off a few days from the French trip to visit Bern. It had to be Bern, he insisted, no substitutions. "Bern is not a tourist city," he said, "and for some reason it does not attract many visitors. But I consider it the greatest city in Switzerland." We gave it a try, old friend, we really did, but the streetcars, the autos, and the street blockades did us in. However, it proved to be one of the best weekends of our lives, thanks to Wichtrach.

The other reason for being in Switzerland was to discover what cross-pollinization of breads there had been in an area so heavily influenced by several cultures. The language of the Bernese was mostly German, while the city of Neuchâtel, less than a hundred kilometers away, was the capital of a French-speaking Protestant district.

We had not yet met Rolf Thomas when Frau Steffen-Liechti brought rolls from his bakery to our table for our first breakfast at the Hotel Kreuz. I knew right away we had made no mistake in forsaking Bern for a charming country *Gasthof* that served breads such as these. There were two kinds in the wicker basket—*weggliteig* (which we thereafter called button rolls) and *gipfelteig,* a kind of croissant. The buttons or small peaks came from scissor-cuts along the top of the roll made just before it went into the oven. The *gipfelteig* was a smaller, more tightly rolled croissant. It was not as buttery nor as flaky as the French ones. But tasty.

When I walked up the street to meet Rolf Thomas a short while later, I knew firsthand (or first-taste) that he was an excellent baker, and one whose recipes for at least two breads should be in my collection.

Rolf's reputation as a top-notch baker had spread far beyond the immediate neighborhood and the 120 families for whom he baked. There were probably another thirty customers, farm families higher up the slopes, who came to the bakery twice a week either on their way to the doctor nearby or to the post office. There was little walk-in trade at the Thomas bakery. Roadside advertising is prohibited in Switzerland and he could not even have a small arrow at the main road junction pointing to the *Bäckerei.* But that had its good points, he explained.

"My business is not seasonal. Each day I know exactly how many loaves I will bake and sell. There's never unsold bread."

Busy as he was six days a week with his regular clientele, Rolf had found time to develop a specialty item that he ships by air to as far away as California. It is *Haselnusslebkuchen*, a butter-and-nut-rich cake baked in the shape of the Swiss bear. At the moment, he was working on an order for thirty of the solid one-pound hazelnut cakes to be given to dealers attending a showing of new automobile models in Bern.

There had been considerable change in the bakery since they bought it. The picture window, to be sure, was unchanged, but the old wood-fired oven, which he still used, had been converted to bottled gas. There was no steam for the oven and breads got their steam when Rolf bounced a stream of water from a hand-held plastic bottle off the hot oven bricks just inside the oven door. New mixing and shaping machines had been installed to make it possible for Rolf to operate what he called his "man-and-a-half" shop. He was referring to himself and his apprentice, a local lad. He was not counting Verena, who snipped the buttons on the rolls and also managed the small adjoining shop on which she could keep an eye from the family kitchen, just behind. The family living quarters were on the second floor and one entire wall included display cases filled with Rolf's collection of Swiss butter molds.

My wife asked Verena why they weren't living in the charming 500-year-old thatched-roofed chalet next door, which they had bought a few years ago.

"They are charming to look at, right enough, but on the inside . . ." She wrinkled her nose and shook her apron. "They are dirty. They smell like cows. The roof leaks. The only people who will live in them are the foreign families who have come to Switzerland to work. They accept it because it is cheap.

"But to live in it, never! We'll tear it down someday and build a modern house with some of the good features of the old—the overhanging roof and the ample balconies, with many flowerboxes."

Boulanger Rolf Thomas takes crusty country loaves from his oven with a *pelle*.

WEGGLITEIG ✤ BUTTON ROLLS

[ABOUT TWO DOZEN]

Weggliteig *is a delicious breakfast roll and a specialty of Herr Thomas's* Bäckerei. *It is a long roll brushed twice with beaten egg and snipped with scissors down the top to produce a sawtooth effect. My grandson saw it differently: "Looks like the buttons on a mother pig."*

The description is not far afield when one considers that some of the good flavor comes from a portion of country lard.

INGREDIENTS	2 cups warm water (105°–115°) 1 cup non-fat dry milk 2 tablespoons sugar 1 tablespoon salt 2 packages dry yeast 5 cups all-purpose flour, approximately 2 tablespoons each lard and vegetable shortening *Glaze:* 1 egg, beaten 1 pinch salt
BAKING SHEET	One greased or Teflon baking sheet.
PREPARATION 12 minutes	In a large bowl, pour the 2 cups water and add the milk, sugar, salt, and yeast. Stir to dissolve. Let rest 3 minutes. Pour in 2 cups all-purpose flour, blend, and add shortening. (Herr Thomas insists half of it be lard if one wishes to duplicate the flavor of his rolls.) When shortening has blended with the heavy batter, add rest of flour, 1/2 cup at a time, until dough is a shaggy mass and can be worked with the hands.
KNEADING 6 minutes	Turn dough from bowl onto flour-dusted work surface. Knead with strong push-turn-fold motion. Add liberal sprinkles of flour to control stickiness. Dough should be soft, elastic, and a pleasure to work. Do not make a hard dough by adding too much flour. Err on the side of less rather than more.
FIRST RISING 2 hours	Return dough to washed, greased bowl, cover with plastic wrap, and leave at room temperature (70°–75°) to double in volume.
SHAPING 20 minutes	Turn dough from bowl and punch down. Divide the dough into 24 pieces and roll each piece into a ball. The balls must be pressed down hard under the cupped palm to force the cut edges and folds to blend into the dough and disappear. (Observe a ball of dough that has not been properly rolled. Very often it can be completely unfolded into

Verena Thomas clips *Weggliteig* while, below, her husband carries a panful of these butter rolls from the oven.

the shape it was when cut.) When each ball is round and cohesive, fashion it into a long roll by pushing it back and forth under the flattened palm with the same pressure as earlier. The roll will be longer than the width of the hand—about 4 or 5 inches.

Place each roll end to end in a line on the baking sheet. Repeat for all pieces. Leave a 3-inch space between the parallel rows.

If there is dough for more rolls than the baking sheet will accommodate, reserve dough and repeat this step when sheet and oven are available.

SECOND RISING
1 hour

Cover rolls with wax paper and leave undisturbed at room temperature (70°–75°) for 40 minutes. Brush each roll with egg-salt mixture. Leave uncovered for remainder of time.

At end of the hour, again brush rolls with egg-salt glaze.

BAKING
375°
35 minutes

Preheat oven 20 minutes before baking.

When rolls have been brushed a second time, face the long side of the rolls. Hold a pair of scissors at a 45° angle and make 5 triangular cuts, about an inch long, down the center of each roll. The points of the triangles will rise, forming the buttons. Dip the scissors into water each time you cut, so the points don't stick to the glaze.

When all the rolls have been cut, place baking sheet on center shelf of oven.

Halfway through the bake period, turn the baking sheet end for end to equalize heat on breads.

Rolls are done when glossy brown. Turn 1 roll over and tap bottom crust to be certain the crust is firm.

FINAL STEP

Place on metal rack to cool. Equally delicious reheated later.

Gipfelteig ❧ Swiss Croissants

[ABOUT FOUR DOZEN CRESCENT ROLLS]

The Gipfelteig *is small (about 1 ounce), rich, and certainly one of the most praiseworthy morsels to be found in the Swiss canton of Bern. Four of Herr Thomas's delicate* Gipfel- teigs *will fit comfortably on the flat of the hand as compared to one French croissant to which it is closely related.*

If there is one different ingredient in this small bread that contributes so much to its extraordinary flavor it is the Schweinefett, *country lard, used in making the dough. It imparts a flavor that cannot be duplicated by any other shortening.*

While there are 55 layers of dough and margarine when all of the turns have been made, the dough is rolled unusually thin—¹/₈ of an inch or less—before the triangles of dough are cut. Herr Thomas agrees that not all the layers are retained in rolling, but enough remain, he believes, to impart a special texture not found in other croissants.

INGREDIENTS
6 cups all-purpose flour, approximately
2 packages dry yeast
4 teaspoons salt
¹/₄ cup sugar
2 cups warm water (105°–115°)
6 tablespoons lard, room temperature
¹/₂ pound (2 sticks) margarine, room temperature

Glaze:
1 egg
1 tablespoon milk

BAKING SHEET
The 4 dozen *Gipfelteigs* will require either two baking sheets or two bake periods with one sheet, greased or Teflon.

PREPARATION
The preparation of the dough before it is cut into triangles is best done the night before baking since the layered dough must be thor- oughly chilled before the final steps.

20 minutes
In a large bowl, mix together 2 cups of flour, the yeast, salt and sugar. Pour the 2 cups of warm water into the bowl and stir to make a smooth batter. Allow this to stand for 15 minutes.

The lard, at room temperature, is added to the batter and blended with 25 strong strokes of a large wooden spoon or rubber scraper. Pour in additional flour, ¹/₂ cup at a time, and stir first with a utensil and then with the hands to make a shaggy mass that cleans the sides of the bowl. Scrape particles from the bowl and incorporate into the dough.

KNEADING
7 minutes
Lift dough to the floured work surface and knead with a strong push- turn-fold rhythm to develop the dough into a soft, elastic mass. Toss down light sprinkles of flour to control stickiness if it develops.

LAYERING   Unlike a French *boulanger* preparing layered croissants, Herr Thomas does not chill margarine before spreading it with his fingers across the rectangle of dough. He puts the dough into the refrigerator later to chill, of course.

20 minutes   Knead the 2 sticks of margarine with a pastry scraper to soften and cream. Set aside.

With rolling pin and fingers, roll and stretch the dough into a rectangle 18 by 14 inches. Let it rest 3 or 4 minutes to retain this shape. With fingers or rubber scraper spread margarine over dough, leaving a 1-inch border of dough around the edges. This will allow the dough to seal together and hold in the fat when rolled.

TURN 1   Fold and overlap the dough lengthwise in three sections—as one would fold a letter. The rectangle now measures about 6 × 14 inches—and is 3 layers deep.

TURN 2   Lightly flour the dough and work surface. Turn the dough so the 6-inch or short sides of the rectangle are at 6 o'clock and 12 o'clock and roll into a new rectangle—12 × 18 inches. Fold again in thirds.

TURN 3   Flour surface. Turn short sides to 6 o'clock and 12 o'clock and roll dough into a 12 × 18-inch rectangle. Fold in thirds.

REFRIGERATION   Wrap the dough in a double thickness of damp towel, so surface of the
3 hours   dough will not dry out. Lay wrapped dough on baking sheet and place
or overnight   in refrigerator.

TURN 4   Unwrap dough and place on floured work surface. Carefully roll out
4 minutes   dough into a 12 × 18-inch rectangle. Fold in thirds. This is the final turn before rolling dough to thin sheet.

SHAPING   Have the work surface sprinkled with flour, so the dough will move
20 minutes   easily under the rolling pin.

Roll the dough into a long rectangle—about 36 × 18 inches—and very thin, 1/8 inch or less. Let the dough rest before cutting with a pastry wheel or the dough will draw back when cut.

With a yardstick as a guide, trim dough and cut into 3 length-wise sections 6 inches wide. The *Gipfelteig* triangles are 4 × 6 inches. Mark each section at 4-inch intervals, alternating on the right and left side of the section, to produce a series of long triangles.

Lay the triangles to one side. If there are too many to bake at one time, reserve the surplus in the refrigerator, separated with small pieces of wax paper.

With rolling pin, roll triangle back and forth once to press it out and make thinner. Hold the point under a finger. With the other hand, roll up the dough toward the point. Place on baking sheet about 1¹/₂ inches apart, with the tip under the body of the *Gipfelteig* to keep it from unrolling in the oven. Shape into a crescent. Repeat with others.

RISING
1 hour

Brush each piece with egg-milk glaze and leave uncovered at room temperature (70°–75°) for 1 hour.

BAKING
375°
25 minutes

Preheat oven 20 minutes before baking.

Brush pieces again with egg-milk glaze before placing sheet on middle shelf of oven. Twenty minutes later, shift baking sheet and quickly inspect *Gipfelteigs*. They are small and brown rapidly the final few minutes of the bake period. If your oven is hotter than it should be, be prepared to take out breads a few minutes early.

FINAL STEP

Remove from oven and cool on metal rack. Serve while warm if possible. To freeze, cool first on rack and package airtight. Thaw before returning to 375° oven for 10 minutes.

NUSSGIPFEL ❧ NUT-FILLED CROISSANTS

[TWO DOZEN CRESCENT ROLLS]

While this nut-filled Gipfelteig *is only a variation of Herr Thomas's fine crescent roll, it deserves special attention for its exceptionally fine taste. Noisette, Haselnuss, or hazelnut is perhaps the principal nut in all kinds of confections in France and, certainly, in the neighboring Swiss canton of Bern. In his small shop, and especially in this recipe, Herr Thomas has elevated the hazelnut to the position of eminence it deserves.*

INGREDIENTS

Dough:
One-half batch of *Gipfelteig* layered dough (page 214).

Filling:
1 cup ground hazelnuts
1 egg
¹/₄ cup sugar
2 tablespoons melted butter
¹/₂ teaspoon vanilla
¹/₂ teaspoon grated orange rind, optional

Glaze:
1 tablespoon apricot or cherry glaze

BAKING SHEET

Baking sheet, greased lightly or Teflon.

PREPARATION Here are the times and steps for the dough (page 214) before the rolls are filled.

Prepare Dough	20 minutes
Kneading	7 minutes
Layering and turning	20 minutes
Refrigeration	3 hours or overnight
4th Turn	4 minutes
Shaping	20 minutes

FILLING
5 minutes
Beforehand, put the hazelnuts (I leave on the skins for color) through the medium blade of a nut grinder. Mix the nuts together in a small bowl with the egg, sugar, melted butter, vanilla, and grated rind. Blend all ingredients but do not cook.

15 minutes
When the triangles have been cut and each has been rolled thinner, spread 2 teaspoons of hazelnut filling near the base of each triangle. Roll up loosely. Do not draw the dough tight. Pieces may be shaped into crescents as they are placed on the prepared baking sheet, or left in the elongated shape. Herr Thomas does both.

Place unused filling, if any, in a plastic container and freeze for future use.

RISING
1 hour
Cover with wax paper and leave at room temperature (70°–75°) for 1 hour.

Prepare glaze by forcing apricot or cherry preserves through sieve or strainer to remove pieces of fruit. Place the thick liquid in a small saucepan and bring to a boil. Remove from fire or hold at warm heat.

BAKING
375°
25 minutes
Preheat oven 20 minutes before baking.

Brush pieces with glaze before placing baking sheet on the middle shelf of the oven. Fifteen minutes later, brush pieces again, and check doneness. These are small and bake rapidly.

FINAL STEP Remove from oven and cool on metal rack. Serve while warm, if possible. To freeze, cool first on rack and package airtight in plastic bag. Thaw in the bag before returning to the oven (375°) to warm. An exceptional breakfast treat.

STOLLE ❧ STOLLEN

[TWO 3-POUND LOAVES]

One of the fine festive breads to come from any kitchen—and for any occasion—is Stolle, a lovely yellow butter-and-egg-rich dough, fairly bursting with candied fruit and nuts. The dough is flattened, folded roughly in half, and baked. Later, before serving, it is topped with a sprinkle of confectioners' sugar to give it a lace-like effect.

This is a larger-than-usual recipe, appropriate for a special brunch or an open house at the holiday season. Of course, there is always the option of cutting the recipe in half.

INGREDIENTS
6^1/$_2$ cups all-purpose flour, approximately
^{1}/$_2$ cup non-fat dry milk
1 package dry yeast
2 teaspoons salt
1^1/$_2$ cups warm water (105°–115°)
1 cup chopped almonds
1^1/$_2$ cups currants or raisins
1 cup candied orange or lemon peel or fruit
1 pound (4 sticks) butter or margarine, room temperature
2 cups sugar
^{1}/$_8$ teaspoon vanilla
2 tablespoons rum or brandy, optional
3 eggs, room temperature
1 tablespoon melted butter, to brush
1 tablespoon confectioners' sugar, to sprinkle

BAKING SHEET
One greased or Teflon baking sheet.

PREPARATION
20 minutes
Place 2 cups of flour in a medium-size bowl and stir in the dry milk, yeast, and salt. Pour in water, stir to make a soft batter. Put aside to rest.

In a separate bowl, mix together the almonds, currants, and candied fruit and set aside.

In a large bowl, cream butter with a wooden spoon or rubber scraper. Add sugar, ^{1}/$_2$ cup at a time, stirring to blend well. Add vanilla (and, if desired, rum or brandy). Break and drop in one egg at a time—beating to blend with the butter-sugar mixture. Add 2 cups of flour and stir to mix ingredients thoroughly. Pour the yeast batter into the large bowl and combine. Add additional flour, ^{1}/$_2$ cup at a time, until dough is a solid mass and can be worked with the hands without sticking. The dough will be slick because of the large quantity of butter.

KNEADING
8 minutes

Turn from the bowl. If there is too much dough to knead comfortably, divide it into 2 pieces. Knead with a strong push-turn-fold motion, occasionally lifting and dropping the dough hard on the work surface to relieve the tedium of kneading.

When the kneading is completed, push and pat dough into a flat oval. Pour half the nut-fruit mixture on the dough and fold in. Knead until the nuts and fruit disappear. Flatten again and add balance of nuts and fruit. Continue to knead until nuts and fruit are distributed evenly throughout the dough.

RISING
2½–3 hours

Return dough to bowl, cover with plastic wrap, and leave at room temperature (70°–75°) to double in volume, about 2½ hours. This is a rich, heavy dough that is slow to rise.

SHAPING
10 minutes

Turn dough onto floured work surface and divide into 2 pieces, or more if you wish smaller loaves. Push and flatten dough into an oval. For a large loaf, this will be about 10 inches in diameter. Fold dough into an off-center envelope—the top about 1½ inches from the bottom edge. Push and pinch top edge to secure it to the bottom dough so it will not pop open during baking. Repeat for other loaves. Place on baking sheet.

REST
15 minutes

Leave the loaves uncovered while oven is preheating.

BAKING
350°
1 hour

Brush loaves with melted butter before placing on the middle shelf of the oven. Midway through the bake period, turn baking sheet around to compensate for temperature variations in oven.

Stolle is done when it is golden brown and the bottom crust sounds hard and hollow when tapped with the forefinger.

FINAL STEP

Brush once again with melted butter and carefully place on metal rack to cool. A large *Stolle* is fragile when hot, so lift with the aid of a spatula. Sprinkle with confectioners' sugar before serving. *Stolle* is better left for a day or two before cutting. Freezes well.

Recipes from Strasbourg

Strasbourg is a French city that loves its croissants and *petits pains*, but it cherishes with equal fervor its *stollen* and *kugelhupf*. It is one of the most epicurean of French cities, yet it is only four kilometers (two and a half miles) from the Rhine River, across which the German influence on food (and a host of other good things as well) has flowed with ease for centuries.

It was almost a hundred years ago that a German physician came to Strasbourg following the occupation of the city in the Franco-Prussian War (1870–71) and became a customer and friend of a young baker, Monsieur Jacques Zimpfer, at 10 Place Broglie, in the old city, near the impressive Théâtre Municipal. His selection of breads was small and the doctor urged the young man to experiment with flour from the whole grain of wheat, ground on millstones, as bakers in Germany had been doing for years with considerable success. The bread was darker, the slice had a roughness about it, and perhaps it didn't have the social standing of white, the doctor explained, but it was good to eat and good for one.

Great-great-grandfather Zimpfer, who agreed to try out a few loaves with the whole wheat flour, could not have known that he was about to set the family business on a course that would come down through a hundred years of baking tradition to rest with the pleasant thirty-five-year-old man standing in the doorway of the most successful *boulangerie* in Strasbourg. It was no small tribute to Monsieur Jean Pierre Scholler that the family bakery (it came to him via his grandmother) today remains one of the finest in a city that has 240 *boulangers*, one for each 1,200 Strasbourg souls.

If there is a fault to be found with Jean Pierre's operation, it would be that he makes a choice difficult by presenting an unbelievable number of breads. In display cases bursting with his products, I took inventory—eighteen different breads and rolls, plus cakes, pies, and tarts. The breads ranged from whole wheat *kugelhupf* to an ordinary white loaf with a delicate braid plaited down one side of the crust.

Successive family *boulangers* never left the path laid down by the elder Zimpfer. With the new whole wheat loaf quickly becoming a favorite, the *boulangerie* began to specialize in other breads made with whole grain flours and other nutritional ingredients. The shop now uses three tons of whole wheat flour (*farine complète*) each week.

To say simply that the Scholler *boulangerie* specializes in diet and health breads would be misleading and would turn off a number of people. But when Jean Pierre calls it the *boulangerie de régime*—diet bakery—people shove to make their way in.

On a bread wrapper is the description of the whole wheat loaf that has come down from his great-great-grandfather. It is called, simply, *pain complet*. Complete.

"This bread has been made with the whole grain grown without fertilizer but vitalized with an organic manuring consisting of a mixture of medicinal plants such as chamomile, valerian, nettle, dandelion and horsetail. The flour is ground on millstones."

Jean Pierre, his pretty wife, Hélène, and I talked late one afternoon (just before his bedtime) in a small room separating the store in front and the bakery in the rear. The lights were out in the bakery and I would have to wait until early the following morning to see where all the marvelous breads were made. We talked about the trend in some French cities toward big commercial *boulangeries,* and soft bread wrapped in plastic. That would never happen in Strasbourg, he said, because he and the other bakers are dedicated to keeping their standards high. An American baker might consider him too diversified, I said, producing too many kinds of bread. Jean Pierre laughed and pointed to a dozen customers standing before the display cases while four women in white smocks rushed to fill orders.

"We give them what they want!"

The Schollers live in a comfortable apartment above the *boulangerie,* where the view is of a bus stop (where all the passengers seem to be carrying Scholler bread) and the city hall across the wide Place Broglie. During our talk, I could occasionally hear the clatter overhead of eight-year-old Matthew, who, said his mother, would someday continue the Zimpfer-Scholler tradition.

The next day, in the early light of a clear spring dawn, I walked across Place Broglie, empty now of people and cars and buses, and slipped through a side door left ajar for me. Having earlier admired the variety of breads produced under the Scholler roof, I had expected to find upwards of a

M. Scholler, a third-generation *boulanger,* is proud of his country loaf.

dozen men at work when I walked into the shop. I was astounded to find only Jean Pierre, two other bakers, and a helper. A total of four. What they may have lacked in numbers, they made up for in energy and skill. Not a movement was lost. When Jean Pierre, with one hand, shook a handful of raisins in a light metal strainer to listen for the hard toc-toc of a wayward stone, he stirred a pan of apricot glaze with the other. When a man walked across the room with a filled pan, he returned with a stack of empties.

One *boulanger* stood in a hip-deep pit in front of the big oven that had three loading doors, one above the other. At that moment, he was bringing dozens of pans of whole wheat bread out of the lower oven. There was no formality about stacking the hot tins. They skidded off his wooden peel into a jumble on the floor, sometimes spilling out, sometimes not. By the time he had finished, loaves and pans were in a mound on the floor as high as his shoulders.

It was about seven o'clock when I said goodbye. The store would open in an hour and the *boulangers'* long night's work would come to an end. Bread was piled everywhere. The table where I had talked with the Schollers the day before held big loaves of *pain de campagne* (country loaves) stacked like logs. Wicker baskets filled with long baguettes were pulled up to the door, looking like a train of railroad cars waiting at a switch-point to be let into the station.

KUGELHUPF ❧ KUGELHUPF

[ONE LARGE LOAF]

There are conflicting stories about who elevated kugelhupf *to its present gastronomic height. Was it Marie Antoinette in the late 1700s (she loved the creation), or Carême, the great chef, who popularized the bread in Paris in the early 1800s? Or was it the skill and devotion of a man named Georges who set up a* pâtisserie-boulangerie *in the rue de Coq in Paris in 1840?*

No matter. Kugelhupf is a triumph large enough to be shared by all three.

There are as many ways to spell kugelhupf *as there are days in the week. Suglhupf, gugelhupf, and kougloff to name but three. And as you might expect, there are even more recipes for this fine yeast-raised bread. This is one of the best.*

Kugelhupf rises elegantly in its own special pan to resemble an almond-studded crown. If no kugelhupf *pan is at hand, a bundt or angel food pan will impart the same* élégance, *especially when sprinkled with a delicate snow of confectioners' sugar.*

INGREDIENTS   *Starter:*
1 package dry yeast
$^1/_2$ cup warm water (105°–115°)
1 pinch salt
$1^1/_4$ cups all-purpose flour

Dough:
$^1/_2$ cup currants or raisins
$^1/_4$ cup dry white wine
$3^1/_2$ cups all-purpose flour, approximately
4 eggs, beaten, room temperature
2 tablespoons warm water (105°–115°)
$^1/_3$ cup sugar
2 teaspoons salt
$^1/_4$ pound (1 stick) butter, room temperature
All of the starter
1 tablespoon cold butter, to coat pan
$^1/_3$ cup slivered almonds, to decorate
1 tablespoon confectioners' sugar, to sprinkle

A circle of whole wheat kugelhupf dough ready for the pan.

The festive bread, warm from the oven, ready to be enjoyed.

BAKING PAN A large, 2-quart *kugelhupf* pan is the choice, although a bundt or angel food pan is a satisfactory substitute. In the event there is too much dough for the *kugelhupf* pan, have a standby prepared such as a large brioche or Charlotte pan.

PREPARATION
5 minutes
6 hours
or overnight

Starter: In a medium-size bowl, dissolve yeast in water. Add pinch of salt and 1 cup all-purpose flour to fashion a rough ball of dough. Add flour if the ball is too sticky to shape with the hands. Cover bowl tightly with plastic wrap and leave at room temperature (70°–75°) for a minimum of 6 hours or overnight. Starter ball will spread across the bowl as it ferments and rises.

BEFOREHAND

Dough: An hour or so before preparing dough, plump currants or raisins in the white wine. The original recipe called for rum or kirsch, but I found either too dominant.

15 minutes

In a large bowl, pour 2 cups all-purpose flour and fashion a well at the bottom. Pour in beaten eggs, water, sugar, and salt. Slowly pull in flour from the sides while stirring with a large wooden spoon or rubber scraper. Cut butter into several pieces and drop into the egg-flour mixture. Beat with 75 strong strokes to completely blend all ingredients. Add additional flour to form a soft mass that can be worked with the hands without sticking.

Uncover starter, punch down, and turn onto floured work surface. Turn out dough and pat and punch into a large flat oval. Place the starter in the center of the oval, fold the dough over the starter, and knead together.

KNEADING
6 minutes
3 minutes

The white starter will gradually blend with the yellow dough as the two become a fine, elastic mass. Add sprinkles of flour if needed.

Let dough rest while currants are drained and patted dry on paper towel. Flatten dough and drop currants in the center. Fold dough over currants and continue kneading until fruit is evenly distributed throughout.

FIRST RISING
2–3 hours

Place dough in a large bowl, cover with plastic wrap, and leave undisturbed at room temperature (70°–75°) until doubled in volume. The starter is slow in the beginning to rise this dough, but then performs admirably in the latter stages.

SHAPING
15 minutes

Turn back plastic covering and punch down dough. Before preparing the *kugelhupf* pan, experiment with the amount of dough needed to fill the mold to the halfway point. This will also indicate if an additional pan is necessary for the balance of the dough, if any.

Put dough aside. With fingers, smear the mold with a film of cold butter to which the slivered almonds will cling. Add almonds and place them uniformly along the bottom and sides of the pan. Reserve some almonds if an additional pan is to be used.

Flatten the ball of dough into an oval roughly the diameter of the *kugelhupf* pan. With fingers, tear and fashion a hole in the center through which the pan tube will slip. Drop dough into place in the pan and push down with the fingers.

If there is dough left, butter an overflow pan, drop in the reserved almonds. Shape remaining dough into a ball and place in pan. Push down with the fingers as above.

SECOND RISING
1–1¹/₂ hours

Tear a hole in a length of wax paper and place over *kugelhupf* tube. Put aside for dough to rise to the edge of pan at room temperature (70°–75°). Cover additional pan, if there is one.

BAKING
400°
1 hour

Preheat oven 20 minutes before baking.

Place pan or pans on the middle shelf. Midway in bake period, change positions of pans so they receive heat equally.

The smaller loaf may be ready in 40 minutes. Check with metal skewer or wooden pick to determine if done.

Test larger loaf to determine when baked. If metal skewer plunged into the heart of the bread comes out clean and free of moist particles, bread is done.

Many *kugelhupf* pans are of shiny metal, which makes it difficult to achieve a deep brown crust. Remove loaf from pan and return to oven for 5 to 8 minutes for a deeper tan.

FINAL STEP

Remove from pan and place on metal rack to cool. While *kugelhupf* may be served as soon as it is cool, *boulangers* suggest allowing the bread to mature for 1 or 2 days before cutting.

Sprinkle *kugelhupf* with confectioners' sugar. It makes a handsome piece for a special breakfast, brunch, or buffet.

Kougelhopf Blanc ❧ White Kougelhopf

[ONE LARGE AND ONE SMALL LOAF]

Two kougelhopfs—this one, made with unbleached white flour, and the one that follows, made with whole wheat flour—are the pride of the Scholler boulangerie.

Kougelhopf blanc *begins with a starter allowed to develop 3 hours before it becomes the base for a dough that is rich with egg, milk, and butter. While all-purpose flour is satisfactory for this recipe, unbleached is recommended because of M. Scholler's dedication to organic ingredients.*

INGREDIENTS

Starter:
$^1/_2$ cup warm milk (100°–110°)
1 package dry yeast
1 cup unbleached flour, approximately

Dough:
All of the starter
1$^1/_2$ cups warm milk (100°–110°)
$^1/_3$ cup sugar
1 teaspoon salt
2$^1/_2$ cups unbleached flour, approximately
1 egg, room temperature
4 ounces (1 stick) butter, room temperature
$^3/_4$ cup raisins, golden preferred

1 tablespoon cold butter, to grease molds
Whole and slivered almonds, to decorate
Confectioners' sugar, to sprinkle

BAKING PANS

The *kougelhopf* pan is the best, certainly. M. Scholler uses only those made of earthenware—which he says gives the loaves a better crust. But a satisfactory substitute is an angel food cake pan or bundt mold for the larger loaf and a fluted brioche or Charlotte pan for the smaller loaf.

This recipe is for 3$^1/_2$ pounds of dough, which can be divided into 2$^1/_2$ pounds for 1 large 9-inch *kougelhopf* pan and 1 pound for a small pan.

"Butter," says M. Scholler, "is very important for greasing the molds. It gives a good flavor."

PREPARATION
5 minutes
3 hours
or overnight

Starter: In a small bowl, mix the warm milk and yeast to dissolve. Stir in flour to make a soft dough that can be kneaded without stickiness. Knead on work surface for 3 minutes. Return to bowl and cover with plastic wrap. Leave at room temperature (70°–75°) for at least 3 hours (or overnight, if more convenient).

Dough: Place starter in a large bowl and pour in warm milk, sugar, and salt. Stir to break up starter dough and dissolve dry ingredients. Add 1 cup of flour, the egg, and butter. Blend with 40 or 50 strokes of a wooden spoon or rubber scraper. Add the additional flour to make a soft dough. Lift from bowl.

KNEADING
8 minutes

Turn dough onto flour-dusted work surface and knead with 1-2-3 rhythm of push-turn-fold. If the dough is sticky, add liberal sprinkles of flour to give it more body. When the dough has been kneaded and is elastic (and not sticky), press flat. Spread raisins on the dough and fold them in. Continue to knead until raisins are distributed throughout.

REST
15 minutes

Cover the dough with the inverted bowl and let it rest while *kougelhopf* pans are prepared. Coat each pan with a film of cold butter. Whole almonds may be placed in a design on bottom of *kougelhopf* pan, which will be the top when baked and turned out. Slivered almonds may be sprinkled on sides where butter will hold them in place. Repeat for other pan.

SHAPING
8 minutes

The *kougelhopf* pans should be filled no more than ³/₄ full. Roll out the dough into a long piece and place carefully in the bottom of the pan—around the tube—so that the ends overlap. Push and smooth with the fingers, so that the dough is uniform.

For pans without tubes, simply lay a ball of dough in the pan and push into the form with the fingers.

RISING
50–60 minutes

Cover pans with wax paper and leave at room temperature (70°–75°) until dough reaches the edge of the pan.

BAKING
360°
50 minutes

Preheat oven 20 minutes before baking.

Place pans on middle shelf of oven. After 30 minutes, open door and turn pans halfway around to equalize temperature variations in oven.

When tops are deep brown, remove pans from oven and test for doneness by plunging a wooden pick, metal skewer, or cake-testing pin into center of each loaf. If pin comes out clean, the loaf is done. If moist particles cling to the pin, return bread to oven for an additional 10 minutes. The small loaf will probably be done in about 40 minutes.

Turn loaves from pans. If pans are shiny bright, the crust of the *kougelhopf* may not be as golden brown as you desire. Return loaves to oven—without pans—for 8 to 10 minutes.

FINAL STEP

Place on metal rack to cool. When completely cool, sprinkle with confectioners' sugar and serve.

Kougelhopf Complet Biologique ❧
Whole Wheat Kougelhopf

[ONE LARGE AND ONE SMALL LOAF]

Flour used for festive loaves has traditionally been white. Happily, Monsieur Scholler has broken with tradition to use whole wheat flour to make a delicious kougelhopf. *While it is difficult to be certain that one is getting flour from wheat organically grown (without chemical fertilizers) such as M. Scholler uses in his* kougelhopf complet biologique, *U.S. and Canadian whole wheat flours do contain all of the elements of the kernel—nothing taken out and nothing added. I believe it is equally good.*

Unrefined cane sugar is in M. Scholler's original recipe, but I have substituted dark brown sugar, which is more easily obtained and is not wholly refined.

INGREDIENTS
4 cups whole wheat flour, approximately
1/3 cup dark brown sugar
2 teaspoons salt
2 packages dry yeast
2 cups milk, warmed (110°–120°)
1 egg, room temperature
3 tablespoons vegetable oil
1/4 cup hazelnuts, coarsely ground
1/2 cup raisins, plumped
1 cup all-purpose flour
1 tablespoon cold butter, to coat pans
Whole and slivered almonds, to decorate
Confectioners' sugar, to sprinkle

BAKING PANS
While a *kougelhopf* pan is best, an angel food cake pan or bundt mold is a satisfactory substitute. For the smaller loaf, use a fluted *brioche* or Charlotte pan. Both pans should be filmed with cold butter.

This recipe is for approximately 3 1/2 pounds of dough—2 1/2 pounds for a large 9-inch *kougelhopf* pan, with 1 pound for a smaller pan.

PREPARATION
12 minutes
Beforehand grind nuts and soak raisins in small bowl of water for 15 minutes. Dry raisins on paper towels.

Into a large bowl, pour 3 cups of whole wheat flour, and the sugar, salt, and yeast. Stir to blend well and add milk. Break egg into the batter add oil, and beat rapidly 40 to 50 strokes to blend thoroughly. Add hazelnuts and raisins. Blend. Add 1 cup of white flour; beat with wooden spoon or rubber scraper. Slowly add more whole wheat flour, perhaps 1 additional cup, mixing well to be certain whole wheat flour has absorbed its fill of moisture before adding final sprinkles of flour to make a solid but elastic mass that can be lifted from the bowl.

KNEADING
8 minutes

Dough that is largely whole wheat is more sticky than all-white dough and it is helpful to have a dough scraper or putty knife at hand to help work the dough and to keep the work surface scraped clean of film. Sprinkles of *white* flour will more quickly control stickiness than will whole wheat. A small addition of white flour will not affect proportions.

Knead the dough vigorously and it soon will become smooth and elastic. Knead for at least 8 minutes.

FIRST RISING
1½–2 hours

Return dough to clean and greased bowl, cover tightly with plastic wrap, and leave undisturbed at room temperature (70°–75°) until doubled in volume.

SECOND RISING
30 minutes

Turn back plastic wrap. Punch down dough with extended fingers; turn it over. Re-cover bowl and leave to rise again.

Prepare *kougelhopf* pans. Coat with a film of cold butter. Whole almonds may be placed in a design on bottom of *kougelhopf* pan, while slivered almonds will be held in place on the sides of the pan by the butter coating. Repeat for other pans.

SHAPING
8 minutes

Fill the *kougelhopf* pans ¾ full. Instead of rolling a long strand of dough to place around the tube, M. Scholler pats the piece of dough into a flat oval, presses hard on the center of the piece, and then tears a hole with his fingertips. He pulls this open so that it will slip over the tube. Carefully, push the dough down into the form. For pans without tubes, lay the ball of dough in the pan and push into the form with the fingers.

THIRD RISING
1 hour

Cover pans with wax paper and leave at room temperature (70°–75°) until dough reaches the edge of the pan.

BAKING
375°
50 minutes

Twenty minutes before baking, preheat oven.

Place pans on middle shelf. Midway in baking, turn the pans around to expose them to different heat variations.

When the tops are deep brown, remove pans from oven and test for doneness with cake-testing pin or metal skewer. If particles cling to the pin when plunged into the bread, return the loaves to the oven for an additional 10 minutes. The smaller loaf will probably be done in 40 minutes.

Turn loaves out of pans. If the crusts are not deep golden brown, return to oven *without* pans for an additional 8 to 10 minutes.

FINAL STEP

Place on metal rack to cool. When completely cool, sprinkle with confectioners' sugar and serve.

Stolle de Noël ❦ Christmas Stollen

[THREE LOAVES]

Often there is a light mantle of snow on the town of Strasbourg and along the banks of the Rhine when Monsieur Scholler begins the annual bake of stolle de Noël, *the Christmas stollen. Almonds, orange and lemon peel, raisins, currants, and schnapps or brandy are the good things that are a part of his special Christmas bread.*

The loaves, which range from ¹/₂ pound to those weighing more than 3 pounds, are brushed with butter the moment they come from the oven. Not only does this enhance the flavor, says M. Scholler, but the stolle *will keep for up to 3 and 4 weeks. When the bread is cooled, M. Scholler sprinkles it lightly with confectioners' sugar.*

A rare Christmas treat—as a gift or to serve to friends.

INGREDIENTS   *Starter:*
¹/₂ cup warm milk (105°–115°)
1 package dry yeast
1 cup unbleached or all-purpose flour, approximately

Dough:
All of the starter
1¹/₂ cups warm milk (105°–115°)
¹/₃ cup sugar
2 teaspoons salt
5¹/₂ cups unbleached or all-purpose flour, approximately
4 ounces (1 stick) butter or margarine
1 tablespoon schnapps or brandy, optional
1 cup chopped almonds
¹/₂ cup candied orange peel
¹/₂ cup candied lemon peel
(1 cup candied mixed fruit may be substituted for orange and
    lemon peel)
³/₄ cup raisins
¹/₄ cup currants

1 tablespoon melted butter, to brush
Confectioners' sugar, to sprinkle

BAKING SHEET   The three stollen will fit on one large (14 × 17) baking sheet, greased or Teflon.

PREPARATION   *Starter:* In a small bowl, mix warm milk and yeast to dissolve. Stir in
5 minutes   flour to make a soft dough that can be kneaded without stickiness.
3 hours   Knead on work surface for 3 minutes. Return to bowl and cover with
or overnight   plastic wrap. Leave at room temperature (70°–75°) for at least 3 hours, or overnight if more convenient.

12 minutes   *Dough:* In a large bowl, place the starter and cover with milk. Stir in sugar, salt, and 2 cups of flour. Divide butter into small pieces and drop into the bowl. Add schnapps or brandy, if desired. With a large wooden spoon or rubber scraper, beat with vigor for about 60 to 70 strokes to cream butter into the thick batter. Dough will begin to pull away from the bowl in heavy strands. This is good. With spoon or fingers, work in additional flour to make a shaggy mass that can be lifted from the bowl.

KNEADING   Dust work surface with flour and turn out dough. Knead with a strong
7 minutes   motion. Don't baby dough. Bang it down hard against the countertop or table to hasten development of the gluten. It is a soft and elastic dough to work. It will be responsive under the hands—and feel alive!

REST   When finished kneading, allow the dough to rest on the work surface
5 minutes   for 5 minutes.

FRUIT-NUTS   Mix the fruit and nuts together in a bowl or on the work surface.
5 minutes   With fingers, punch down dough into an oval and spread half of the fruit-nut mixture over the top. Fold it in, and when it has disappeared, fold in the balance of the mix. Knead for about 4 minutes to distribute thoroughly.

FIRST RISING   While the 3 pieces of dough can be placed individually in smaller bowls
1¼ hours   to rise, M. Scholler puts his on a length of canvas—36 × 18 inches—which is pulled up around each ball of dough to protect it from the air.

    Divide the dough and shape into balls. Place on cloth or in bowls with seam *up.* If on a cloth, separate each ball with a fold of cloth. Prop up end of cloth with a book, pot, or pan. Cover tops of dough balls with wax paper. If dropped into a bowl, cover with plastic wrap.

    Leave undisturbed at room temperature (70°–75°) until balls are light and puffy, about 1¼ hours.

SHAPING   Lift each ball from its cloth pocket and place on flour-dusted work
10 minutes   surface. With rolling pin, roll out ball into an oval about 10 inches long and 8 inches wide—and about ½ inch thick. Brush surface with melted butter. Fold lengthwise almost in half—allowing 1 inch of the lower dough to project. Place on baking sheet. Repeat with other balls of dough.

SECOND RISING   Cover stollen with wax paper and leave at room temperature (70°–75°).
1 hour

BAKING   Preheat oven 20 minutes before baking.
360°   Remove wax paper and place baking sheet on middle shelf of
45 minutes   oven. Turn baking sheet around 30 minutes into the bake. Stollen are done when deep brown on top crust and when bottom crust tapped with forefinger sounds hard and hollow.

FINAL STEP Immediately brush with melted butter when removed from oven and placed on metal rack. When loaves are completely cooled, sprinkle with confectioners' sugar. If the loaves are to be frozen, don't sprinkle until they come out of the freezer and are thawed.

Pain de Seigle Strasbourg ❧ Strasbourg Rye Bread

[TWO LOAVES]

The influence of fine German baking across the Rhine is reflected in this adaptation of the traditional French rye bread made without sugar. It is distant kin of Old Milwaukee Rye, but without the strong molasses flavor (this pain de seigle *has but a small amount) or the distinct spiciness of caraway, which can be added, of course.*

This loaf is solid, moist—an excellent buffet bread.

The shape of a rye loaf in the Scholler boulangerie *in Strasbourg—an oval with a banded effect created by surface cuts—is one of the most popular in France, especially in the cities. Country people favor the round hearth loaf, the* boule.

INGREDIENTS *Starter:*
1 package dry yeast
1^1/$_2$ cups warm water (105°–115°)
2 cups rye flour

Dough:
All of the starter
1 cup warm water (105°–115°)
1 package dry yeast
1 tablespoon salt
1 tablespoon molasses, light or dark
1 tablespoon vegetable shortening
2 cups rye flour
1 cup all-purpose flour, approximately

Glaze:
1 egg
1 tablespoon milk

BAKING SHEET One baking sheet, greased or Teflon.

PREPARATION *Starter:* In a large bowl, stir together yeast, water, and rye flour until a
15 minutes smooth batter. Cover with plastic wrap and leave at room temperature
1–3 days (70°–75°) for at least 1 day. Stir down daily.

12 minutes *Dough:* Uncover bowl, stir down starter, and add water, yeast, salt, molasses, and shortening. Blend with wooden spoon or rubber scraper. Pour in 2 cups rye flour, ^{1}/$_2$ cup at a time, stirring each addition to

blend it into the batter. Add all-purpose flour at first with implement and then with hands as mass absorbs the white flour. When it can be lifted from the bowl with the hands, it is ready to be kneaded.

KNEADING
6 minutes

Turn dough onto floured work surface. Predominately rye dough is sticky and tenacious. It smears. The best instrument for subduing rye dough in the early stages is a dough scraper or putty knife. Push-turn-fold with the scraper, while adding liberal sprinkles of white flour to control stickiness.

Rye dough will be soft and velvety, but it will not have the elasticity of white dough.

FIRST RISING
30 minutes

Dough is left to rise for a surprisingly short time. Leave on work surface and cover with inverted bowl.

SHAPING
15 minutes

Knead dough briefly for 1 or 2 minutes. Divide the ball into 3 pieces for 1-pound loaves (or 2 pieces for 1¹/₂-pound loaves).

(See instructions on *Les Benoîtons,* page 103, if you want to put aside a portion of this dough for raisin rolls.)

Shape each of the pieces into a round ball, pulling down with cupped hands to keep the surface of the dough taut. Press with both hands to elongate the ball to a length at least twice its width. Roll gently once or twice to help achieve an oval loaf.

A Strasbourg rye bread with banded effect created by surface cuts in the dough.

SECOND RISING
25 minutes

Cover loaves with wax paper and leave at room temperature (70°–75°) for a relatively short period—25 minutes.

BAKING
400°
45 minutes

Preheat oven 20 minutes before baking.

Uncover loaves and brush with egg-milk glaze. With a razor, carefully make ¹/₂-inch-deep cuts across loaf, beginning near one end, cutting at 1-inch intervals to the other end—a total of 6 or 8 cuts in all. Place loaves on baking sheet in oven. Halfway through the bake period, turn the baking sheet around to compensate for temperature variations in the oven.

The oval loaf will be about 10 inches long and 5 inches wide. When it is done, it will be well browned. Turn 1 loaf over and tap with finger. If it sounds hard and hollow, bread is baked.

FINAL STEP

Remove from oven and place on metal rack to cool. This loaf will freeze well.

RECIPES FROM CHARLEVILLE-MÉZIÈRES

Charleville-Mézières is a big industrial town in the Ardennes, not far from the Belgium-Luxembourg borders, where I found a small bakery at a time when I wanted peace, quiet, and a loaf of good bread. We had been traveling constantly, a different hotel every other night. I had never felt so overpowered by the automobile—mine and theirs. I was tired. To unwind, I had walked a dozen blocks from the hotel to a small park I had seen as we drove into town. An old church, Saint Lie de Mohon, was across the street.

I pushed against the worn wooden panel of the church door. It opened quietly. There was no one inside. The big chamber was surprisingly light, yet quiet and cool. Very close to heaven for a travel-weary person, I thought. Saint Lie had been a shepherd in the fields above the town once upon a time and now I blessed him for this sanctuary. When I entered the church, I was weary and tired of the noise, the congestion, and the oily smell of traffic. For an hour or more, I sat there. A splash in a cold mountain stream could not have been more refreshing.

Time passed and I remembered that I had seen a *boulangerie* across from the church as I entered. I went outside. It was cooler now, and quieter.

In the *boulangerie*, a cheerful lady stood behind a counter stacked with a dozen or more loaves of *pain de ménage,* family bread. It was from the last bake of the day and still warm. As she wrapped the loaf, I told her I was an American who had a great interest in baking and that I was impressed with the handsome *pains de ménage.*

Her smile broadened and she called to several other customers in the shop. "He is an American and he likes our bread," she said with a delighted laugh. In a body, they rushed to shake my hand and to affirm, yes, *madame* and her husband did make the best bread in all of France.

Madame was more modest. She explained that, while the bread was *pain ordinaire,* it was the unusual design cut into the ball of dough that allowed a beautiful crust to develop.

I propped my loaf of *pain de ménage* against the front door of Saint Lie and took its picture. It seemed the fitting thing to do.

The church door of Saint Lie de Mohon is the backdrop for *pain de ménage* from a neighboring bakery.

Pain de Ménage ❧ Family Loaf

[TWO ROUND LOAVES]

There was nothing elaborate about the pain de ménage *I found in the small* boulangerie *near the church in Charleville-Mézières. It was simply good bread—handsomely presented in a round* boule *that the* boulanger *had deftly cut with eight strokes of his sharp* lame *or blade. In the oven, the loaf opened up along the cuts like a flower in bloom.*

INGREDIENTS One batch, about 3 pounds, of *pain ordinaire* dough (page 163). This loaf can also be made with dough for *pain de campagne* (page 74) with equally good results.

BAKING SHEET One baking sheet, greased or Teflon.

PRIOR STEPS Here are the steps and times for the *pain ordinaire* dough (page 163) before the loaves are shaped:

Prepare Dough	18 minutes
First Rising	2 hours

SHAPING
5 minutes Remove plastic wrap and punch down dough. Turn out on lightly dusted work surface and knead for a moment or two to press out the bubbles. The dough will be light and elastic.

Divide the dough into 2 pieces and shape each into a round ball.

SECOND RISING
1 hour Place at diagonal corners of the baking sheet and leave to rise at room temperature (70°–75°) covered with wax paper or a cloth.

BAKING
450°
400°
45–50 minutes Place broiler pan on the bottom shelf of the oven. Preheat oven 20 minutes before baking. Five minutes before baking, pour 1 cup hot tap water into the broiler pan. Be careful of the burst of steam.

Uncover loaves. With a sharp knife, razor blade, or *lame*, make 4 quartering cuts $1/4$ inch deep from the top of the loaf to the bottom edge. In each quarter, midway between the cuts and centered up and down, make a 2-inch-long cut. This will make a total of 8 cuts for each loaf. Repeat for the second loaf.

Place bake sheet in the oven. Immediately reduce heat to 400°. Halfway through the bake period, shift the loaves so they are exposed equally to the oven's temperature variations.

When baked, the loaves will be golden brown. Turn over 1 loaf and tap with a forefinger. If it is hard and sounds hollow, the bread is done.

FINAL STEP Place on metal rack to cool.

LES PISTOLETS ❧ SPLIT ROLLS

[FOUR DOZEN 1¹/₂-OUNCE ROLLS]

While the pistolet, *a split roll, is made from a special dough in most* boulangeries, *it is the manner in which the roll is formed that commands attention. The dough is shaped into a ball often no larger than a golf ball, sprinkled with rye flour (to keep it from sticking), and split almost in two with a length of broomstick or a dowel, or a blow of the side of the palm! After the split, the roll is placed upside down to rise—and then turned right-side up on a baking sheet for the oven.*

The pistolet *is little known in Paris, but it is at home in the eastern regions of France, and much appreciated in Belgium.*

Malt syrup or extract, much used in French baking, gives the dough a lovely light tan color.

INGREDIENTS
7 cups hard-wheat bread flour or all-purpose flour, approximately
4 teaspoons salt
2 packages yeast
3 tablespoons sugar
¹/₂ cup non-fat dry milk
3 cups warm water (105°–115°)
2 teaspoons plain malt syrup
4 ounces (1 stick) butter, room temperature
1 cup rye flour, for dusting

BAKING SHEETS
Four dozen *pistolets* will fill two baking sheets, greased or Teflon. Two shelves in the oven can be used if the baking sheets are changed once or twice during the final 10 minutes of the bake period; otherwise, reserve the dough in a covered bowl until the baking sheet and oven are available for the second batch.

PREPARATION
12 minutes
Pour 4 cups of flour into a large bowl and stir in the salt, yeast, sugar, and dry milk. Form a well in the bottom of the bowl and pour in 3 cups of water. With rubber scraper or a large wooden spoon, pull in flour from the sides of the bowl to form a heavy batter. Add malt syrup. Break butter into small pieces and stir into the batter. Blend with 50 strong strokes. Add rest of flour, ¹/₂ cup at a time, first stirring with a utensil and then with hands. Dough will be rough and shaggy.

KNEADING
7 minutes
Lift the dough to the floured work surface and knead with strong push-turn-fold motion, adding liberal sprinkles of white flour if dough remains sticky. Dough will become pleasant to work—soft, elastic, and responsive under the hands.

FIRST RISING
3–4 hours
Return dough to the bowl, which has been cleaned and greased. Cover tightly with plastic wrap and leave undisturbed at room temperature

Les pistolets, split with a stick, rise and bake into an interesting shape.

(70°–75°). Dough will more than *triple* in volume during the lengthy rising, during which time it matures and develops an exceptionally fine taste.

SECOND RISING
45 minutes

Turn back plastic wrap and punch down dough with extended fingers. Turn dough over, re-cover bowl. Leave to rise again.

SHAPING
20 minutes

Divide the dough into 2 pieces. Place half on floured work surface. Keep other piece covered and in reserve.

Determine the size of the *pistolet* you desire. I like to make them 1^{1}/$_{2}$ ounces, about the size of an egg. Others like them larger, about twice that size. For young appetites, yes. For a tea party or special buffet, the smaller size.

A ^{3}/$_{4}$-inch wooden dowel (at any hardware store) or broom handle, cut to a 12-inch length, is an ideal dough-splitter. (I sand the piece of dowel and then rub it with vegetable oil.)

Cut the dough into pieces with a knife or dough scraper. Roll into tight balls under cupped palms—pressing hard against the work surface to force the dough into a ball without seams or edges. Place balls together at one side. Repeat with balance of dough if you can accommodate all of them at one time; otherwise reserve.

REST
20 minutes

Cover balls with a length of wax paper and leave while you prepare splitting gear—oiled stick, rye flour, and the floured work surface (countertop or bread board) on which *pistolets* will rise before going into the oven.

SHAPING
20 minutes

Take one ball at a time from under the wax paper and place it before you on the work surface. Dust top lightly with rye flour to prevent it from sticking to itself when folded during final rising. Place oiled stick across center of ball, press down, dividing ball almost in half, leaving a ^{1}/$_{4}$-inch strip of dough between the two sides.

Lift the *pistolet,* place thumbs in the trough and stretch gently to elongate the roll. Remove thumbs and allow sides to come together. Don't press, however. Place *seam down* on prepared work surface. Repeat with other pieces.

THIRD RISING
30 minutes

Cover *pistolets* with wax paper and leave for 30 minutes.

BAKING
425°
25–30 minutes

Pistolets must be baked in steam, a moist oven. Place broiler pan filled with 1^{1}/$_{2}$ cups of hot tap water in oven 20 minutes before bake period. Preheat to 425°, a hot oven.

Carefully lift *pistolets* and place on baking sheet—*seam up!* Place on middle shelf of oven if a single baking sheet; otherwise, use middle and top shelves and alternate sheets during final 10 minutes of baking.

Pistolets are done when they are golden brown and feel hard and hollow to the touch, not soft.

FINAL STEP Place rolls on metal rack to cool. Prepare to bake reserved dough. These freeze well.

Chapelure et Croutons ❧ Breadcrumbs and Croutons

It has been said by almost every home baker that there are no mistakes in bread baking, only more breadcrumbs.

Breadcrumbs have a dozen uses in a kitchen, from coating a cutlet to sharing with Parmesan cheese the mission of covering a breast of chicken for suprêmes. *While most cookbooks overlook rye and whole wheat crumbs, both can add a new flavor to a dish that will delight if not puzzle a dinner guest.*

Breadcrumbs can be made from dry, stale bread if they are to be used within a few days—or toasted and kept sealed for an indefinite period. Don't use festive breads with fruit and nut ingredients.

Chapelure is crushed bread that has been dried very slowly. I have a large bowl in a warm place over a range in which I toss broken pieces of loaves or slices (white, rye, and whole wheat, to be sorted later) that don't measure up to what good bread should be. Perhaps it was too dense, too crusty, over-baked, under-baked, too fat, too lean, not pretty, and on and on.

For white crumbs, cut or pull off the crusts. Reserve the crusts for "golden" crumbs. The rye and whole wheat in the bowl are separated, but the crusts are left on. The color doesn't matter that much.

WHITE CRUMBS
200°
1 hour

Regardless of how dry they seem, spread the pieces on a baking sheet and place them in the oven for an hour. Do not let them brown. They are to remain white. Take them from the oven and, when cool, place them in a cloth and roll them under a rolling pin, or put them through a fine or medium blade of a food grinder.

GOLDEN CRUMBS
250°
1–2 hours

These are the white bread crusts. Place them in the oven to toast lightly. Do not burn them. Watch the oven carefully. When toasted, crush as above.

Both white and golden crumbs may be stored in tightly closed glass or plastic containers or bags—or frozen.

WHOLE WHEAT
AND RYE CRUMBS
250°
1–2 hours

Proceed as with crumbs above.

DRIED BREAD FOR SOUPS
250°
1 hour
350°
10 minutes

Loaves to be discarded can be sliced and shaped into thin ovals to be dried in the oven at 250° and served with soup later. Before serving, brush with melted butter or olive oil and if desired, sprinkle with cheese. Place in oven for 10 minutes.

Serve.

CROUTONS

Croutons for a wide range of garnishes, from soup to salads, can be made from thin slices of bread cut into many shapes and fried in butter, grilled, or oven-dried.

If the occasion merits, bake bread specially for croutons; otherwise, select discards and, before the bread has dried, cut it into small 1/4-inch cubes or into other shapes—hearts, spades, diamonds, clubs, stars, etc., with fancy aspic or jelly cutters.

A crumb or a crouton can be something very important. Give a bagful as a gift.

RECIPES FROM THE S.S. *FRANCE*

The passenger liner S.S. *France* is remembered by me for many things, but none are held in my memory more tenaciously or with greater affection than three golden morsels from her pastry and bake shops on A Deck. The flaky *croissant*, the lovely egg-and-butter-rich *brioche*, and that marvelous miniature loaf, the crispy *petit pain*, of which 5,000 a day were carried forth in baskets and on platters to the Versailles and Chambord dining rooms.

The *France*, with some 1,500 paying guests aboard served by some 1,000 crew, had made her maiden voyage Le Havre–New York in the pre-jumbo jet year of 1962, and now, twelve years later, this was her last season. She would soon return to France to be retired from service.

The French government had decided it could no longer support the vessel with a multimillion-dollar subsidy, and there was already a cutback in some of the amenities aboard. The legendary five-pound tin of caviar ($100 a pound), resting in a carved block of ice and passed freely around the Versailles dining room, was out. A first-class passenger could order a large spoonful from the kitchen, but that was the limit. There was still a bottle of red and a bottle of white wine on first-class tables, but second-class was having to get by with red only. The ship had been ordered to conserve precious fuel by cutting down her speed. Her 160,000 horses now were throttled back and would no longer gulp one ton of fuel every 120 seconds while running at 32 knots. Because she was traveling slower, we were enjoying a full day longer at sea. The extra food for us cost less than the black gold that poured into her engines.

Several months earlier when troublesome little items began to appear in print about the possibility of the *France* being retired from service, I decided I wanted to sail on her before it happened. I wanted to write down some of the great recipes from her bake and pastry shops before she was laid up forever, and her bakers and pastry cooks scattered from Le Havre to Cannes.

Fortunately, when a French Line executive in New York learned of my interest and wrote that "the bread of the *France* is one of the most enjoyed and talked about foods aboard. Its recognition is long overdue," I was to be given free run of the *boulangerie* and *pâtisserie*.

I was scarcely aboard and anxious to begin a quasi-apprenticeship in the galley when I discovered a curious separation of duties between the *boulangerie*, presided over by Monsieur Yves Sauvignon, and the *pâtisserie*, the domain of Pastry Chef Leon Tardy. M. Sauvignon and his eight *boulangers*, all of whom had been together as a team for eight years, worked in shifts around the clock every day of the week, baking only bread—*petits pains*, the larger loaves for the crew, and bread for toast. The bakers wore skull-tight toques and white cotton short-sleeve pullover shirts. Chef Tardy's men, in contrast, wore the traditional towering white chef hats and starched jackets, buttoned to the collar. In the *pâtisserie*, the work was divided between men who worked through the night making brioches and croissants for breakfast and others who came to work later in the morning and were responsible for the delicate petits fours, cakes, ice cream, ices, and the beautiful *pièces montees,* wide ribbons of pulled colored sugar tied in great bows.

I had expected all three delicacies—*petits pains,* brioches, and croissants—to be made in the same shop. But not so.

The dominant feature of the bakery, apart from two large electric ovens built into one bulkhead, was an eight-foot-square beechwood table (never oiled, only scrubbed) around which the nine bakers worked. Only the mixing and kneading were done by machine. The bread dough for *petits pains* was cut by one baker, slicing furiously with a dough blade held in one hand, while tossing away the little pieces of dough with the other. Each piece landed unerringly in front of another baker, who quickly rolled it into a tight little ball for the second rise. It occurred to me then that perhaps this was the last large bakery left in the world—nine bakers feeding 2,500 people—that relied so heavily on hand labor. (Even in the village *boulangeries* in France, the machine has taken over cutting and shaping.)

While bread was the product of nine bakers working together at intervals around the clock, croissants and brioches were almost entirely one man's effort between midnight and six o'clock in the morning.

He was Monsieur Marcel Gousse, *pâtissier,* small, lean, and untiring.

"He does not like the hustle and bustle during the day and he prefers to work alone in the early morning hours when he can think his thoughts and be undisturbed," explained Chef Tardy. "He makes them so beautifully that we must let him have his way."

M. Gousse had a small team of three or four young men assigned to help him, but he trusted no one but himself to do the knife work involved in cutting the croissant dough to precise triangles. And it was he alone who presided over the cutting of a spectacular six-foot-long roll of brioche dough into small pieces for the fluted pans.

Each man, *boulanger* and *pâtissier,* was a dedicated craftsman. M. Tardy awoke each morning, excited to be going to the *pâtisserie.* He said he had felt that way since his youth when he decided against a career in other parts of the kitchen because he hated the smell of fish. He opted for the *pâtisserie.* "I loved the delicate aroma and feel of things made with sugar."

The voyage had been six days from New York to Le Havre. During those days and nights at sea, I spent hours learning from those gracious men, both *boulangers* and *pâtissiers.* Again and again, they applauded my clumsy efforts and I loved them for it. It was mid-morning of our last full day at sea when the telephone rang. It was Chef Tardy. Could I come to the *pâtisserie* at eleven o'clock? "Certainly," I replied, for I welcomed any excuse to go again to the galley. When I stepped over the small threshold into the pastry shop, I was somewhat surprised to see M. Tardy and eight of his *pâtissiers* assembled around the large worktable in the center of the room. Work had ceased. A bottle of Scotch stood on the table and around it, a cluster of water glasses. Chef Tardy handed me a glass and then poured it more than half full. The bottle was passed to each man who poured himself a stiff drink.

Aboard S.S. *France*, M. Sauvignon shows the author how to shape *petits pains*.

"To *Monsieur* Clayton," the chef exclaimed, raising his glass. "You are our friend!"

While a half-glass of Scotch, taken neat in the forenoon, is a half-glass more than I have ever taken at that hour, I was infinitely pleased with the honor.

In turn, I can do no less than to honor them by reproducing here their recipes and describing their techniques as best I can.

To my friends aboard the *France*, wherever you now are—*Merci!*

Petits Pains S.S. *France* ❦ Rolls S.S. *France*

[TWO DOZEN ROLLS, 5 INCHES LONG, OR FOUR 1-POUND LOAVES]

The anchor of the cuisine aboard the S. S. France *was French bread in its least compli-cated form—flour, yeast, salt, and water. These four basic ingredients became some-thing very special in the hands of its nine* boulangers.

Can it be the French flour that makes the difference, I wanted to know? For a long moment, Monsieur Sauvignon studied the dough he was shaping.

"Non, Monsieur, American flour can be used if one understands that it must be treated with deference. Permit it to relax. Don't rush it or it will get stubborn. There is more gluten in American flour and it will fight back when it has been kneaded too aggressively. Like so." He crashed a large piece of dough down hard against the table top.

"Now I walk away for a while," he said.

Monsieur Sauvignon had another caution. Don't pour hot water into flour because it will toughen the dough. Use water that is baby-bottle warm, he suggested, and I took that to mean about 97°.

One surprising practice in the France *bakery that can be adapted by the home baker is to use a piece of an old well-laundered wool blanket to cover the dough as it rises. The bakers aboard the* France *had cut 6-foot-by-3-foot strips from wonderfully soft white blankets that in earlier times had been used by the stewards to tuck around passengers taking their ease in deck chairs. The names of famous French Line ships and the years the blankets had gone into service, some before World War II, were woven into many. Now they were keeping dough warm, not passengers.*

If not a wool blanket, then use any cloth that will allow some air to reach the dough to form a light crust before it goes into the oven. I have since cut up an old Army blanket to use in my kitchen and have discovered that even the soft doughs will not stick to the wool.

The France *bakers were constantly scattering light sprinkles of flour on the work surface and dough before them. The flour was kept on the big table in three or four small wooden boxes, perhaps 5 inches square and 4 inches deep, which seemed to be bottomless reservoirs of flour! Any container, of course, will work as long as it is sturdy and won't tip over.*

To allow the dough to grow and mature and to become more flavorful, the France *recipe calls for the dough to rise three times and to rest for one 15-minute interval.*

The petit pain *or small bread is nothing more than an elongated roll about 5 inches in length and 1¹/₂ inches in girth. It is golden brown and crusty on the outside, white and soft inside. The dough can also be made into four 1-pound loaves of bread.*

INGREDIENTS 2 packages dry yeast
$^1/_4$ cup warm water (95°–100°)
7 cups all-purpose flour, approximately
1 tablespoon salt
3 cups warm water (95°–100°)

BAKING SHEET One baking sheet, greased or Teflon. (*Petits pains* can also be baked in the traditional French bread pan. Place 3 *petits pains* end to end where the long loaf would customarily go.)

PREPARATION Dissolve the yeast in the small amount of warm water. Place 6 cups
20 minutes of flour in a large bowl and form a well in the center (a fountain, M. Sauvignon called it). Pour the dissolved yeast mixture into the well. With a spoon, mix in a little of the flour to make a thicker mixture. Let it bubble for 10 minutes.

Dissolve the salt in the 3 cups of warm water and pour it gradually over the yeast mixture, slowly stirring in a portion of flour from the sides. Beat the soft batter 25 or 30 strokes each time after a portion of flour is added. When the dough is firm and can no longer be stirred, use hands to blend in an additional cup of flour, if needed. The dough will be soft but should not stick to the hands if it is sprinkled lightly with flour.

KNEADING Turn out on the countertop and begin kneading—push down with
8 minutes force with heels of hands, draw back, give the dough a quarter turn, fold it in half, push down with force, draw back, turn the dough again and fold it, and so continue. If the dough is sticky, toss sprinkles of flour over the dough and on the work surface. This is a lean dough (no shortening), so it will have a tendency to stick. A dough scraper or a broad putty knife is useful to turn the dough. Knead for about 8 minutes or until dough is a soft, velvety ball—elastic to the touch but not solid or too firm. If the latter, work in a little water (2 tablespoons).

FIRST RISING Wash and rinse the bowl in hot water. Coat lightly with shortening.
$1^1/_2$ hours Drop in the ball of dough, turning it so all of it is filmed with grease. Cover the bowl lightly with plastic wrap. Put aside to double in volume at room temperature (70°–75°).

REST Punch down the dough. Cover again and let rest.
15 minutes

SHAPING Turn the dough onto the work surface. With a sharp knife or dough
15 minutes scraper, cut off small 3-ounce pieces slightly larger than a large egg. Once you have established the size, be consistent. Use a scale, if necessary.

These pieces are rolled into balls to be placed on a baking sheet, bread board, or left on the work surface to rise. Form the balls by compressing the small piece of dough between the thumb and forefinger, while tucking together the cut surfaces with the other hand— or roll between the palms.

The *France* bakers form the pieces on the workbench, pressing down hard and rolling the dough in a circular fashion under a cupped palm. Both hands at once.

SECOND RISING
1 hour

Place the balls about an inch apart and cover with a piece of wool blanket or cloth. Leave for 1 hour.

SHAPING
10 minutes

Place each ball in front of you on the work surface. Flatten and then fold in half. With the palms of both hands, roll back and forth to form a *petit pain* about 5 inches long and 1 inch thick, tapered to the ends. Place on baking sheet with seam down.

If you wish, some may be shaped as round rolls. Flatten dough and reshape into a ball. Place on baking sheet.

(The *France* bakers use this same dough to make large loaves eaten by the officers and men. Divide the dough into 4 pieces, shape into loaves; place on baking sheet. After third rising, slash tops of loaves diagonally 4 or 5 times with a razor blade and bake 35 to 40 minutes.)

THIRD RISING
1 hour

Cover with wool blanket or other cloth and leave at room temperature (70°–75°) for 1 hour.

BAKING
440°
20–25 minutes

Twenty minutes prior to the bake period, place broiling pan or other container (for $1/2$ cup hot water) on lower oven rack. The middle rack will be for the bread. Preheat oven to 440°.

With a razor blade, make a $1/2$-inch-deep cut $3/4$ of the length of each *petit pain*, or across the roll.

Carefully pour $1/2$ cup of hot water into the broiler pan. Slip the baking sheet into the oven. Close the oven door.

Check bread in 20 minutes. If the *petits pains* along the edge of the baking sheet appear done, remove them and bake the balance for another 5 minutes.

FINAL STEP

When baked, remove from oven and place on rack to cool. Delicious when served warm or reheated. Because they are made of lean dough, they will soon begin to dry out. They freeze well, however, for a later meal.

BRIOCHES S.S. *FRANCE* ❧ BRIOCHES S.S. *FRANCE*

[ABOUT SIXTY PIECES]

While the brioche may take many forms—en couronne *(crown) or* mousseline *(tall and cylindrical) and a score more—none is more familiar at the breakfast table than the yellow, buttery* brioche à tête *baked in a small fluted tin and sporting a golden top-knot. And I have found no recipe more delicious, more buttery, or more light and eggy than this one for the brioche served aboard the S. S.* France.

The brioche was shaped by Monsieur Gousse, chief pâtissier *of the* France, *in a way that permits a shortcut of the traditional technique of shaping the lower body and piercing the dough to accept a separate tear-shaped piece for the head.*

"Time-consuming and unnecessary," Monsieur Gousse said, as he clustered before him a half hundred small fluted pans and an equal number of balls he had rolled from chilled brioche dough a few minutes before.

"Attention!" he said, and gently rested the side of his palm on one of the balls, not midway, but at the edge so that about a quarter of the dough was on one side of the palm and three-quarters on the other side. He pressed down and rolled the dough back and forth (perhaps three times) until there was only a small neck (about ³/4 of an inch thick) connecting the two pieces. He lifted the dough by the small end and lowered the bottom into a fluted tin. Then, with his fingers still in position, he forced the smaller ball of dough into the larger piece, his fingertips pushing to the bottom of the tin. The final result—perfect brioches à tête.

The first time I did it, I feared that I had pushed the dough out of shape forever, but miraculously the rising dough covered my imperfect efforts.

This large recipe can be divided in half.

INGREDIENTS 8 cups all-purpose flour
¹/4 cup non-fat dry milk
4 teaspoons salt
¹/3 cup sugar
2 packages dry yeast
¹/3 cup warm water (105°–115°)
12 eggs, room temperature
1 pound (4 sticks) butter, room temperature
(Additional water if needed—see below)

Glaze:
1 egg, beaten
1 tablespoon milk

BAKING TINS AND BAKING SHEET Small fluted brioche or muffin tins, greased; a baking sheet on which to place the small tins for the oven.

PREPARATION
15 minutes

Keep in mind that the dough is soft and elastic—never firm. It will stick to the hands as you blend the ingredients, but slowly it will begin to pull away from the sides of the bowl and the hands. With the final addition of flour, the dough can be kneaded.

Normally in bread recipes, a specific volume of liquid is indicated, with the amount of flour left approximate. M. Gousse suggested that for his brioche the procedure be reversed—a specific amount of flour, with water added only as necessary to keep the dough "very soft, full-bodied, and elastic."

Because brioche dough must be well chilled in the refrigerator, plan to make the dough in the late afternoon or evening to bake the following forenoon.

Measure 4 cups of the flour, the non-fat dry milk, salt, and sugar into a large bowl and mix together. Form a well in the flour and pour in yeast and 1/3 cup of water. Stir to dissolve and leave for 3 minutes. Beat in one egg at a time, pulling in flour from the sides of the bowl. When all the eggs have been added, beat 100 strong strokes. Gradually add 2 cups additional flour. When it is well blended, add butter (cut into 1-inch chunks). When butter has been absorbed, add 1 cup of flour. This will be a heavy mass to stir with a wooden spoon, so use the hands to mix and blend butter and flour. If dough is solid and has lost its elasticity, add 1 or 2 tablespoons of water.

KNEADING
5 minutes

Turn dough onto countertop and work with hands and dough scraper. Pour the final cup of flour near the dough and pull in small amounts as needed. The dough will be soft, but not sticky. It will become firm later when refrigerated.

FIRST RISING
1 hour

Cover bowl with plastic wrap, tightly drawn. Put in a warm place (80°–85°) for 1 hour or until dough has doubled in volume.

REFRIGERATED RISING
2 hours

Uncover bowl, push down dough with fingers and fist. Turn dough over. Drape a moist cloth over the dough to keep crust from forming. Place bowl in refrigerator for 2 hours.

SECOND RISING
2 hours

Remove bowl from refrigerator, turn back cloth, punch down chilled dough, and leave at room temperature for 2 hours.

SECOND REFRIGERATED RISING
overnight

Again, use fingers and fist to punch down dough. Cover with moist cloth and return to the refrigerator overnight.

SHAPING
30 minutes

Grease tins.

Remove dough from refrigerator. Divide dough (it will weigh about 5 pounds) into 2 or 3 pieces to make the work easier. Return all but one to refrigerator. Slowly work 1 piece into a 3-foot-long roll, 1¹/₂ inches in diameter. Use a yardstick and press a mark at 1-inch intervals. With a knife or dough scraper, cut the 1-inch pieces from the long roll. Each will weigh about 2 ounces.

Cup the palm of the hand and roll each piece in a circular fashion to form a ball about the size of a large egg. Try doing one under each hand at the same time.

Follow M. Gousse's technique for shaping the brioche and topknot (page 249). Place each in a brioche or muffin tin as described. When you begin, take the first ball through the process to be certain the shaped brioche is the right size for the tin. It should fit into the lower half, with the topknot at the level of the edge. If fingertips should stick, dust with flour.

If brioches are to be made over a period of time because of a shortage of either tins or oven space, cover the unused dough and place in the refrigerator until tins are forthcoming.

FINAL RISING
1¹/₂ hours

Leave brioches in their tins on countertop to rise. Do not cover. Mix egg and milk and carefully brush brioche dough, topknot and body. This will keep dough moist during the rise, as well as help give it its golden color later when baked.

The chilled dough must be allowed time to warm and rise—about 1¹/₂ hours. When the finger marks in the body of the brioche disappear, the brioche is ready for a second egg-milk wash and to be placed in the oven.

BAKING
450°
18–20 minutes

Twenty minutes before the bake period, preheat the oven. M. Gousse recommends that the baking sheet on which the brioche tins are carried to and placed in the oven be preheated for 10 minutes. This hot plaque or baking sheet gives the dough a big push in the oven, M. Gousse explained.

Fill the preheated baking sheet with brioche tins and place in the oven.

Check on brioches after 10 minutes. Don't let them get too brown in this hot, fast oven. The brioches will be done when the topknots are well raised, and they are rich deep brown in color.

FINAL STEP

Serve brioches warm from the oven, reheat later, or freeze. They are delicious whenever served!

In the bakery of S.S. *France,* M. Gousse feeds croissant dough into an automatic rolling machine.

CROISSANTS S.S. *FRANCE* ✤ CROISSANTS S.S. *FRANCE*

[THREE TO FOUR DOZEN CRESCENT ROLLS]

Aboard the S.S. France at 3:30 in the morning, there were men at work only on the bridge, in the engine room, and in the pâtisserie. Outside, in the cool September air, the ocean was calm but black under a moonless sky. In the pastry shop, however, the lights were bright as M. Marcel Gousse and his helpers placed dozens of trays of fresh-cut croissants on every conceivable resting place in the room.

The tables were blanketed with the crescent-shaped breads, while two trays perched atop the ice cream machine. Several were tucked out of the way on shelves high overhead. Everywhere croissants.

Finally, when the filled trays began to nudge even into the small work space kept open for M. Gousse, the morning's quota was pronounced filled. Two apprentices, meanwhile, were moving past the uncovered trays to brush each croissant with the first of the two egg-and-milk coatings they would get during the hour's rising time.

Four hours later, when M. Gousse and his men at last were in their bunks, the first of 2,000 warm, tender, and flaky croissants were carried to the first arrivals in the dining rooms.

Two impressions are most vivid in memory of the early morning hours I spent in the pâtisserie with M. Gousse and his helpers. The first is of thousands of croissants rising. The other is the use of dampened cloths in evidence everywhere in the room during the hours the dough was being prepared.

"One must not allow the skin of the dough to become dry or a crust will form, which will make it difficult later to work the dough smoothly," M. Gousse explained as he stepped into a walk-in refrigerator with a large pan of dough covered with a moist cloth.

M. Gousse, like other professionals who work with this type of dough, cautions the home baker to return the dough to the refrigerator if it begins to ooze butter while it is being worked and rolled.

"The cold will correct many mistakes," he said.

This is a large recipe (8 cups of flour), so for fewer croissants—or if it is your first time to make them and the bulk concerns you—divide the recipe and cut all ingredients in half.

INGREDIENTS 8 cups all-purpose flour, approximately
4 teaspoons salt
$^1/_4$ cup sugar
$^1/_2$ cup non-fat dry milk
1 package dry yeast
$3^1/_2$ cups warm water (105°–115°)
1 pound butter (1 piece preferably), chilled

Glaze:
1 egg, beaten
1 tablespoon milk

BAKING SHEET One or more baking sheets or trays. Caution: Do not use a flat baking sheet without sides or one open at the corners unless you form
a liner of aluminum foil with $^1/_2$-inch sides to retain butter, which
otherwise might drip below and burn.

PREPARATION This is not a difficult dough. It is the mechanics of layering dough and
15 minutes butter that make it sound so. But, taken step by step, it is relatively
easy, and highly rewarding.

The butter should be chilled. It is easier to work with 1 block of
butter rather than 4 sticks.

Blend in a large bowl 4 cups of flour, the salt, sugar, nonfat dry
milk, and yeast. Stir in $3^1/_2$ cups warm water. Beat 100 strokes. Stir
in additional flour, a cup at a time, to make a soft dough that will
become firm only when chilled. There is no kneading, which would
toughen the otherwise tender dough. Only a thorough blending of
all ingredients.

If it is difficult to stir this large mass, divide and stir or work each
portion on the work surface with hands and dough scraper for 2 to
3 minutes. Dough will be soft and slightly sticky. Do not knead.

REFRIGERATED This begins the process of cooling the dough and at the same time
REST allowing it to rise. Cover bowl with plastic wrap and place in refrig-
1–1$^1/_2$ hours erator for 1 to 1$^1/_2$ hours.

INTERLAY With a rolling pin, beat the block of butter between pieces of wax
20 minutes paper until it is a sheet 6 inches by 12 inches, and about $^1/_4$ inch thick.

Set aside in the refrigerator while the dough is rolled.

Place the chilled dough on a floured work surface and, with a
heavy rolling pin, roll into a rectangle about 8 × 20 inches. Remove
the chilled butter from the refrigerator and place on the upper two-
thirds of the rolled-out dough. There should be about an inch-wide
border of dough around the edges to allow the dough to be sealed
without the interference of butter.

FIRST AND SECOND TURNS Fold the lower (and unbuttered) third over the center third. Bring the upper third down on top of the center—as one would fold a letter into thirds. There should now be a layering of dough-butter-dough-butter-dough. Turn so that the open ends are at 6 o'clock and 12 o'clock. Roll gently and firmly into a 12 × 36-inch rectangle.

Don't hurry the rolling process or the butter may break instead of spreading beneath the layers of dough. If the butter comes through the dough, patch the tear with a sprinkle of flour. Refrigerate 10 to 15 minutes if the butter softens and oozes out between the folds.

Again fold the length of dough into three as one would a letter. Turn. Roll. Then fold in thirds again.

REFRIGERATION **2 hours** Wrap tightly in a cloth (an old tea towel is fine) that has been soaked in cold water and wrung dry. Lay wrapped dough on baking sheet and place in the refrigerator. If the refrigerator is frost-free, wrap wax paper, plastic wrap, or foil around the damp cloth to prevent the defrost action from pulling the moisture out of the cloth and dough. If the surface of the dough is allowed to dry, it will separate into less than attractive pieces as the dough is rolled and stretched.

THIRD AND FOURTH TURNS Remove from refrigerator and place on floured work surface. Unwrap, roll out, and fold in three as before. Give a half-turn on work surface. Roll out, then fold in three again.

REFRIGERATION **overnight** Dampen cloth again and wrap tightly around the dough, which will also restrain the rising. Again protect the damp cloth against drying out with a plastic or foil wrapping. Place in the refrigerator overnight.

THE FOLLOWING DAY Have ready the egg-milk wash, a knife or pastry cutter, baking sheets, and a wooden yardstick.

SHAPING **20 minutes** Remove dough from the refrigerator and, while still wrapped in cloth, gently flatten somewhat by pressing down with both hands.

Sprinkle work surface with flour. Unwrap. Roll dough until it is 10 inches wide and 44 to 48 inches long—and about ¼ inch thick. If the work surface is small, the dough can be cut in half. One piece can be refrigerated while rolling out the other. Trim irregularities to make strip 10 inches wide. Cut the strip in half lengthwise to make two 5-inch pieces. Keep the work surface dusted with flour to prevent stickiness if butter should be pressed out. First, mark the strips in 5-inch triangles and then, using the yardstick as a guide, cut through the dough with a pastry or pizza wheel. Separate the triangles.

Any time the butter softens and sticks, place the triangles in the refrigerator until they are chilled again.

Moisten baking sheet with a damp cloth and set aside.

Place the first triangle on the work surface, point away. Roll with a rolling pin from the broad side to the point to stretch and flatten the dough. The triangle will be longer, wider, and thinner.

With the fingers, roll the triangle from the bottom to the point, stretching the dough as it is rolled. Place roll on the baking sheet. Touch the tip of the point to the pan, but do not place underneath the body of the croissant. Bend into a crescent shape. Repeat until the sheet is filled.

GLAZE Brush each croissant with egg-milk glaze when tray is filled. Do not cover.

RISING
2–2^1/$_2$ hours Croissants will double in volume in 72° room in 2 to 2^1/$_2$ hours. (Some of those aboard the S.S. *France* raised while very near open portholes.)

BAKING
450°
18–22 minutes Ten minutes before bake period, preheat oven; brush croissants with egg-milk glaze again.

Place in oven. Check after 10 minutes, since this is a hot, fast oven. Parisians like their croissants a deep brown. You may wish to take them out earlier if you plan to freeze, reheat, and brown additionally later.

FINAL STEP Place on cooling rack immediately, so they will not absorb any butter left on the baking sheet.

Glossary

Acide ascorbique: Ascorbic acid. Because of its close affinity with Vitamin C, it is the only chemical additive allowed in France. It improves the strength and tolerance of the dough, thereby making it possible to obtain larger loaves. Used in minute amounts.

Apprêt: The final rising of the dough after the loaves have been shaped.

Apprêt sur couche: Placing the pieces of dough between folds of a length of cloth for a final rising or *apprêt*.

Baguette: The classic French loaf. It can weigh between $3/4$ pound and $1^1/2$ pounds, is about 2 feet long, and is usually carried unwrapped in the hand, under the arm, or strapped to a bicycle seat.

Bannetons: Woven wicker baskets of various sizes in which the dough makes its final rise.

Bassinage: Thinning of dough, if necessary, by adding water during kneading.

Bâtard: A stubby loaf, it weighs about $1^1/2$ pounds and is 12 to 14 inches long.

Blé: Wheat.

Boulanger: Baker of bread.

Boulangerie: Bakery or bake shop.

Chapelure: Breadcrumbs.

Chef: Piece of dough taken from the last kneading of the daily batch to be used as the basis for the fermentation of the next day's bake.

Clé: The seam in the dough when the loaf has been molded. The key.

Contre-frase: Addition of flour to give more body to the dough, if necessary, during kneading.

Couche: The cloth in which loaves are placed between folds for the final rising.

Coupe-pâte: Dough knife or scraper. A putty knife with a wide blade is an excellent substitute.

Couper le pâton: To slit the risen dough with a blade as the loaf is readied for the oven. It may be done with a blade called a *lame* or with a razor blade to allow the loaf to expand.

Coups de lame: The slits made in the risen dough.

Couronne: A crown-shaped loaf formed in a basket that has a center tube.

Epi: A long loaf cut with scissors, each cut piece angled to the side to resemble heads of wheat (*épis*) on a stalk.

Farine: Flour.

Farine supérieure: Bread flour made from American hard wheat.

Fer à cheval: A horseshoe achieved by shaping dough for a long loaf, then curving it to accommodate the baking sheet.

Ficelle: A "string;" a long, thin loaf of bread that weights slightly less than $1/3$ pound and is 8 to 12 inches long.

"Fines lames": The nickname given to those bakers' assistants (called *brigadiers*) who are known for their skill in slitting the loaf.

Fleurage: The thin coating of a material to prevent the dough from sticking to the peel or paddle when it is thrust into the oven to drop the loaves on the oven floor. In France, it can range from cornmeal to powdered rice husks to ground sawdust!

Flûte: A long and very slender loaf—less than a pound and 15 to 20 inches long.

Fougasse: In Paris, a milk roll. Elsewhere, dough cut and formed into fanciful shapes.

Frasage: The mixing of ingredients into dough.

Galette: A loaf traditionally baked to commemorate Twelfth Night.

Gâteau: A rich, filled loaf as well as other specialty breads, such as *gâteaux au poivre,* pepper cakes.

Jet: The swelling or bulge in the surface of the loaf resulting from slitting it before baking.

Lame: One of several special blades used to make slits in the dough.

Languette: The tongue or point of a croissant.

Levain: A leaven of dough.

Levare: Yeast.

Mie: The crumb or mie is the bread beneath the crust; *pain de mie* is a white loaf baked in an enclosed pan to produce a bread that is almost all crumb with a thin crust.

Oreille: The upper side of the slit in the crust as it opens in the heat of the oven. The ear.

Pain: A loaf.

Pain complet: Whole wheat loaf.

Pain de Beaucaire: A table bread noted for its good taste, as well as the unusual way the dough is placed in the oven to bake.

Pain de campagne: A country loaf, customarily a round hearth loaf weighing several pounds. Usually it will last a farm family a week until the next bake.

Pain de gruau: White loaf made with the finest flour from premium wheat that is usually imported from the U. S. or Canada.

Pain de ménage: A loaf for the family, same as *pain ordinaire.*

Pain de mie: Known also as *pain anglais,* English bread. It is a white, thin-crusted loaf that is used chiefly for sandwiches, toast, and hors d'oeuvres.

Pain de seigle: Rye loaf.

Pain italien: Italian bread.

Pain ordinaire: Everyday bread.

Pain sans sel: Salt-free bread.

Pain saucisson: Sausage bread. So called because it resembles a large sausage when the dough is slit across the width of the loaf rather than diagonally or lengthwise.

Pâte bâtarde: Ordinary white dough for making *pain ordinaire.*

Pelle: Wooden paddle or peel on which the loaves are moved in and out of large ovens.

Petites galettes saleés: Small salted biscuits or crackers.

Petit pain: A small loaf, a roll.

Pétrissage: Kneading.

Pistolet: Split roll.

Plaque: Baking sheet.

Pogne: A rich brioche-like bread.

Pointage: The first rising of the dough after kneading and before shaping.

Pompe: A loaf traditionally served during the holidays in Provence.

Poolish: A thin batter-like starter. It is like a U. S. sourdough starter.

Tourte: A round country loaf, originally raised in the large wicker basket used on the farm in pressing oil from sunflower seeds.

Viennoiserie: Breads and pastries brought to France generations ago by workers from Vienna.

U.S., British, and Metric Equivalent Weights and Measures

The British are officially on the metric system, but British recipes written before the early 1970s may use an "Imperial" unit of measurement, which differs from U.S. Standard measurements. A British measuring cup holds 10 fluid ounces, a U.S. measuring cup 8 fluid ounces.

Fluid measure can be used not only for liquids, such as water and milk, but also for ingredients such as flour, sugar, and shortenings. Greater accuracy is assured by weighing ingredients. In the following table of ingredients used by home bakers, most British measurements are indicated by weight and U.S. measurements by cups and spoons, following customary U.S. usage and that of the recipes in this book.

FLUID MEASURE EQUIVALENTS

METRIC	UNITED STATES	BRITISH
1 liter	4$^1/_4$ cups *or* 1 quart 2 ounces	1$^3/_4$ pints
1 demiliter ($^1/_2$ liter)	2 cups (generous) *or* 1 pint (generous)	$^3/_4$ pint (generous)
1 deciliter ($^1/_{10}$ liter)	$^1/_2$ cup (scant) *or* $^1/_4$ pint (scant)	3–4 ounces

WEIGHT MEASURE EQUIVALENTS

METRIC	UNITED STATES	BRITISH
1.00 gram	.035 ounce	.035 ounce
28.35 grams	1 ounce	1 ounce
100.00 grams	3.5 ounces	3.5 ounces
114.00 grams	4 ounces (approx.)	4 ounces (approx.)
226.78 grams	8 ounces	8 ounces
500.00 grams	1 pound 1.5 ounces	1 pound 1.5 ounces
1.00 kilogram	2.21 pounds	2.21 pounds

COMPARATIVE WEIGHTS AND MEASURES
FOR INGREDIENTS IMPORTANT TO HOME BAKERS

INGREDIENT	METRIC	UNITED STATES	BRITISH
Baking powder (also soda)	4.3 grams	1 teaspoon	1 teaspoon
Breadcrumbs (dry)	90 grams	1 cup	3 1/4 ounces
Butter	15 grams 125 grams 500 grams	1 tablespoon 1/2 cup 2 cups	1/2 ounce 4 ounces 1 pound (generous)
Cheese	500 grams	1 pound (generous)	1 pound (generous)
Cheese (grated hard type)	100 grams	1 cup (scant)	4 ounces (scant)
Cornstarch	10 grams	1 tablespoon	1/3 ounce
Flour (unsifted)	35 grams 70 grams 142 grams 500 grams	1/4 cup 1/2 cup 1 cup 3 1/2 cups	1 1/4 ounces 2 1/2 ounces 4 3/4 ounces 1 pound
Pepper (ground)	30 grams	4 tablespoons	1 ounce (generous)
Raisins (seedless)	10 grams 160 grams 500 grams	1 tablespoon 1 cup 3 cups	1/3 ounce 5 1/3 ounces 1 pound
Salt	15 grams	1 tablespoon	1/2 ounce
Spices (ground)	2.5 grams 15 grams	1 teaspoon 2 tablespoons	1/12 ounce 1/2 ounce
Sugar (granulated)	5 grams 15 grams 60 grams 240 grams	1 teaspoon 1 tablespoon 1/4 cup 1 cup	1/6 ounce 1/2 ounce 2 ounces 8 ounces
Sugar (confectioners')	35 grams 70 grams 140 grams	1/4 cup 1/2 cup 1 cup	1 ounce (generous) 2 1/4 ounces (scant) 4 1/2 ounces (scant)
Sugar (brown)	10 grams 80 grams 160 grams	1 tablespoon 1/2 cup 1 cup	1/3 ounce 2 2/3 ounces 5 1/3 ounces

INDEX

A

The Agriculture, 190
Albert I, Prince, 137
All-purpose flour, 4
Almonds
    Christmas Stollen, 230–32
    Kugelhupf, 222–25
    Spice Bread, 60–61
    Stollen, 218–19
Angoulême, 108–12
Apprêt sur couche, 14
Arrobia, 122
Atomizer, 17, 19
Avignon, 152, 157

B

Bacharan, Madame A., 127–28
Bagels, 48–54
    Jo Goldenberg's Bagels, 49–52
    Salted Sesame Bagels, 52–54
Bagels de Jo Goldenberg, les, 49–52
Baking sheet, 14, 23
Baking stone, 14–15, 24
Bannetons, 13
Basque breads, 113–24
Basque Cake, 122–24
Basque Pumpkin Bread, 119–20
Batterie de cuisine, 22–23
Bayeux, 6, 73, 85–92
Bayonne, 113–20
Beaucaire, 157–59
Beaucaire Bread, 157–59
Benoîtons, les, 103
Bern, 209, 214, 216
Bichet, Gaston, 93–95, 97
Biscuits
    Corn Biscuits, 115–16

Little Salted Biscuits, 169–71
    Biscuits au maïs, 115–16
Bourbonnais, 203
Bowls, 12
Bracieux, 93–107
Bran flakes, 22
    Bran Diet Bread, 62–63
    Nut Bread, 38–40
Breadcrumbs, 241
Bread knife, 17, 24
Brewer's yeast, 8
Brioche
    Brioches S.S. *France*, 249–51
    Brioche with Prune Filling, 104–6
    Cheese Brioche Loaf, 69–71
    Crescent-Shaped Brioches, 46–48
    Mousseline Brioche, 79–81
    Nanterre Brioche Loaf, 65–68
    Parisian Brioche Loaf, 65–68
    Raisin Brioche Loaf, 69–71
    Vendéenne Brioche, 110–12
Brioche au fromage, 69–71
Brioche aux pruneaux, 104–6
Brioche aux raisins secs, 69–71
Brioche mousseline, 79–81
Brioche Nanterre, 65–68
Brioche parisienne, 65–68
Brioche vendéenne, 108–12
Budapest, 125
Bun de Montélimar, le, 176–77
The Bun of Montélimar, 176–77
Burrenne, Monsieur, 122
Button Rolls, 211–13

C

Calvel, Raymond, 46, 157
Cambo-les-Bains, 121–26
Carcas, Dame, 127

Carcassonne, 27, 127–30, 131
Carême, 163, 222
Chambord, 93, 94, 95
Chapelure, 241–42
Charamnac, Monsieur, 202
Charlemagne, 127
Charles d'Andigne, Count and Countess, 172, 173–74
Charleville-Mézières, 235–42
Cheese
    Cheese Brioche Loaf, 69–71
    Gannat Cheese Bread, 200–201
    Gannat Clabber Bread, 192–95
Chef, 5, 155
Cherry preserves
    Basque Cake, 122–24
Chocolate-Filled Rolls, 106–7
Christmas Stollen, 230–32
Clabber Bread, Gannat, 192–95
Clamart, 41
Coconut
    Fauchon's Hawaiian Bread, 36–37
Coffee cans, 15–16
Columbus, Christopher, 113
Cooling rack, 17
Coquet, Georges, 180–81, 184, 187, 188
Corn, history of, 113
Cornmeal, 5
    Basque Pumpkin Bread, 119–20
Corn Biscuits, 115–16
Corn Cake, 113–14
Corn Sandwich Muffins, 117–18
Côte d'Azur, 152
Cottage cheese
    Gannat Clabber Bread, 192–95
Couches, 14
Coupe-pâte, 13
Coups de lame, 16–17
Cracklings
    Crackling Bread, 197–99
    making, 197
Crescent-Shaped Brioches, 46–48
Croissants
    Crescent-Shaped Brioches, 46–48
    Croissants S.S. *France*, 253–56

Flaky Croissants, 82–84
    history of, 82
    Nut-Filled Croissants, 216–17
    rolling out, 13
    Swiss Croissants, 214–16
    tips for, 82
    Unlayered Croissants, 125–26
Croissants briochés, 46–48
Croissants Cambo, 125–26
Croissants feuilletés, 82–84
Croutons, 241, 242
Crust, problems with, 30–31
Currants
    The Bun of Montélimar, 176–77
    Christmas Stollen, 230–32
    Currant Rolls, 178–79
    Kugelhupf, 222–25
    Raisin Brioche Loaf, 69–71
    Spice Bread, 60–61
    Stollen, 218–19

D
A Daily Loaf, 163–65
David, André, 3, 43, 72–73, 74, 75
Deauville, 65
Diet breads
    Bran Diet Bread, 62–63
    Gluten Diet Bread, 135–36
    Persian Flatbread, 55–56
    Salt-Free Bread, 63–64
    Whole Wheat Health Bread, 57–59
Dough
    freezing, 28
    kneading, 8–9
    problems with, 29–30
    rising, 9–10
    volume, 11
Dough knife, 13
Doz, Madame, 161–62, 165–66

E
Eau de fleur d'oranger
    about, 22, 181
    Romans Loaf, 181–84
Eisenhower, Dwight D., 93

Equipment
    sources for, 22–24
    types of, 12–19
Escoffier, Auguste, 137

F
Family Loaf, 237
Fauchon, 35–36, 38
Fauchon's Hawaiian Bread, 36–37
Ficelle de Romans, la, 187–89
Finest Wheaten Bread, 139–42
Flaky Croissants, 82–84
Flatbread, Persian, 55–56
Flour
    amount of, 3–4
    gluten in, 4
    sources of, 20–21
    types of, 3, 4–5, 20
Fougasse, 152, 153–54
Fraisage, 8
France, S.S., 243–56
Freezing, 28
Fromage blanc
    Gannat Clabber Bread, 192–95
    making, 191
Fruit, candied
    Christmas Stollen, 230–32
    Italian *Panettone,* 141–45
    Stollen, 218–19

G
Galette de Dame Carcas, 127–30
Galette de Gannat, 200–201
Galette persane, 55–56
Gannat, 25, 26, 190–201
Gannat Cheese Bread, 200–201
Gannat Clabber Bread, 192–95
Gâteau au maïs, 113–14
Gâteau basque, 121–24
Gâteau de Gannat, 191, 192–95
Gâteaux au poivre, 131–34
Gautier, Bernard, 85–87, 90
Gipfelteig, 209, 214–16
Gluten, 4
Gluten Diet Bread, 135–36

Gluten flour, 135
Goldenberg, Jo, 48, 49, 52
Gousse, Marcel, 244, 249, 250, 251, 252, 253
Grace, Princess, 137
Grasse, 152
Grenoble, 25, 160–71
Gugelhupf. See Kugelhupf

H
Haselnusslebkuchen, 210
Hawaiian Bread, Fauchon's, 36–37
Hazelnuts
    Fauchon's Hawaiian Bread, 36–37
    Nut-Filled Croissants, 216–17
    Whole Wheat *Kougelhopf,* 228–29
Honey
    Spice Bread, 60–61
    Whole Wheat Health Bread, 57–59
Honfleur, 3, 43, 65, 72–84, 88
Honfleur Country Bread, 74–76

I
Italian Bread, 146–48
Italian *Panettone,* 141–45

K
Ka'achei sumsum, 52–54
Kneading, 8–9, 13
Knives
    bread, 17, 24
    dough, 13
Kougelhopf blanc, 226–27
Kougelhopf complet biologique, 228–29
Kougloff. See Kugelhupf
Kugelhupf, 222–25
White *Kougelhopf,* 226–27
Whole Wheat *Kougelhopf,* 228–29

L
Ladder Bread, 153–54
Lallemand, Roger, 190
Lames, 16–17, 22
La Petite Marquise, 54, 55, 57
Leavening, 5, 8
Le Borghèse, 40

Le Havre, 65–71, 243, 244
L'Epi d'Or, 137–38, 139
Le Relais, 93–95
Les Halles, 35
Levain, 5
Limoux, 131–36
Little Salted Biscuits, 169–71
Loaf shapes, 10
Lucerne, 208
Lutetia Concorde Hotel, 40

M

Madame Doz' Peasant Loaf, 165–68
Malleret, Louis, 190–91, 192
Malt syrup, 21
Marie Antoinette, 222
Maslin Stone-Ground Rye or Pumpernickel
    Bread, 77–78
Méture au potiron basquais, 119–20
Milk Rolls, 97–99
Mixer, electric, 12–13
Monaco, 137–51
Montélimar, 174, 176
Morel, Pierre, 161, 163, 165–66
Moureau, Fernand, 157
Mousseline Brioche, 79–81
Muffin de Montélimar, le, 174–75
Muffins
    Corn Sandwich Muffins, 117–18
    The Muffin of Montélimar, 174–75

N

Nanterre Brioche Loaf, 65–68
Napoleon, 152, 174
Neuchatel, 209
Normandy Beaten Bread, 88–90
Nussgipfel, 216–17
Nuts. *See also individual nuts*
    grinding, 18
Nut Bread, 38–40
Nut-Filled Croissants, 216–17

O

Olney, Richard, 172–73
Orange flower water. *See Eau de fleur*
    d'oranger

Oranges
    Twelfth-Night Cake of Dame Carcas,
        129–30
Ordonneau, Yves, 109–10
Ovens
    baking on floor of, 18
    steam in, 19
    temperature of, 18–19, 31
    types of, 18

P

Pain anglais, 149
Pain aux noix, 38–40
Pain brié, 72–73, 85, 88–90
Pain complet, 57–59
Pain de Beaucaire, 157–59
Pain de campagne
    Honfleur, 74–76
    Madame Doz, 165–68
    Poilane, 43–46
Pain de gruau, 139–42
Pain de ménage, 235–37
Pain de méteil, 77–78
Pain de mie de Monaco, 149–51
Pain d'epice, 60–61
Pain de régime gluten, 135–36
Pain de seigle Sisteron, 155–56
Pain de seigle Strasbourg, 232–34
Pain de son—régime, 62–63
Pain hawaiien Fauchon, 36–37
Pain italien, 146–48
Pain ordinaire Carême, 163–65
Pain ordinaire de M. Gautier, 90–92
Pain sans sel, 63–64
Pains de régime. See Diet breads
Pain seigle, 100–102
Panettone, 141–45
Pans
    coffee cans as, 15–16
    conventional bread, 16
    French bread, 15, 22
    size of, 11, 30
    sources of, 22, 23
    stovepipe, 15
Paris, 3, 7, 25, 27, 35–64, 65, 93, 129, 157, 238
Parisian Brioche Loaf, 65–68

Pastry wheel, 18
Pear Bread, 195–97
Peel, 17
Pepper Cakes, 131–34
Persian Flatbread, 55–56
Petites galettes salées, 169–71
Petits pains au beurre, 185–86
Petits pains au chocolat, 106–7
Petits pains au lait, 96–99
Petits pains aux oeufs, 185
Petits pains S.S. France, 246–48
Phillippi, Wendell, 172
Phillips, Albert, 137–38, 139, 141, 146,
        147, 149
Piquenchagne, 195–97
Pistolets, les, 238–41
Pizza cutter, 18
Place Victor Hugo, 54
Pogne de Romans, 174, 180–84
Poilane, Pierre, 3, 7, 18, 36, 38, 40–42, 43, 46
Poilane's Peasant Bread, 43–46
Pompe au fromage, 192
Pompe aux gratons, 197–99
Poolish, 5
Potatoes
        Salt-Free Bread, 63–64
Proofing, 8
Provence, 152, 155
Prune Filling, Brioche with, 104–6
Pumpernickel Bread, Maslin Stone-
        Ground, 77–78
Pumpkin Bread, Basque, 119–20

R

Rainier III, Prince, 137
Raisins
        The Bun of Montélimar, 176–77
        Christmas Stollen, 230–32
        Italian *Panettone*, 141–45
        Kugelhupf, 222–25
        Raisin Brioche Loaf, 69–71
        Rye Rolls with Raisins, 103
        Sandwich Bread, 149–51
        Spice Bread, 60–61
        Stollen, 218–19

Vendéenne Brioche, 110–12
        White *Kougelhopf*, 226–27
        Whole Wheat *Kougelhopf*, 228–29
Rebolledo, Roger, 131–32, 133, 135
Record II, 160–61, 163, 165
Rhône Valley, 172–79
Rising, 9–10, 30
Rochefort-Montagne, 26, 202–7
Rolling pin, 13
Rolls
        Button Rolls, 211–13
        Chocolate-Filled Rolls, 106–7
        Currant Rolls, 178–79
        Finest Wheaten Bread, 139–42
        Milk Rolls, 97–99
        Rolls S.S. *France*, 246–48
        Rye Rolls with Raisins, 103
        Small Sandwich Rolls, 96–97
        Split Rolls, 238–41
Romans Loaf, 181–84
Romans-sur-Isère, 180–89
Rostand, Edmond, 122
Round Country Loaf, 203–4
Rye Bread, 100–102
        crumbs, 241
Maslin Stone-Ground Rye Bread, 77–78
Rye Country Loaf, 205–7
Rye Rolls with Raisins, 103
Sisteron Rye Bread, 155–56
Strasbourg Rye Bread, 232–34
Rye flour, 4–5

S

Saint Emilion, 108
Salt, 29
Salted Sesame Bagels, 52–54
Salt-Free Bread, 63–64
Sandwich Bread, 149–51
Sauvignon, Yves, 243, 245, 246
Schneckes, 178–79
Scholler, Hélène, 220–22
Scholler, Jean Pierre, 220–22, 226, 228,
        230, 232
Sesame Bagels, Salted, 52–54
Shaping, 10

Shelling, 31
Sisteron, 152–56
Sisteron Rye Bread, 155–56
Small Braided Breads of Romans, 187–89
Small Butter Loaves, 185–86
Small Sandwich Rolls, 96–97
Solliès-Toucas, 172
Soumoulou, 26
Soups, dried bread for, 242
Sources, 20–24
Spice Bread, 60–61
Split Rolls, 238–41
Sponges, 5
Starters, 5
Steam, 17, 19
Stolle, 218–19
Stolle de Noël, 230–32
Stollen, 218–19
Christmas Stollen, 230–32
Vendéenne Brioche, 110–12
Stollen-brioche, 110–12
Storing, 28
Stovepipe pans, 15
Strasbourg, 6, 220–34
Strasbourg Rye Bread, 232–34
Suglhupf. See Kugelhupf
Sumsum, 52–54
Swiss Croissants, 214–16
Switzerland, 208–19

T
Taloa, 117–18
Tardy, Leon, 243, 244
Thermometers, 18
Thomas, Rolf, 208–10, 211, 212, 214, 216
Thomas, Verena, 208–9, 210, 212

Tourte, la, 203–4
Tourte de seigle, la, 205–7
Troubleshooting, 29–31
Trouville, 65
Twelfth-Night Cake of Dame Carcas, 129–30

U
Unlayered Croissants, 125–26
Utensils. *See* Equipment

V
Vendéenne Brioche, 110–12
Vevey, Claude, 152–53
Villesavin, 104
Vizille, 161–62

W
Walnuts
Currant Rolls, 178–79
Nut Bread, 38–40
Water temperatures, 8
Weggliteig, 209, 211–13
Wheat, hard vs. soft, 4, 20, 139
White *Kougelhopf*, 226–27
Whole wheat flour, 4
Whole Wheat Health Bread, 57–59
Whole Wheat *Kougelhopf*, 228–29
Wichtrach, 6, 208–19
Work surfaces, 12

Y
Yeast, 5, 8

Z
Zimpfer, Jacques, 220